The Little SAS® Book

a primer

SECOND EDITION

Lora D. Delwiche and *Susan J. Slaughter*

SAS Publishing

The correct bibliographic citation for this manual is as follows: Delwiche, Lora D., and Susan J. Slaughter. 1998. *The Little SAS® Book: A Primer, Second Edition.* Cary, NC: SAS Institute Inc.

The Little SAS Book: A Primer, Second Edition

ISBN 1-58025-239-7

SAS Institute Inc., SAS Campus Drive, Cary, North Carolina 27513.

1st printing, October 1998
2nd printing, April 1999
3rd printing, October 1999
4th printing, June 2000
5th printing, September 2000
6th printing, October 2001
7th printing, February 2003

SAS Publishing provides a complete selection of books and electronic products to help customers use SAS software to its fullest potential. For more information about our e-books, e-learning products, CDs, and hard-copy books, visit the SAS Publishing Web site at **support.sas.com/pubs** or call 1-800-727-3228.

CONTENTS

Chapter 3 Working with Your Data

Chapter 4 Sorting, Printing, and Summarizing Your Data

Chapter 5 Modifying and Combining SAS Data Sets

Chapter 6 Writing Flexible Code with the SAS Macro Facility

Chapter 7 Using Basic Statistical Procedures

Chapter 8 Debugging Your SAS Programs

Appendices

Index   **245**

Acknowledgments

As hard as we have worked on this book, we could never have done it without the help of many people, both inside and outside SAS Institute.

We are grateful to all the people at SAS Institute who helped make this book what it is. Working with beta software is a challenge, and we often felt like we were exploring uncharted territory as we attempted to discover which of the hundreds of new features in Version 7 of the SAS System would be useful to our readers and which, however wonderful, are too esoteric for this book. We would particularly like to thank our editor and frontier guide Julie Platt. The hard work of Nancy Mitchell, our production specialist; Cate Parrish and Laurin Smith, our designers; and Caroline Brickley, our copy editor, was also critical.

Many reviewers provided invaluable and insightful comments greatly improving the book: Darrell Barton, Michelle Buchecker (who also reviewed the first edition and was brave enough to do it again!), Dina Fiorentino, Todd Folsom, Jake Jacobs, Paul Kent, Kathy Kiraly, Carol Linden, Ted Meleky, Chevell Parker, Kent Reeve, and Lorilyn Russell. Many people outside SAS Institute also contributed to this book. We are grateful to the many readers who answered a survey telling us what changes and additions would be most useful. Ginger and Helen Carey helped us revise the appendix "Coming to SAS from SPSS." Michael Delwiche wrote the C++ program in appendix D. David Slaughter photographed the authors. Most of all we would like to thank our families for their understanding and support.

Introducing SAS® Software

The SAS System is used by people all over the world—in 120 countries, at over 31,000 sites, by an estimated 3.5 million users. SAS (pronounced sass) is both a company, SAS Institute, and software, the SAS System. When people say SAS, they sometimes mean the software running on their computers and sometimes mean the company. In this book, SAS means the software, and the company is referred to as SAS Institute.

SAS products The roots of SAS software reach back to the 1970s when it started out as a software package for statistical analysis, but SAS didn't stop there. By the early 1980s SAS had already branched out into graphics, spreadsheets, and online data entry. Today the SAS family tree includes products as diverse as compilers for the C programming language, software for geographic information systems, and tools for building interfaces to the World Wide Web. Appendix C, "An Overview of SAS Products," lists the products available at the time this book was written. Just as AT&T is now more than telephones and telegraphs, SAS is more than statistics.

While SAS Institute has a diverse family of products, most of these products are integrated; that is, they can be put together like building blocks to construct a seamless system. For example, in one day you might read your data using base SAS, run a statistical analysis using SAS/STAT, and then display the results with SAS/GRAPH, all without leaving the SAS interactive windowing environment. Another time you might use SAS/ACCESS to read data stored in an external data base such as DB2 or ORACLE and analyze it using SAS/OR (operations research and project management), SAS/QC (quality improvement), or SAS/ETS (business planning, forecasting, and decision support), all in a single computer program.

Operating environments Other software packages often behave differently from one operating environment to another, but not SAS. You can take a program written on a personal computer and run it on a mainframe after changing only the operating-environment-specific file-handling statements. And because SAS programs are as portable as possible, SAS programmers are as portable as possible too. If you know SAS in one operating environment, you can switch to another operating environment without having to relearn SAS.

SAS Institute is committed to making SAS products available for all major computer operating environments. To facilitate this, SAS software is designed using a Multi-Vendor Architecture, meaning the software is written in as portable a way as possible. Only that small part of the software dealing with host-specific operations such as file handling must be customized for each individual operating environment. The remainder of the computer code for SAS software is the same on all systems. As new operating environments emerge, SAS software can be ported quickly and so be available quickly to users.

Licensing SAS products Some people (especially microcomputer users) are surprised to learn that SAS software cannot be owned, only licensed. Licensing software is like leasing it; once a year you pay your rent. Licensing has one important advantage when compared with buying: you automatically get each new release without an extra charge. Since SAS software is continually being improved and new versions released, licensing is helpful. For information about licensing SAS products, contact the Institute.

SASware Ballot SAS Institute puts a high percentage of its revenue into research and development, and each year SAS users help determine how that money will be spent by voting on the SASware Ballot. The ballot is a list of suggestions for new features and enhancements. All SAS users are eligible to vote and thereby influence the future development of SAS software. You can even make your own suggestions for the SASware Ballot by mailing them to SAS Institute or by sending electronic mail to `ballot@sas.com`. If you have other software suggestions that are not specifically for the SASware Ballot, you are welcome to send them to suggest@sas.com.

About This Book

Who needs this book This book is for all new SAS users in business, government, and academia, or for anyone who will be conducting data analysis using the SAS System. You need no prior experience with SAS software, but if you have some experience you may still find this book useful for learning techniques you missed or for reference.

What this book covers This book introduces you to the SAS language with lots of practical examples, clear and concise explanations, and as little technical jargon as possible. Most of the features covered here come from base SAS, which contains the core of features used by all SAS programmers. One exception is Chapter 7 which includes some procedures from SAS/STAT software. Another exception is section 2.18 which covers options from SAS/ACCESS for PC File Formats for importing data from spreadsheets and databases.

We have tried to include every feature of base SAS that a beginner is likely to need. Some of you will be surprised that certain topics, such as macros, are included because macros are normally considered advanced. But they appear here because sometimes new users need them. However, that doesn't mean that you need to know everything in this book. On the contrary, this book is designed so you can read just those sections you need to solve your problems. Even if you read this book from cover to cover, you may find yourself returning to refresh your memory as new programming challenges arise.

What this book does not cover To use this book you need no prior knowledge of SAS, but you must know something about your local computer and operating environment. The SAS System behaves virtually the same from one operating environment to another, but some differences are unavoidable. For example, every operating environment has a different way of storing and accessing files. Some operating environments have more of a capacity for interactive computing than others. Your employer may have rules limiting the size of files you can print. This book addresses operating environments as much as possible, but no book can answer every question about your local system. You must have either a working knowledge of your operating environment or someone you can turn to with questions.

This book is not a replacement for the SAS System Help, online documentation, Companions for your operating environment, or the many other SAS manuals. Sooner or later you'll need to go to these sources to learn details not covered in this book.

We cover only a few of the many SAS statistical procedures. Fortunately, the statistical procedures share many of the same statements, options, and output, so these few can serve as an introduction to the others. Once you have mastered the procedures in this book, the other statistical procedures should feel familiar.

Unfortunately, a book of this type cannot provide a thorough introduction to statistical concepts such as degrees of freedom, or crossed and nested effects. There are underlying assumptions about your data that must be met for the tests to be valid. Experimental design and careful selection of the models are critical. Interpretation of the results can often be difficult and subjective. We assume that readers who are interested in statistical computing already know something about statistics. People who want to use statistical procedures but are unfamiliar with these concepts should consult a statistician, seek out an introductory statistics text, or, better yet, take a course in statistics.

Versions of SAS This book was written using Release 7.0 of the SAS System under the Windows 95 operating environment, but all of the material covered here should apply to future releases.

Modular sections Our goal in writing this book is to make learning SAS as easy and enjoyable as possible. Let's face it—SAS is a big topic. You may have already spent some time scratching your head in front of a shelf full of SAS manuals, or staring at a screen full of online documentation until your eyes become blurry. We can't condense all of SAS into this little book, but we can condense topics into short, readable sections.

This entire book is composed of two-page sections, each section a complete topic. This way, you can easily skip over topics which do not apply to you. Of course, we think *every* section is important, or we would not have included it. You probably don't need to know everything in this book, however, to complete your job. By presenting topics in short digestible sections, we believe that learning SAS will be easier and more fun—like eating three meals a day instead of one giant meal a week.

Graphics Wherever possible, graphic illustrations either identify the contents of the section or help explain the topic. A box with rough edges indicates a raw data file, and a box with nice smooth edges indicates a SAS data set. The squiggles inside the box indicate data—any old data—and a period indicates a missing value. The arrow between boxes of these types means that the section explains how to get from data that look like the one box to data that look like the other. Some sections have graphics which depict printed output. These graphics look like a stack of papers with variable names printed on the top of the page and observation numbers shown on the left.

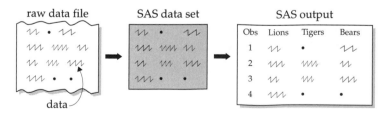

Typographical conventions SAS doesn't care whether your programs are written in upper or lowercase, so you can write your programs any way you want. In this book, we have used upper and lowercase to tell you something. The statements on the left below show the syntax, or general form, while the statements on the right show an example of actual statements as they might appear in a SAS program.

Syntax

```
PROC PRINT DATA = data-set-name;
   VAR variable-list;
```

Example

```
PROC PRINT DATA = bigcats;
   VAR Lions Tigers;
```

Notice that the keywords PROC PRINT, DATA, and VAR are the same on both sides and that the descriptive terms *data-set-name* and *variable-list* on the syntax side have been replaced with an actual data set name and variable names in the example.

In this book, all SAS keywords appear in uppercase letters. A keyword is an instruction to SAS and must be spelled correctly. Anything written in lowercase italics is a description of what goes in that spot in the statement, not what you actually type. Anything in lowercase or mixed case (and not in italics) is something that the programmer has made up such as a variable name, a name for a SAS data set, a comment, or a title. See section 1.2 for further discussion of the significance of case in SAS names.

Indention This book contains many SAS programs, each complete and executable. Programs are formatted in a way which makes them easy for you to read and understand. You do not have to format your programs this way, as SAS is very flexible, but attention to some of these details will make your programs easier to read. Easy-to-read programs are time-savers for you, or the consultant you hire at $100 per hour, when you need to go back and decipher the program months or years later.

The structure of programs is shown by indenting all statements after the first in a step. This is a simple way to make your programs more readable, and it's a good habit to form. SAS doesn't really care where statements start or even if they are all on one line. In the following program, the INFILE and INPUT statements are indented, indicating that they belong with the DATA statement:

```
* Read animals' weights from file. Print the results.;

   DATA animals;

      INFILE 'c:\MyRawData\Zoo.dat';

      INPUT Lions Tigers;

   PROC PRINT DATA = animals;

   RUN;
```

Last, we have tried to make this book as readable as possible and, we hope, even enjoyable. Once you master the contents of this small book you will no longer be a beginning SAS programmer.

What's New

New in Version 7 Version 7 is a major new release of the SAS System. There are many changes with Version 7, and we can't begin to cover them all in this book. We have tried to cover every new feature that we think new users would need to know, or find useful. Of course, there are many other useful features included in Version 7. For a complete list, see your online documentation or visit the SAS Web site at www.sas.com. The following is a list of the new features in Version 7 that we do cover.

Section	Feature
1.2	**Variable and data set member names** can be up to 32 characters long, and the case of variable names is preserved in your SAS output.
1.2	**Character data values** can be up to 32,767 bytes.
1.6	**The Explorer window** gives you quick access to your SAS files.
1.6,1.9	**The Results window** gives you more control over viewing and printing your SAS output.
1.9	**Viewing your output with an internet browser** is now possible in some operating environments.
2.17, 2.18	**PROC IMPORT** allows you to write simple SAS programs to import delimited files (as well as Excel, Lotus, and dBase files if you have SAS/ACCESS for PC File Formats).
2.19	**PROC EXPORT** allows you to write simple SAS programs to export delimited files (as well as Excel, Lotus, and dBase files if you have SAS/ACCESS for PC File Formats).
2.20	**The DSD and DLM= options** are now available in the FILE statement.
2.8, 4.1	**Labels** can now have up to 256 characters.
2.9	**Direct referencing of permanent SAS data sets** is now possible. You no longer need a LIBNAME statement in most situations.
2.11	**Viewtable** is a new interactive method of entering and editing data in a SAS data set.
3.7	**The YEARCUTOFF= system option** default value is now 1920.
4.9	**The MEANS** procedure has several new options including MEDIAN.
4.15	**Using ODS** (the Output Delivery System) you can now easily create HTML files from your output.
4.16	**The ODS TRACE and OUTPUT** statements allow you to save results from SAS procedures into SAS data sets.

7.9   **The Analyst application** was available as an add-on to Release 6.12, but is now included with Version 7. Analyst provides a graphical user interface to many of the SAS statistical procedures.

8.3   **The DATASTMTCHK=** system option checks for SAS keywords in DATA statements.

New terminology   With Version 7, SAS is adopting some new terminology. SAS data sets are now also called tables. Variables can be called columns, and observations can be called rows. This terminology is consistent with relational databases. One term you will find missing from this book is Display Manager. Display Manager has been replaced with the SAS windowing environment.

Missing topic   One of the major changes with Version 7 of SAS is that SAS data sets are now more portable. You can read Version 7 SAS data sets created in other operating environments without conversion (except for CMS and OS/390 bound libraries). You can directly access SAS data sets created in another operating environment but residing on your shared network. Or, you can transfer SAS data sets between operating environments using binary transfer. Because it takes more resources to read a SAS data set created in a different operating environment it is also possible, using Cross Environment Data Access (CEDA), to write SAS data sets in the format of an operating environment other than your own. For more information on this topic, see your online documentation. Because SAS data sets are now so portable, you will rarely need to use the tools for transporting SAS data sets (the CPORT procedure and the XPORT data engine). Therefore, this topic is no longer covered in this book.

New to this book   Some topics are not new to Version 7, but are nonetheless new to this book. You may want to look for these topics that we added in this edition.

Section	Feature
2.18	**Dynamic Data Exchange**, or DDE, allows you to read data directly from other applications in the Windows operating environment.
4.12, 4.13	**PROC TABULATE** provides a powerful way to present data in a tabular format.
6.1-6.7	**Macros** are now the topic of a complete chapter.
8.10	**DATA step debugger** provides an interactive way to find logic errors in DATA steps.

Future topic   The Enhanced Editor was not ready at the time this book was written, but we do mention it in section 8.1 because we think you will really like it.

1

> "An honest tale speeds best being plainly told."

WILLIAM SHAKESPEARE, *KING RICHARD III*

CHAPTER 1

Getting Started Using SAS® Software

1.1 The SAS Language

Many software applications are either menu driven, or command driven (enter a command—see the result). SAS is neither. With SAS, you use statements to write a series of instructions called a SAS program. The program communicates what you want to do and is written using the SAS language. There are some menu-driven front ends to SAS, SAS/ASSIST software for example, which make SAS appear like a point-and-click program. However, these front ends still use the SAS language to write programs for you. You will have much more flexibility using SAS if you learn to write your own programs using the SAS language. Maybe learning a new language is the last thing you want to do, but be assured that although there are parallels between SAS and languages you know (be they English or FORTRAN), SAS is much easier to learn.

SAS programs A SAS program is a sequence of statements executed in order. A statement gives information or instructions to SAS and must be appropriately placed in the program. An everyday analogy to a SAS program is a trip to the bank. You enter your bank, stand in line, and when you finally reach the teller's window, you say what you want to do. The statements you give can be written down in the form of a program:

```
I would like to make a withdrawal.
   My account number is 0937.
   I would like $200.
   Give me five 20s and two 50s.
```

Note that you first say what you want to do, then give all the information the teller needs to carry out your request. The order of the subsequent statements may not be important, but you must start with the general statement of what you want to do. You would not, for example, go up to a bank teller and say, "Give me five 20s and two 50s." This is not only bad form, but would probably make the teller's heart skip a beat or two. You must also make sure that all the subsequent statements belong with the first. You would not say, "I want the largest box you have" when making a withdrawal from your checking account. This statement belongs with "I would like to open a safe deposit box." A SAS program is an ordered set of SAS statements like the ordered set of instructions you use when you go to the bank.

SAS statements As with any language, there are a few rules to follow when writing SAS programs. Fortunately for us, the rules for writing SAS programs are much fewer and simpler than those for English.

The most important rule is

Every SAS statement ends with a semicolon.

This sounds simple enough. But while children generally outgrow the habit of forgetting the period at the end of a sentence, SAS programmers never seem to outgrow forgetting the semicolon at the end of a SAS statement. Even the most experienced SAS programmer will at least occasionally forget the semicolon. You will be two steps ahead if you remember this simple rule.

Layout of SAS programs There really aren't any rules about how to format your SAS program. While it is helpful to have a neat looking program with each statement on a line by itself and indentions to show the various parts of the program, it isn't necessary.

- ♦ SAS statements can be in upper- or lowercase.

- ♦ Statements can continue on the next line (as long as you don't split words in two).

- ♦ Statements can be on the same line as other statements.

- ♦ Statements can start in any column.

So you see, SAS is so flexible that it is possible to write programs so disorganized that no one can read them, not even you. (Of course, we don't recommend this.)

Comments To make your programs more understandable, you can insert comments into your programs. It doesn't matter what you put in your comments—SAS doesn't look at it. You could put your favorite cookie recipe in there if you want. However, comments are usually used to annotate the program, making it easier for someone to read your program and understand what you have done and why.

There are two styles of comments you can use: one starts with an asterisk (*) and ends with a semicolon (;). The other style starts with a slash asterisk (/*) and ends with an asterisk slash (*/). The following SAS program shows the use of both of these style comments:

```
* Read animals' weights from file;
DATA animals;
   INFILE 'c:\MyRawData\Zoo.dat';
   INPUT Lions Tigers;
PROC PRINT DATA = animals;   /* Print the results */
RUN;
```

Since some operating environments interpret a slash asterisk (/*) in the first column as the end of a job, be careful when using this style of comment not to place it in the first column. For this reason, we chose the asterisk-semicolon style of comment for this book.

Errors People who are just learning a programming language often get frustrated because their programs do not work correctly the first time they write them. To make matters worse, SAS errors often come up in bright red letters, and for the poor person whose results turn out more red than black, this can be a very humbling experience. You should expect errors. Most programs simply don't work the first time, if for no other reason than that you are human. You forget a semicolon, misspell a word, have your fingers in the wrong place on the keyboard. It happens. Often one small mistake can generate a whole list of errors. Don't panic if you see red.

1.2 SAS Data Sets

Before you run an analysis, before you write a report, before you do anything with your data, SAS must be able to read your data. Before SAS can read your data, the data must be in a special form called a SAS data set.[1] Getting your data into a SAS data set is usually quite simple as SAS is very flexible and can read almost any data. Once your data have been read into a SAS data set, SAS keeps track of what is where and in what form. All you have to do is specify the name and location of the data set you want, and SAS figures out what is in it.

Variables and observations Data, of course, are the primary constituent of any data set. In traditional SAS terminology the data consist of variables and observations. Adopting the terminology of relational databases, SAS data sets are also called tables, observations are also called rows, and variables are also called columns. Below you see a rectangular table containing a small data set. Each line represents one observation, while Id, Name, Height, and Weight are variables. The data point Charlie is one of the values of the variable Name and is also part of the second observation.

Variables (Also Called Columns)

		Id	Name	Height	Weight
	1	53	Susie	42	41
	2	54	Charlie	46	55
Observations (Also Called Rows)	3	55	Calvin	40	35
	4	56	Lucy	46	52
	5	57	Dennis	44	.
	6	58		43	50

Data types Raw data come in many different forms, but SAS simplifies this. In SAS there are just two data types: numeric and character. Numeric fields are, well, numbers. They can be added and subtracted, can have any number of decimal places, and can be positive or negative. In addition to numerals, numeric fields can contain plus signs (+), minus signs (-), decimal points (.), or E for scientific notation. Character data are everything else. They may contain numerals, letters, or special characters (such as $ or !) and can be up to 32,767 characters long.

If a variable contains letters or special characters, it must be character data. However, if it contains only numbers, then it may be numeric or character. You should base your decision on how you will use the variable.[2] Sometimes data that consist solely of numerals make more sense as character data than as numeric. ZIP codes, for example, are made up of numerals, but it just doesn't make sense to add, subtract, multiply, or divide ZIP codes. Such numbers make more sense as character data. In the previous data set, Name is obviously a character variable, and Height and Weight are numeric. Id, however, could be either numeric or character. It's your choice.

---

[1] There are exceptions. If your data are in a format written by another software product, you may be able to read your data directly without creating a SAS data set. For database management systems and spreadsheets, you may be able to use SAS/ACCESS. See section 2.18 for more information. For SPSS you can use the SPSS data engine. See appendix D.

[2] If disk space is a problem, you may also choose to base your decision on storage size. You can use the LENGTH statement, discussed in section 8.15, to control the storage size of variables.

Missing data Sometimes despite your best efforts, your data may be incomplete. The value of a particular variable may be missing for some observations. In those cases, missing character data are represented by blanks, and missing numeric data are represented by a single period (.). In the data set above, the value of Weight for observation 5 is missing, and its place is marked by a period. The value of Name for observation 6 is missing and is just left blank. The use of a period for missing numeric data turns out to be very useful, as you will see.

Size of SAS data sets SAS can handle up to 32,767 variables in a single data set. The number of observations, on the other hand, is limited only by your computer's capacity to handle and store them.

Rules for SAS names The rules for naming SAS data sets and variables changed considerably with Version 7 of SAS software. Prior to Version 7, names could be only 8 characters long; now many names can be longer. These are the rules for variable names and data set member names:

- ◆ Names must be 32 characters or fewer in length.[3]

- ◆ Names must start with a letter or an underscore (_).

- ◆ Names can contain only letters, numerals, or underscores (_). No %$!*&#@, please.[4]

- ◆ Names can contain upper- and lowercase letters.

This last point is an important one. SAS is insensitive to case so you can use uppercase, lowercase or mixed case—whichever looks best to you. SAS doesn't care. The data set name heightweight is the same as HEIGHTWEIGHT or HeightWeight. Likewise, the variable name BirthDate is the same as BIRTHDATE and birThDaTe. However, there is one difference for variable names. SAS remembers the case of the first occurrence of each variable name and uses that case when printing results. That is why, in this book, we use mixed case for variable names but lowercase for other SAS names.

Documentation stored in SAS data sets In addition to your actual data, SAS data sets contain information about the data set such as its name, the date that you created it, and the version of SAS you used to create it. SAS also stores information about each variable, including its name, type (numeric or character), length (or storage size), and position within the data set. This information is sometimes called the descriptor portion of the data set, and it makes SAS data sets self-documenting.

---

[3] Librefs, filerefs, and format names must be 8 characters or fewer in length; informat names must be 7 characters or fewer, and member names for versioned data sets must be 28 characters or fewer.

[4] It is possible to use special characters, including spaces, in variable names if you use the system option VALIDVARNAMES=ANY and a name literal of the form '*variable-name*'N. See the online documentation for details.

1.3 ▸ The Two Parts of a SAS Program

SAS programs are constructed from two basic building blocks: DATA steps and PROC steps. A typical program starts with a DATA step to create a SAS data set and then passes the data to a PROC step for processing. Here is a simple program that converts miles to kilometers in a DATA step and prints the results with a PROC step:

DATA step
```
DATA distance;
    Miles = 26.22;
    Kilometer = 1.61 * Miles;
```

PROC step
```
PROC PRINT DATA = distance;
RUN;
```

DATA and PROC steps are made up of statements. A step may have as few as one or as many as hundreds of statements. Most statements work in only one type of step—in DATA steps but not PROC steps, or vice versa. A common mistake made by beginners is to try to use a statement in the wrong kind of step. You're not likely to make this mistake if you remember that DATA steps read and modify data while PROC steps analyze data, perform utility functions, or print reports.

DATA steps start with the DATA statement, which starts, not surprisingly, with the word DATA. This keyword is followed by a name that you make up for a SAS data set. The DATA step above produces a SAS data set named DISTANCE. In addition to reading data from external, raw data files, DATA steps can include DO loops, IF-THEN/ELSE logic, and a large assortment of numeric and character functions. DATA steps can also combine data sets in just about any way you want, including concatenation and match-merge.

Procedures, on the other hand, start with a PROC statement in which the keyword PROC is followed by the name of the procedure (PRINT, SORT, or PLOT, for example). Most SAS procedures have only a handful of possible statements. Like following a recipe, you use basically the same statements or ingredients each time. SAS procedures do everything from simple sorting and printing to analysis of variance and 3D graphics. Other SAS procedures perform utility functions such as importing data files and data entry.

A step ends when SAS encounters a new step (marked by a DATA or PROC statement), a RUN statement, or, if you are running in batch mode, the end of the program.[1] RUN statements tell SAS to run all the preceding lines of the step and are among those rare, global statements that are not part of a DATA or PROC step. In the program above, SAS knows that the DATA step has ended when it reaches the PROC statement. The PROC step ends with a RUN statement, which coincides with the end of the program.

---

[1] If you use SAS long enough, you may run into an exception. Steps can also terminate with a QUIT, STOP, or ABORT statement.

While a typical program starts with a DATA step to input or modify data and then passes the data to a PROC step, that is certainly not the only pattern for mixing DATA and PROC steps. Just as you can stack building blocks in any order, you can arrange DATA and PROC steps in any order. A program could even contain only DATA steps or only PROC steps.

To review, the table below outlines the basic differences between DATA and PROC steps:

DATA steps	PROC steps
▶ begin with DATA statements	▶ begin with PROC statements
▶ read and modify data	▶ perform specific analysis or function
▶ create a SAS data set	▶ produce results or report

As you read this table, keep in mind that it is a simplification. Because SAS is so flexible, the differences between DATA and PROC steps are, in reality, more blurry. The table above is not meant to imply that PROC steps never create SAS data sets (many do), or that DATA steps never produce reports (they can). Nonetheless, you will find it much easier to write SAS programs if you understand the basic functions of DATA and PROC steps.

1.4 The DATA Step's Built-in Loop

DATA steps read and modify data, and they do it in a way that is flexible, giving you lots of control over what happens to your data. However, DATA steps also have an underlying structure, an implicit, built-in loop. You don't tell SAS to execute this loop: SAS does it automatically. Memorize this:

DATA steps execute line by line and observation by observation.

This basic concept is rarely stated explicitly. Consequently, new users often grow into old users before they figure this out on their own.

The idea that DATA steps execute line by line is fairly straightforward and easy to understand. It means that, by default, SAS executes line one of your DATA step before it executes line two, and line two before line three, and so on. That seems common sense, and yet new users frequently run into problems because they try to use a variable before they create it. If a variable named Z is the product of X and Y, then you better make sure that the statements creating X and Y come before the statements creating Z.

What is not so obvious is that while DATA steps execute line by line, they also execute observation by observation. That means SAS takes the first observation and runs it all the way through the DATA step (line by line, of course) before looping back to pick up the second observation. In this way, SAS sees only one observation at a time.

Imagine a SAS program running in slow motion: SAS reads observation number one from your input data set. Then SAS executes your DATA step using that observation. If SAS reaches the end of the DATA step without encountering any serious errors, then SAS writes the current observation to a new, output data set and returns to the beginning of the DATA step to process the next observation. After the last observation has been written to the output data set, SAS terminates the DATA step and moves on to the next step, if there is one. End of slow motion; please return to normal megahertz.

This diagram illustrates how an observation flows through a DATA step:

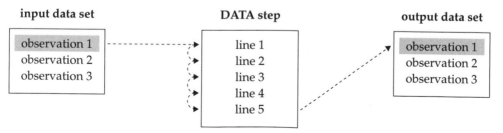

SAS reads observation number one and processes it using line one of the DATA step, then line two, and so on until SAS reaches the end of the DATA step. Then SAS writes the observation in the output data set. This diagram shows the first execution of the line-by-line loop. Once SAS finishes with the first observation, it loops back to the top of the DATA step and picks up observation two. When SAS reaches the last observation, it automatically stops.[1]

Here is an analogy. DATA step processing is a bit like voting. When you arrive at your polling place, you stand in line behind other people who have come to vote. When you reach the front of the line you are asked standard questions: "What is your name? Where do you live?" Then you sign your name, and you cast your vote. In this analogy, the people are observations, and the voting process is the DATA step. People vote one at a time (or observation by observation). Each voter's choices are secret, and peeking at your neighbor's ballot is definitely frowned upon. In addition, each person completes each step of the process in the same order (line by line). You cannot cast your vote before you give your name and address. Everything must be done in the proper order.

---

[1] If this seems a bit too structured, don't worry. You can override the line-by-line and observation-by-observation structure in a number of ways. For example, you can use the RETAIN statement, discussed in section 3.9, to make data from the previous observation available to the current observation. You can also use the OUTPUT statement, discussed in sections 5.11 and 5.12, to control when observations are written to the output data set.

1.5 Choosing a Mode for Submitting SAS Programs

So far we have talked about writing SAS programs, but simply writing a program does not give you any results. Just like writing a letter to your representative in Congress does no good unless you mail it, a SAS program does nothing until you submit or execute it. You can execute a SAS program several ways, but not all methods are available for all operating environments. Check in the SAS Companion for your operating environment or with your SAS site representative to find out which methods are available to you. The method you choose for executing a SAS program will depend on your preferences and on what is most appropriate for your application and your environment. If you are using SAS at a large site with many users, then ask around and find out which is the most accepted method of executing SAS. If you are using SAS on your own personal computer, then choose the method that suits you.

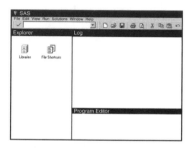

SAS windowing environment If you type SAS at your system prompt, or click on the SAS icon, you will most likely get into the SAS windowing environment (also called interactive SAS). In this environment, formerly called display manager, you can write and edit SAS programs, submit programs for processing, and view and print your results. In addition, there are many SAS windows for performing different tasks such as managing SAS files, customizing the interface, accessing SAS Help, and importing or exporting data. Exactly what your windowing environment looks like depends on the type of computer or terminal you are using, the operating environment on the computer, and what options are in effect when you start up SAS. If you are using a personal computer, then the SAS windowing environment will look similar to other programs on your computer, and many of the features will be familiar to you.

Non-interactive mode Non-interactive mode is where your SAS program statements are in a file on your system, and you start up SAS specifying that you want to execute that file. SAS immediately starts to process your file and ties up your computer, or window, until it is finished. The results are usually placed in a file or files, and you are returned to your system prompt.

Non-interactive mode is useful in many situations. This mode is good if you want your program to execute immediately, but you do not want to or cannot use a windowing environment. Non-interactive mode is usually started by typing SAS at your system prompt (shown here as $), followed by the filename containing your program statements:

```
$ SAS MyFile.sas
```

Batch or background mode With batch or background mode, your
SAS program is in a file. You submit the file for processing with SAS.
Your SAS program may start executing immediately, or it could be put in
a queue behind other jobs. Batch processing is used a lot on mainframe
computers, which are capable of executing many processes at one time.
You can continue to work on your computer while your job is being
processed, or better yet, you can go to the baseball game and let the
computer work in your absence. Batch processing is usually less
expensive than other methods and is especially good for large jobs which
can be set up to execute at off hours when the rates are at their lowest.
When your job is complete, the results will be placed in a file or files, which you can display or
print at any time.

Batch processing may not available for your operating environment. Check in the SAS Companion
for your operating environment to see if it is available, then check with your SAS site representative to find out how to submit SAS programs for batch processing. Even sites with the same
operating environment may have different ways of submitting jobs in batch mode.

Interactive line mode This mode is mentioned only because you
might see it in the SAS documentation, and you might get into it by
accident. In interactive line mode, you are prompted for SAS statements
one line at a time. There is no easy way to correct mistakes once you
have entered them, so unless you are an excellent typist, and an
excellent programmer, interactive line mode is exceedingly frustrating.

If you do find yourself in this mode (you will know when you get a 1?
as a prompt), you can get out by typing ENDSAS; and pressing ENTER.
For example

```
1? ENDSAS;
```

Seek assistance from your SAS site representative to find out why you got into line mode and how
to avoid it in the future.

1.6▶ Windows and Commands in the SAS Windowing Environment

It used to be that SAS looked pretty much the same on all platforms, and you couldn't change its appearance. But now SAS adopts the look and feel of your operating environment, and there are many ways in which you can customize your SAS environment. This is good for you because many aspects of the SAS windowing environment will be familiar, and if you don't like the default view, you can change it. It makes writing about it more difficult, because we can't tell you exactly what your SAS session will look like and how it will behave. However, there are many common elements between the various operating environments, and you will probably already be familiar with those elements which are different.

The SAS Windows

There are five basic SAS windows: the Results and Explorer windows, and three programming windows: Program Editor, Log, and Output. It is possible to bring up SAS without all these windows, and sometimes the windows are not immediately visible (for example, in the Windows operating environment, the Output window comes up behind the Program Editor and Log windows), but all these windows do exist in your SAS session. There are also many other SAS windows that you may use for tasks such as getting help, changing SAS system options, and customizing your SAS session. The following figure shows the default view for a Microsoft Windows 95 SAS session, with pointers to the five main SAS windows.

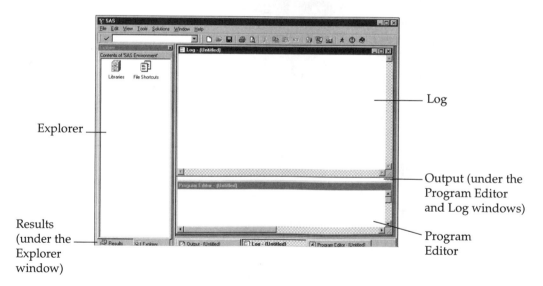

Program Editor This window is a text editor. You can use it to type in, edit, and submit SAS programs as well as edit other text files such as raw data files.

Log The Log window contains notes about your SAS session, and after you submit a SAS program, any notes, errors, or warnings associated with your program as well as the program statements themselves will appear in the Log window.

Output If your program generates any printable results, then they will appear in the Output Window.

Results The Results window is like a table of contents for your Output window; the results tree lists each part of your results in an outline form.

Explorer The Explorer window gives you easy access to your SAS files and libraries.

The SAS Commands

There are SAS commands for performing a variety of tasks. Some tasks are probably familiar, such as opening and saving files, cutting and pasting text, and accessing Help. Other commands are specific to the SAS System, such as submitting a SAS program, or starting up a SAS application. You may have up to three ways to issue commands: menus, the tool bar, or the SAS command bar (or command line). The following figure shows the location of these three methods of issuing SAS commands in the Windows operating environment default view.

Menus Most operating environments will have pull-down menus located either at the top of each window, or at the top of your screen. If your menus are at the top of your screen, then the menus will change when you activate the different windows (usually by clicking on them). You may also have, for each window, context-sensitive pop-up menus that appear when you press the right or center button of your mouse.

Tool bar You will probably see the tool bar only if you are working in a highly graphical system, such as a personal computer or UNIX system running X Windows. The tool bar gives you quick access to commands that are already accessible through the pull-down menus.

SAS command bar The command bar is a place that you can type in SAS commands. In some operating environments the command bar is located with the tool bar (as shown here); in other operating environments you may have a command line with each of the SAS windows (usually indicated by `Command=>`). Most of the commands that you can type in the command bar are also accessible through the pull-down menus or the tool bar.

Controlling your windows The Window pull-down menu gives you choices on how the windows are placed on your screen. You can also activate any of the programming windows by selecting it from the Window pull-down menu, typing the name of the window in the command line area of your SAS session, or simply clicking on the window.

1.7 Submitting a Program in the SAS Windowing Environment

Naturally after going to the trouble of writing SAS programs, you want to see some results. As we have already discussed, there are several ways of submitting your SAS programs. If you are using SAS in a windowing environment, such as Windows or UNIX, then you will probably want to submit your programs from within the SAS windowing environment.

Getting your program into the Program Editor   The first thing you need to do is get your program into the Program Editor window. You can either type your program into the Program Editor, or you can bring the program into the Program Editor window from a file. The commands for editing in the Program Editor and for opening files should be familiar. SAS tries to follow conventions that are common for your operating environment. For example, to open a file in the Program Editor, you can select Open from the File pull-down menu. For some operating environments you may have an Open icon on your tool bar, and you may also have the option of pasting your file into the Program Editor from the clipboard.

Submitting your program   Once your program appears in the Program Editor, you execute it using the SUBMIT command. Depending on your operating environment, you have a few choices on how to execute the SUBMIT command.

 Use the Submit icon on the tool bar.

 Make the Program Editor window active and enter SUBMIT in the command line area of your SAS session.

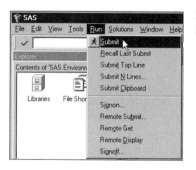 Make the Program Editor window active and select Submit from the Run pull-down menu.

The figure shows a program in the Program Editor ready to be submitted using the Submit icon on the tool bar (Windows 95).

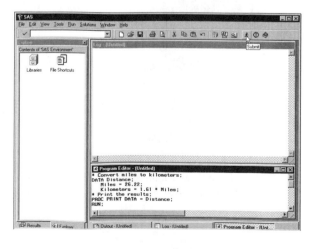

Viewing the SAS Log and Output   After you submit your program, it is cleared from the Program Editor window, and the results of your program go into the Log and Output windows. At first it may be a shock for you to see your program disappear in front of your eyes. Don't worry; the program you spent so long writing is not gone forever. If your program produced any output, then you will also get new entries in your Results window (your Results window may not be visible if you do not have the SAS Explorer window active). The Results window is like a table of contents for your SAS output and is discussed in more detail in section 1.9. The figure is an example of what your screen might look like after you submit a program.

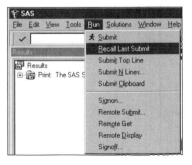

You may not see all three of the programming windows (Program Editor, Log, and Output) at the same time. In some operating environments, the windows are placed one on top of the other. You can bring a window to the top by clicking on it, typing its name in the command line area, or selecting it from the Window menu.

Getting your program back

Unfortunately for most of us, our programs do not run perfectly every time. If you have an error in your program, you will most likely want to edit the program and run it again. To get your program back in the Program Editor window, use the RECALL command. You have two choices for executing the RECALL command.

Make the Program Editor the active window, then enter RECALL in the command line area of your SAS session.

Make the Program Editor the active window, then select `Recall Last Submit` from the Run pull-down menu.

The RECALL command will bring back the last block of statements you submitted. If you use the RECALL command again, it will insert the block of statements submitted before the last one, and so on and so on, until it retrieves all the statements you submitted.

1.8 Reading the SAS Log

Every time you run a SAS job, SAS writes messages in your log. Many SAS programmers ignore the SAS log and go straight to the output. That's understandable, but dangerous. It is possible—and sooner or later it happens to all of us—to get bogus results that look fine in the output. The only way to know they are bad is to check the SAS log. Just because it runs doesn't mean it's right.

Where to find the SAS log The location of the SAS log varies depending on the operating environment you use, the mode you use (SAS windowing environment, non-interactive, or batch), and local settings. If you submit a program in the windowing environment, you will, by default, see the SAS log in your Log window as in the following figure.

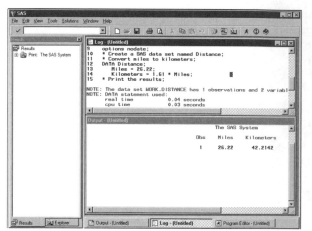

If you submit your program in batch or non-interactive mode, the log will be written to a file that you can view or print using your operating environment's commands for viewing and printing. The name given to the log file is generally some permutation of the name you gave the original program. For example, if you named your SAS program Marathon.sas, then it is a good bet that your log file will be Marathon.log. At some installations the log and output files are written to a single file, so don't be surprised if you find them together.

What the log contains People tend to think of the SAS log as either a rehash of their program or as just a lot of gibberish. OK, we admit, there is some technical trivia in the SAS log, but there is also plenty of important information. Here is a simple program that converts miles to kilometers and prints the result:

```
* Create a SAS data set named distance;
* Convert miles to kilometers;
DATA distance;
   Miles = 26.22;
   Kilometers = 1.61 * Miles;
* Print the results;
PROC PRINT DATA = distance;
RUN;
```

If you run this program, SAS will produce a log similar to this:

```
❶ NOTE: Copyright (c) 1998 by SAS Institute Inc., Cary, NC, USA.
   NOTE: SAS (r) Proprietary Software Version 7 BETA  (TS B1)
         Licensed to XYZ Inc., Site 0098541001.
   NOTE: This session is executing on the WIN_95  platform.

   NOTE: SAS initialization used:
         real time           24.00 seconds

❷ 1    * Create a SAS data set named distance;
   2    * Convert miles to kilometers;
   3    DATA distance;
   4       Miles = 26.22;
   5       Kilometers = 1.61 * Miles;
   6    * Print the results;
❸ NOTE: The data set WORK.DISTANCE has 1 observations and 2 variables.
   NOTE: DATA statement used:
         real time            2.80 seconds

❷ 7    PROC PRINT DATA = distance;
   8    RUN;

❹ NOTE: PROCEDURE PRINT used:
         real time            1.30 seconds
```

The SAS log above is a blow-by-blow account of how SAS executes the program.

❶   It starts with notes about the version of SAS and the SAS site number.

❷   It contains the original program statements with line numbers added on the left.

❸   The DATA step is followed by a note containing the name of the SAS data set created (WORK.DISTANCE), and the number of observations (1) and variables (2). A quick glance is enough to assure you that you did not lose any observations or accidentally create a lot of unwanted variables.

❹   Both DATA and PROC steps produce a note about the computer resources used. At first you probably won't care in the least. But if you run on a multi-user system or have long jobs with large data sets, these statistics may start to pique your interest. If you ever find yourself wondering why your job takes so long to run, a glance at the SAS log will tell you which steps are the culprits.

If there were error messages, they would appear in the log, indicating where SAS got confused and what action it took. You may also find warnings and other types of notes which sometimes indicate errors and other times just provide useful information.

1.9 ▶ Viewing and Printing the SAS Output

How you view or print your output depends on how you submit your programs. If you submit your program in the SAS windowing environment, then your output will, by default, go to the Output window. If you choose another way to submit your programs, either batch or non-interactive, then your output will probably be in a file on your computer. Use your operating environment's commands to view and print the output (also called listing) files. For example, if you execute your SAS program in non-interactive mode on a UNIX system, then your output will be in a file with an extension .lst. To view the file, you can use either the cat or more commands, and to print the file you would use your system's command for printing files (usually you would type either lp or lpr).

The Output window   After submitting your program in the SAS windowing environment, your results will go to your Output window. If you have the SAS Explorer option turned on (some operating environments have this turned on by default, while others do not), then you will also see a listing of the different parts of your output in your Results window. The following figure shows what your screen might look like after submitting a simple program under Windows 95.

Printing or saving the contents of the Output window   If you want to print or save the entire contents of the Output window, first activate the Output window by clicking in it, then select either Print or Save As from the File pull-down menu. If you are not using a personal computer, then your environment may not be set up for printing from within SAS. If you cannot print from within SAS, then save the output to a file and use your system's command for printing files.

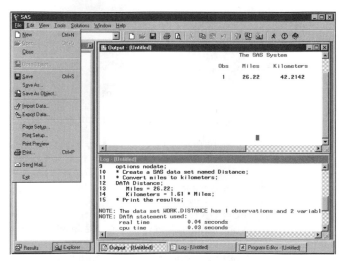

The Results window   When you have a lot of output, the Results window can be very helpful. The Results window is like a table of contents for your output. It lists each procedure that produces output, and if you open, or expand, the procedure in the Results tree, you can see each part of the procedure output. The following figure shows what your screen might look like if you ran the Analysis of Variance (ANOVA) procedure.

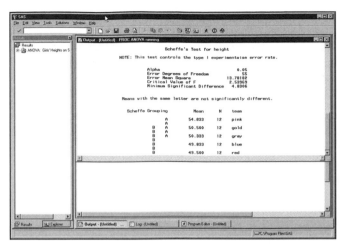

There is one entry in the Results window for the ANOVA procedure. Notice that in the Output window, you see the end of the procedure's output. If you expand the ANOVA procedure in the results tree, by clicking on the plus (+) signs, then you will see all the different parts of the ANOVA output. Double click on the output you want to see, and it will appear at the top of the Output window. The following figure shows what your screen would look like after you double click on the Overall ANOVA item in the Results window.

Printing or saving parts of the output

Using the Results window, it is possible to print or save just the parts of the output you want. First highlight the item you want in the Results window, then bring up the context-sensitive menu. In the Windows operating environment you do this with the right mouse button; in other operating environments, it may be the middle or right mouse button. Then select either Print or Save As from the pop-up menu. You may also be able to print or save from the File pull-down menu once you highlight the output part you want. If your

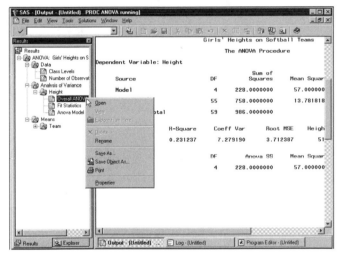

SAS environment is not set up for printing from within SAS, then save your results to a file and use your operating environment's command for printing files.

Viewing your output using a browser

PC users,[1] you can change your output destination from the standard listing in the Output window to an internet browser such as Internet Explorer or Netscape. In Windows operating environments, make this change in the Results tab of the Preferences window. Access the Preferences window from the Options item in the Tools pull-down menu.

---

[1] At the time this book was written, this feature was available only for PC users, but it may also be availabe for UNIX users in future releases.

1.10 Using SAS System Options

System options are parameters you can change that affect the SAS System—how it works, what the output looks like, how much memory is used, error handling, and a host of other things. The SAS System makes many assumptions about how you want it to work. This is good. You do not want to specify every little detail each time you use SAS. However, you may not always like the assumptions SAS makes. System options give you a way to change some of these assumptions.

A long list of system options can be found in your online documentation for the SAS language. The options are grouped by the following general areas:

Communications	Log and procedure output control
Environment control	Macro
Files	Sort
Input control	System administration
Graphics	

Not all options are available for all operating environments. A list of options specific to your operating environment appears in the SAS Companion documentation for your operating environment. You can see a list of system options and their current values by opening the SAS System Options window or by using the OPTIONS procedure. To use the OPTIONS procedure, submit the following SAS program and view the results in the SAS log:

```
PROC OPTIONS;
RUN;
```

There are four ways to specify system options. Some options can be specified only by using some of these methods. The SAS Companion documentation tells you which methods are valid for each system option:

1. Your system administrator (this could be you if you are using a PC) can create a SAS configuration file which contains settings for the system options. This file is accessed by the SAS System every time SAS is started.

2. Specify system options at the time you start up SAS from your system's prompt (called the invocation).

3. Change selected options in the SAS System Options window if you are using the SAS windowing environment.

4. Use the OPTIONS statement as a part of your SAS program.

The methods are listed here in order of increasing precedence; method 2 will override method 1, method 3 will override method 2, and so forth. If you are using the SAS windowing environment, methods 3 and 4, the SAS System Options window and OPTIONS statement will override each other—so whichever was used last will be in effect. Only the last two methods are covered here. The first two are very system dependent; to find out more about these methods see the SAS Companion documentation for your operating environment.

OPTIONS statement The OPTIONS statement is part of a SAS program and affects all steps that follow it. It starts with the keyword OPTIONS and follows with a list of options and their values. For example

```
OPTIONS LINESIZE = 80 NODATE;
```

The OPTIONS statement is one of the special SAS statements which do not belong to either a PROC or a DATA step. This global statement can appear anywhere in your SAS program, but it usually makes the most sense to let it be the first line in your program. This way you can easily see which options are in effect. If the OPTIONS statement is in a DATA or PROC step, then it affects that step and the following steps. Any subsequent OPTIONS statements in a program override previous ones.

The SAS System Options

window You can view and change SAS system options through the SAS System Options window. Open it by either typing OPTIONS in the command line area on your screen, or by selecting it from the Tools pull-down menu. To change the value of an option, first locate the option by clicking on the appropriate category on the left side of the screen. A list of options and their current values will appear on the right side of the screen. Right click on the option itself to modify the value or set it to the default.

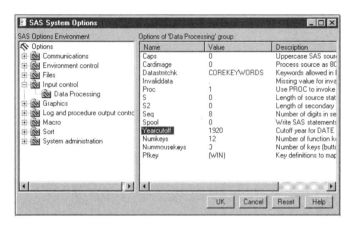

Common options The following are some common system options you might want to use:

CENTER	NOCENTER	This option works as a switch. CENTER centers your output on the page. NOCENTER left justifies your output.
DATE	NODATE	This is also a switch. With DATE, today's date will appear at the top of each page of output; with NODATE it will not.
NUMBER	NONUMBER	This switch controls whether or not page numbers appear on each page of SAS output.
LINESIZE = *n*	With LINESIZE you can control the maximum length of output lines. Possible values for *n* are 64 to 256.
PAGESIZE = *n*	PAGESIZE controls the maximum number of lines per page of output. Possible values for *n* are 15 to 32767.
PAGENO = *n*	Starts numbering output pages with *n*.
YEARCUTOFF = *yyyy*	Specifies the first year in a hundred-year span for interpreting two-digit dates.

2

" **P**ractice is the best of all instructors. "

Publius Syrus, *circa* 42 b.c.

" We all learned by doing, by experimenting (and often failing), and by asking questions. "

Jay Jacob Wind, SAS® user since 1980

CHAPTER 2

Getting Your Data into the SAS® System

2.1 Methods for Getting Your Data into the SAS System

Data can be in many different forms. Your data may be handwritten on a piece of paper, or typed into a raw data file on your computer. Perhaps your data are in a database file on your personal computer, or in a database management system (DBMS) on the mainframe computer at your office. Wherever your data reside, there is a way for SAS to use them. You may need to convert your data from one form to another, or SAS may be able to use your data in their current form. This section outlines several methods for getting your data into the SAS System. Most of these methods are covered in this book, but a few of the more advanced methods are merely mentioned so that you know they exist. We do not attempt to cover all methods available for getting your data into SAS, as new methods are continually being developed, and creative SAS users can always come up with clever methods that work for their own situations. But there is at least one method of getting your data into the SAS System explained in this book that will work for you.

Methods for getting your data into the SAS System can be put into four general categories:

♦ entering data directly into SAS data sets

♦ creating SAS data sets from raw data files

♦ converting other software's data files into SAS data sets

♦ reading other software's data files directly.

Naturally, the method you choose will depend on where your data are located, and what software tools are available to you. Some of the methods discussed here require that you have additional SAS products such as the SAS/ACCESS or SAS/FSP. But even if you don't have these products, you will still be able to get your data into the SAS System (it just may not be as easy).

Entering data directly into SAS data sets Two methods for entering your data directly into SAS data sets are the Viewtable window and SAS/FSP.

♦ The Viewtable window, discussed in section 2.11, is included with base SAS. Viewtable allows you to enter your data into a table form. You can define variables, or columns, and give them attributes such as names, lengths, and type (character or numeric).

♦ SAS/FSP, short for Full Screen Product, allows you to design custom data entry screens. It also has the capability for detecting data entry errors as they happen. The SAS/FSP product is licensed separately from base SAS, and is not covered in this book.

Creating SAS data sets from raw data files Most of this chapter is devoted to reading raw data files (also referred to as text, ASCII, sequential, or flat files). You can always read a raw data file since the DATA step is an integral part of base SAS. And, if your data are not already in a raw data file, chances are you can convert your data into a raw data file. There are two general methods for reading raw data files: the DATA step, and the IMPORT procedure or Import wizard.

♦ The DATA step is so versatile that it can read almost any type of raw data file. This method is covered in this chapter starting with section 2.2.

♦ The IMPORT procedure and the Import wizard, covered in section 2.17, are currently not available for all operating environments. These are simple methods for reading particular types of raw data files including Comma Separated Value (CSV) files, and other delimited files.

Converting other software's data files into SAS data sets Each software application has its own form for data files. While this is useful for software developers, it is troublesome for software users. Especially when your data are in one application, but you need to analyze them with another. There are several options for converting data from some applications into SAS data sets.

♦ Dynamic Data Exchange (DDE), covered in section 2.18, is available only for those working in a Windows operating environment. To use DDE, you must have the other Windows application (Excel for example) running on your computer at the same time as SAS. Then using DDE and the DATA step, you can convert data into SAS data sets.

♦ The IMPORT procedure and the Import wizard can be used to convert Excel, Lotus, dBase, and Microsoft Access files into SAS data sets if you have SAS/ACCESS for PC File Formats installed on your computer. This is covered in section 2.18.

♦ If you don't have SAS/ACCESS and you cannot use DDE, then you can always create a raw data file from your application and read the raw data file with either the DATA step or the IMPORT procedure. Many applications can create CSV files, which are easily read using the IMPORT procedure (covered in section 2.17) or the DATA step (covered in section 2.16).

Reading other software's data files directly Under certain circumstances you may be able to read data in your application's special form without converting to a SAS data set. This method is particularly useful when you have many people updating data files, and you want to make sure that you are using the most current data.

♦ The SAS/ACCESS products allow you to read data without converting your data into SAS data sets. In addition to SAS/ACCESS for PC File Formats already mentioned, there are SAS/ACCESS products for most of the popular database management systems including ORACLE, DB2, INGRES, and SYBASE. This method of data access is not covered in this book.

♦ There are also data engines that allow you to read data directly but are part of base SAS. The SPSS engine is covered in Appendix D. There are also engines for OSIRIS, old versions of SAS data sets, and SAS data sets in transport format. Check the online documentation for your operating environment for a complete list of available engines.

Given all these methods for getting your data into the SAS System, you are sure to find at least one method that will work for you, and you may end up using several different methods depending on circumstances and the nature of your data.

2.2 Telling SAS Where to Find Your Raw Data

Before you can analyze your data with SAS software, your data must be in a form that SAS can read. If your data are in raw data files (also referred to as text, ASCII, sequential, or flat files), you can use the DATA step to read the data and create a SAS data set. Your raw data may be either internal to your SAS program, or in a separate file. Either way, you must tell SAS where to find your data.

A raw data file can be viewed using simple text editors or system commands. For PC users, raw data files will either have no program associated with them, or they will be associated with simple editors like Notepad. In some operating environments, you can use commands to list the file, such as the cat or more commands in UNIX. Spreadsheet files are examples of data files that are not raw data. If you try using a text editor to look at a spreadsheet file, you will probably see lots of funny special characters you can't find on your keyboard. It may cause your computer to beep and chirp, making you wish you had that private office down the hall. It looks nothing like the nice neat rows and columns you see when you use your spreadsheet software to view the same file. Most personal computers these days will save you the embarrassment, and refuse to open a spreadsheet file in a text editor.

Internal raw data If you put your raw data directly in your SAS program, then your data are internal. You may want to do this when you have small amounts of data, or you are testing a program with a small test data set. Use the DATALINES statement to indicate internal data. The DATALINES statement must be the last statement in the DATA step. All lines in the SAS program following the DATALINES statement are considered data until SAS encounters a semicolon. The semicolon can be on a line by itself or at the end of a SAS statement which follows the data lines. Any statements following the data are part of a new step. If you are old enough to remember punching computer cards, you might like to use the CARDS statement instead. The CARDS statement and the DATALINES statement are synonymous. The following SAS program illustrates the use of the DATALINES statement. (The INPUT statement in the program tells SAS how to read the data. The INPUT statement is discussed in sections 2.3 through 2.7.)

```
* Read internal data into SAS data set uspresidents;
DATA uspresidents;
   INPUT President $ Party $ Number;
   DATALINES;
Adams      F  2
Lincoln    R 16
Grant      R 18
Kennedy    D 35
   ;
RUN;
```

External raw data files Usually you will want to keep your data in external files, separating the data from the program. This eliminates the chance that your data will accidentally be altered when you are editing your SAS program. Use the INFILE statement to tell SAS the filename and path, if appropriate, of the external file containing the data. The INFILE statement follows the DATA statement and must precede the INPUT statement. After the INFILE keyword, the file path and name are enclosed in single quotes. Examples from several operating environments follow:

Windows, NT, OS/2:	`INFILE 'c:\MyDir\President.dat';`
UNIX:	`INFILE '/home/mydir/president.dat';`
OpenVMS, VMS:	`INFILE '[username.mydir]president.dat';`
CMS:	`INFILE 'presiden data a';`
OS/390:	`INFILE 'MYID.PRESIDEN.DAT';`

Suppose the following data are in a file called President.dat in the directory MyRawData on the C drive (Windows, NT, OS/2):

```
Adams     F   2
Lincoln   R  16
Grant     R  18
Kennedy   D  35
```

The following program shows the use of the INFILE statement to read the external data file:

```
* Read data from external file into SAS data set;
DATA uspresidents;
   INFILE 'c:\MyRawData\President.dat';
   INPUT President $ Party $ Number;
RUN;
```

The SAS log Whenever you read data from an external file, SAS gives some very valuable information about the file in the SAS log. The following is an excerpt from the SAS log after running the previous program. Always check this information after you read a file as it could indicate problems. A simple comparison of the number of records read from the infile with the number of observations in the SAS data set can tell you a lot about whether or not SAS is reading your data correctly.

```
NOTE: The infile 'c:\MyRawData\President.dat' is:
      File Name=c:\MyRawData\President.dat,
      RECFM=V,LRECL=256
NOTE: 4 records were read from the infile 'c:\MyRawData\President.dat'.
      The minimum record length was 13.
      The maximum record length was 13.
NOTE: The data set WORK.USPRESIDENTS has 4 observations and 3 variables.
```

Long records In some operating environments, SAS assumes external files have a record length of 256 or less. (The record length is the number of characters, including spaces, on a data line.) If your data lines are long, and it looks like SAS is not reading all your data, then use the LRECL= option in the INFILE statement to specify a record length at least as long as the longest record in your data file.

```
INFILE 'c:\MyRawData\President.dat' LRECL=2000;
```

Check the SAS log to see that the maximum record length is as long as you think it should be.

2.3 Reading Raw Data Separated by Spaces

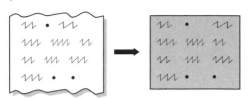

If the values in your raw data file are all separated by at least one space,[1] then using list input (also called free formatted input) to read the data may be appropriate. List input is an easy way to read raw data into SAS, but with ease come a few limitations. You must read all the data in a record—no skipping over unwanted values. Any missing data must be indicated with a period. Character data, if present, must be simple: no embedded spaces, and no values greater than eight characters in length.[2] If the data file contains dates or other values which need special treatment, then list input may not be appropriate. This may sound like a lot of restrictions, but a surprising number of data files can be read using list input.

The INPUT statement, which is part of the DATA step, tells SAS how to read your raw data. To write an INPUT statement using list input, simply list the variable names after the INPUT keyword in the order they appear in the data file. Generally, variable names must be 32 characters or fewer, start with a letter or an underscore, and contain only letters, underscores, or numerals. If the values are character (not numeric) then place a dollar sign ($) after the variable name. Leave at least one space between names, and remember to place a semicolon at the end of the statement. The following is an example of a simple list style INPUT statement.

```
INPUT Name $ Age Height;
```

This statement tells SAS to read three data values. The $ after Name indicates that it is a character variable, whereas the Age and Height variables are both numeric.

Example Your hometown has been overrun with toads this year. A local resident, having heard of frog jumping in California, had the idea of organizing a toad jump to cap off the annual town fair. For each contestant you have the toad's name, weight, and the jump distance from three separate attempts. If the toad is disqualified for any jump, then a period is used to indicate missing data. Here is what the data file ToadJump.dat looks like:

```
Lucky 2.3 1.9 . 3.0
Spot 4.6 2.5 3.1 .5
Tubs 7.1 . . 3.8
Hop 4.5 3.2 1.9 2.6
Noisy 3.8 1.3 1.8
1.5
Winner 5.7 . . .
```

This data file does not look very neat, but it does meet all the requirements for list input: the character data are eight characters or fewer and have no embedded spaces, all values are separated by at least one space, and missing data are indicated by a period. Notice that the data for Noisy have spilled over to the next data line. This is no problem since, by default, SAS will go to the next data line to read more data if there are more variables in the INPUT statement than there are values in the data line.

---

[1] SAS can read files with other delimiters such as commas or tabs using list input. This is shown in sections 2.16 and 2.17.

[2] It is possible to override this constraint using the LENGTH statement, discussed in section 8.13, which can change the length of character variables from the default of 8 to anything between 1 and 32767.

Here is the SAS program that will read the data:

```
* Create a SAS data set named toads;
* Read the data file ToadJump.dat using list input;
DATA toads;
    INFILE 'c:\MyRawData\ToadJump.dat';
    INPUT ToadName $ Weight Jump1 Jump2 Jump3;
* Print the data to make sure the file was read correctly;
PROC PRINT DATA = toads;
    TITLE 'SAS Data Set Toads';
RUN;
```

The variables ToadName, Weight, Jump1, Jump2, and Jump3 are listed after the keyword INPUT in the same order as they appear in the file. A dollar sign ($) after ToadName indicates that it is a character variable; all the other variables are numeric. A PROC PRINT statement is used to print the data values after reading them to make sure they are correct. The PRINT procedure, in its simplest form, prints the values for all variables and all observations in a SAS data set. The TITLE statement after the PROC PRINT tells SAS to put the text enclosed in quotes on the top of each page of output. If you had no TITLE statement in your program, SAS would put the words "The SAS System" at the top of each page.

The output will look like this:

```
                           SAS Data Set Toads                          1

              Toad
       Obs    Name      Weight    Jump1    Jump2    Jump3

        1     Lucky      2.3       1.9       .        3.0
        2     Spot       4.6       2.5      3.1       0.5
        3     Tubs       7.1        .        .        3.8
        4     Hop        4.5       3.2      1.9       2.6
        5     Noisy      3.8       1.3      1.8       1.5
        6     Winner     5.7        .        .         .
```

Because SAS had to go to a second data line to get the data for Noisy's final jump, the following note appears in the SAS log:

```
NOTE: SAS went to a new line when INPUT statement reached past the end of a line.
```

If you find this note in your SAS log when you didn't expect it, then you may have a problem. If so, look in section 8.4 which discusses this note in more detail.

2.4   Reading Raw Data Arranged in Columns

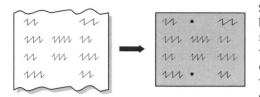

Some raw data files do not have spaces (or other delimiters) between all the values or periods for missing data—so the files can't be read using list input. But if each of the variable's values is always found in the same place in the data line, then you can use column input as long as all the values are character or standard numeric. Standard numeric data contain only numbers, decimal points, plus and minus signs, and E for scientific notation. Dates or numbers with embedded commas, for example, are not standard.

Column input has the following advantages over list input:

♦   spaces are not required between values

♦   missing values can be left blank

♦   character data can have embedded spaces

♦   you can skip unwanted variables.

Survey data are good candidates for column input. Most answers to survey questionnaires are single digits (0 through 9). If a space is entered between each value, then the file will be twice the size and require twice the typing of a file without spaces. Data files with street addresses, which often have embedded blanks, are also good candidates for column input. The street Martin Luther King Jr. Boulevard should be read as one variable not five, as it would be with list input. Data which can be read with column input can often also be read with formatted input or a combination of input styles (discussed in sections 2.5, 2.6, and 2.7).

With column input, the INPUT statement takes the following form: after the INPUT keyword, list the first variable's name. If the variable is character, leave a space; then place a $. After the $, or variable name if it is numeric, leave a space; then list the column or range of columns for that variable. The columns are positions of the characters or numbers in the data line and are not to be confused with columns like those you see in a spreadsheet. Repeat this for all the variables you want to read. The following shows a simple INPUT statement using column style.

```
INPUT Name $ 1-10 Age 11-13 Height 14-18;
```

The first variable, Name, is character and the data values are in columns 1 through 10. The Age and Height variables are both numeric, since they are not followed by a $, and data values for both of these variables are in the column ranges listed after their names.

Example   The local minor league baseball team, the Walla Walla Sweets, is keeping records about concession sales. A ballpark favorite are the sweet onion rings which are sold at the concession stands and also by vendors in the bleachers. The ballpark owners have a feeling that in games with lots of hits and runs more onion rings are sold in the bleachers than at the concession stands. They think they should send more vendors out into the bleachers when the game heats up, but need more evidence to back up their feelings.

For each home game they have the following information: name of opposing team, number of onion ring sales at the concession stands and in the bleachers, the number of hits for each team, and the final score for each team. The following is a sample of the data file named Onions.dat. For your reference, a column ruler showing the column numbers has been placed above the data:

```
----+----1----+----2----+----3----+----4
Columbia Peaches      35  67  1 10   2  1
Plains Peanuts       210      2  5   0  2
Gilroy Garlics       151035 12 11   7  6
Sacramento Tomatoes  124  85 15  4   9  1
```

Notice that the data file has the following characteristics, all making it a prime candidate for column input. All the values line up in columns, the team names have imbedded blanks, missing values are blank, and in one case there is not a space between data values. (Those Gilroy Garlics fans must really love onion rings.)

The following program shows how to read these data using column input:

```
* Create a SAS data set named sales;
* Read the data file Onions.dat using column input;
DATA sales;
   INFILE 'c:\MyRawData\Onions.dat';
   INPUT VisitingTeam $ 1-20 ConcessionSales 21-24 BleacherSales 25-28
         OurHits 29-31 TheirHits 32-34 OurRuns 35-37 TheirRuns 38-40;
* Print the data to make sure the file was read correctly;
PROC PRINT DATA = sales;
   TITLE 'SAS Data Set Sales';
RUN;
```

The variable VisitingTeam is character (indicated by a $) and reads the visiting team's name in columns 1 through 20. The variables ConcessionSales and BleacherSales read the concession and bleacher sales in columns 21 through 24 and 25 through 28, respectively. The number of hits for the home team, OurHits, and the visiting team, TheirHits, are read in columns 29 through 31 and 32 through 34, respectively. The number of runs for the home team, OurRuns, is read in columns 35 through 37, while the number of runs for the visiting team, TheirRuns, is in columns 38 through 40.

The output will look like this:

```
                        SAS Data Set Sales                              1

                     Concession Bleacher  Our Their  Our Their
    Obs    VisitingTeam      Sales     Sales  Hits  Hits Runs  Runs

     1   Columbia Peaches      35        67     1    10    2    1
     2   Plains Peanuts       210         .     2     5    0    2
     3   Gilroy Garlics        15      1035    12    11    7    6
     4   Sacramento Tomatoes  124        85    15     4    9    1
```

2.5 Reading Raw Data Not in Standard Format

Sometimes raw data are not straightforward numeric or character. For example, we humans easily read the number 1,000,001 as one million and one, but your trusty computer sees it as a character string. While the embedded commas make the number easier for us to interpret, they make the number impossible for the computer to recognize without some instructions. In SAS, informats are used to tell the computer how to interpret these types of data.

Informats are useful anytime you have non-standard data. (Standard numeric data contain only numbers, decimal points, minus signs, and E for scientific notation.) Numbers with embedded commas or dollar signs are examples of non-standard data. Other examples include data in hexadecimal or packed decimal formats. SAS has informats for reading these types of data as well.

Dates[1] are perhaps the most common non-standard data. Using date informats, SAS will convert conventional forms of dates like 10-31-2001 or 31OCT99 into a number, the number of days since January 1, 1960. This number is referred to as a SAS date value. (Why January 1, 1960? Who knows? Maybe 1960 was a good year for the SAS founders.) This turns out to be extremely useful when you want to do calculations with dates. For example, you can easily find someone's current age by subtracting the birth date from today's date and dividing by the number of days per year [(today's date - birth date)/365.25].

There are three general types of informats: character, numeric, and date. A table of selected SAS informats appears in section 2.6. The three types of informats have the following general forms:

Character	**Numeric**	**Date**
$informatw.	informatw.d	informatw.

The $ indicates character informats, INFORMAT is the name of the informat, *w* is the total width, and *d* is the number of decimal places (numeric informats only). Two informats do not have names: $*w*., which reads standard character data, and *w.d*, which reads standard numeric data. The period in an informat is very important because it distinguishes an informat from a variable name, which, by default, cannot contain any special characters except the underscore.

Use informats by placing the informat after the variable name in the INPUT statement; this is called formatted input. The following INPUT statement is an example of formatted input.

```
INPUT Name $10. Age 3. Height 5.1 BirthDate MMDDYY10.;
```

The columns read for each variable are determined by the starting point and the width of the informat. SAS always starts with the first column; so the data values for the first variable, Name, which has an informat of $10., are in columns 1 through 10. Now the starting point for the second variable is column 11, and SAS reads values for Age in columns 11 through 13. The values for the third variable, Height, are in columns 14 through 18. The five columns include the decimal place and the decimal point itself (150.3 for example). The values for the last variable, BirthDate, start in column 19 and are in a date form.

---

[1] Using dates in SAS is discussed in more detail in section 3.7.

Example This example illustrates the use of informats for reading data. The following data file, Pumpkin.dat, represents the results from a local pumpkin-carving contest. Each line includes the contestant's name, age, type (carved or decorated), the date the pumpkin was entered, and the scores from each of five judges.

```
Alicia Grossman   13 c 10-28-1999 7.8 6.5 7.2 8.0 7.9
Matthew Lee        9 D 10-30-1999 6.5 5.9 6.8 6.0 8.1
Elizabeth Garcia  10 C 10-29-1999 8.9 7.9 8.5 9.0 8.8
Lori Newcombe      6 D 10-30-1999 6.7 5.6 4.9 5.2 6.1
Jose Martinez      7 d 10-31-1999 8.9 9.5 10.0 9.7 9.0
Brian Williams    11 C 10-29-1999 7.8 8.4 8.5 7.9 8.0
```

The following program reads these data. Please note there are many ways to input these data, so if you imagined something else, that's OK.

```
* Create a SAS data set named contest;
* Read the file Pumpkin.dat using formatted input;
DATA contest;
    INFILE 'c:\MyRawData\Pumpkin.dat';
    INPUT Name $16. Age 3. +1 Type $1. +1 Date MMDDYY10.
        (Score1 Score2 Score3 Score4 Score5) (4.1);
* Print the data set to make sure the file was read correctly;
PROC PRINT DATA = contest;
    TITLE 'Pumpkin Carving Contest';
RUN;
```

The variable Name has an informat of $16., meaning that it is a character variable 16 columns wide. Variable Age has an informat of three, is numeric, three columns wide, and has no decimal places. The +1 skips over one column. Variable Type is character, and it is one column wide. Variable Date has an informat MMDDYY10. and reads dates in the form 10-31-1999 or 10/31/1999, each 10 columns wide. The remaining variables, Score1 through Score5, all require the same informat, 4.1. By putting the variables and the informat in separate sets of parentheses, you have only to list the informat once. Here are the results:

```
                  Pumpkin Carving Contest                          1

 Obs     Name       Age Type  Date²  Score1 Score2 Score3 Score4 Score5

   1  Alicia Grossman   13  c   14545   7.8    6.5    7.2    8.0    7.9
   2  Matthew Lee        9  D   14547   6.5    5.9    6.8    6.0    8.1
   3  Elizabeth Garcia  10  C   14546   8.9    7.9    8.5    9.0    8.8
   4  Lori Newcombe      6  D   14547   6.7    5.6    4.9    5.2    6.1
   5  Jose Martinez      7  d   14548   8.9    9.5   10.0    9.7    9.0
   6  Brian Williams    11  C   14546   7.8    8.4    8.5    7.9    8.0
```

---

[2] Notice that these dates are printed as the number of days since January 1, 1960. Section 4.5 discusses how to format these values into readable dates.

2.6 Selected Informats

Definitions of commonly used informats[1] along with the width range and default width.

Informat	Definition	Width range	Default width
Character			
$CHAR*w*.	Reads character data—does not trim leading or trailing blanks	1-32767	8 or length of variable
$HEX*w*.	Converts hexadecimal data to character data	1-32767	2
$*w*.	Reads character data—trims leading blanks	1-32767	none
Date, Time, and Datetime[2]			
DATE*w*.	Reads dates in form: *ddmmmyy* or *ddmmmyyyy*	7-32	7
DATETIME*w*.	Reads datetime values in the form: *ddmmmyy hh:mm:ss.ss*	13-40	18
DDMMYY*w*.	Reads dates in form: *ddmmyy* or *ddmmyyyy*	6-32	6
JULIAN*w*.	Reads Julian dates in form: *yyddd* or *yyyyddd*	5-32	5
MMDDYY*w*.	Reads dates in form: *mmddyy* or *mmddyyyy*	6-32	6
TIME*w*.	Reads time in form: *hh:mm:ss.ss* (hours:minutes:seconds—24-hour clock)	5-32	8
Numeric			
COMMA*w.d*	Removes embedded commas and $, converts left parentheses to minus sign	1-32	1
HEX*w*.	Converts hexadecimal to floating-point values if *w* is 16. Otherwise, converts to fixed-point.	1-16	8
IB*w.d*	Reads integer binary data	1-8	4
PD*w.d*	Reads packed decimal data	1-16	1
PERCENT*w*.	Converts percentages to numbers	1-32	6
w.d	Reads standard numeric data	1-32	none

[1] Check the online documentation for a complete list of informats.

[2] SAS date values are the number of days since January 1, 1960. Time values are the number of seconds past midnight, and datetime values are the number of seconds past midnight January 1, 1960.

Examples using the selected informats.

Informat	Input data	INPUT statement	Results
Character			
$CHAR*w*.	my cat 　my cat	INPUT Animal $CHAR10.;	my cat 　my cat
$HEX*w*.	6C6C	INPUT Name $HEX4.;	11　(ASCII)or %%　(EBCDIC)[3]
$*w*.	my cat 　my cat	INPUT Animal $10.;	my cat my cat
Date, Time, and Datetime			
DATE*w*.	1jan1961 1 jan 61	INPUT Day DATE10.;	366 366
DATETIME*w*.	1jan1960 10:30:15 1jan1961,10:30:15	INPUT Dt DATETIME18.;	37815 31660215
DDMMYY*w*.	01.01.61 02/01/61	INPUT Day DDMMYY8.;	366 367
JULIAN*w*.	61001 1961001	INPUT Day JULIAN7.;	366 366
MMDDYY*w*.	01-01-61 01/01/61	INPUT Day MMDDYY8.;	366 366
TIME*w*.	10:30 10:30:15	INPUT Time TIME8.;	37800 37815
Numeric			
COMMA*w.d*	$1,000,001 (1,234)	INPUT Income COMMA10.;	1000001 -1234
HEX*w*.	F0F3	INPUT Value HEX4.;	61683
IB*w.d*	▨[4]	INPUT Value IB4.;	255
PD*w.d*	▨[4]	INPUT Value PD4.;	255
PERCENT*w*.	5% (20%)	INPUT Value PERCENT5.;	0.05 -0.2
w.d	1234 -12.3	INPUT Value 5.1;	123.4 -12.3

---

[3] The EBCDIC character set is used on most IBM mainframe computers, while the ASCII character set is used on most other computers. So, depending on the computer you are using, you will get one or the other.

[4] These values cannot be printed.

2.7 Mixing Input Styles

Each of the three major input styles has its own advantages. List style is the easiest; column style is a bit more work; and formatted style is the hardest of the three. However, column and formatted styles do not require spaces (or other delimiters) between variables and can read embedded blanks. Formatted style can read special data such as dates. Sometimes you use one style, sometimes another, and sometimes the easiest way is to use a combination of styles. SAS is so flexible that you can mix and match any of the input styles for your own convenience.

Example The following raw data contain information about U.S. national parks: name, state (or states as the case may be), year established, and size in acres.

```
Yellowstone              ID/MT/WY 1872     4,065,493
Everglades               FL 1934           1,398,800
Yosemite                 CA 1864             760,917
Great Smoky Mountains NC/TN 1926            520,269
Wolf Trap Farm           VA 1966                 130
```

You could write the INPUT statement for these data in many ways—that is the point of this section. The following program shows one way to do it:

```
* Create a SAS data set named nationalparks;
* Read a data file Park.dat mixing input styles;
DATA nationalparks;
   INFILE 'c:\MyRawData\Park.dat';
   INPUT ParkName $ 1-22 State $ Year @40 Acreage COMMA9.;
PROC PRINT DATA = nationalparks;
   TITLE 'Selected National Parks';
RUN;
```

Notice that the variable ParkName is read with column style input, State and Year are read with list style input, and Acreage is read with formatted style input. The output looks like this:

```
                    Selected National Parks                    1

     Obs    ParkName                State      Year    Acreage

      1     Yellowstone             ID/MT/WY   1872    4065493
      2     Everglades              FL         1934    1398800
      3     Yosemite                CA         1864     760917
      4     Great Smoky Mountains   NC/TN      1926     520269
      5     Wolf Trap Farm          VA         1966        130
```

Sometimes programmers run into problems when they mix input styles. When SAS reads a line of raw data it uses a pointer to mark its place, but each style of input uses the pointer a little differently. With list style input, SAS automatically scans to the next non-blank field and starts reading. With column style input, SAS starts reading in the exact column you specify. But with formatted input, SAS just starts reading—wherever the pointer is, that is where SAS reads. Sometimes you need to move the pointer explicitly, and you can do that by using the column pointer, @*n*, where *n* is the number of the column SAS should move to.

In the preceding program, the column pointer @40 tells SAS to move to column 40 before reading the value for Acreage. If you removed the column pointer from the INPUT statement, as shown in the following statement, then SAS would start reading Acreage right after Year:

```
INPUT ParkName $ 1-22 State $ Year Acreage COMMA9.;
```

The resulting output would look like this:

```
                    Selected National Parks                       1

    Obs     ParkName                State      Year     Acreage

     1      Yellowstone             ID/MT/WY   1872       4065
     2      Everglades              FL         1934        .
     3      Yosemite                CA         1864        .
     4      Great Smoky Mountains   NC/TN      1926        5
     5      Wolf Trap Farm          VA         1966        .
```

Because Acreage was read with formatted input, SAS started reading right where the pointer was. Here is the data file with a column ruler for counting columns at the top and asterisks marking the place where SAS started reading the values of Acreage:

```
----+----1----+----2----|----3----+    4     +----5
Yellowstone             ID/MT/WY 1872 *  4,065,493
Everglades              FL 1934 *        1,398,800
Yosemite                CA 1864 *          760,917
Great Smoky Mountains   NC/TN 1926 *       520,269
Wolf Trap Farm          VA 1966 *              130
```

The COMMA9. informat told SAS to read nine columns, and SAS did that even when those columns were completely blank.

The column pointer, @n, has other uses too and can be used anytime you want SAS to skip backwards or forwards within a data line. You could use it, for example, to skip over unneeded data, reading some of the data but not all.

2.8 Listing the Contents of a SAS Data Set

To use a SAS data set, all you need to do is tell SAS the name and location of the data set you want, and SAS will figure out what is in it. SAS can do this because SAS data sets are self-documenting, which is another way of saying that SAS automatically stores information about the data set (also called the descriptor portion) along with the data. You can't display a SAS data set on your computer screen using a word processor. However, there is an easy way to get a description of a SAS data set; you simply run the CONTENTS procedure.

PROC CONTENTS is a simple procedure. In most cases you just type the keywords PROC CONTENTS and specify the data set you want with the DATA= option:

```
PROC CONTENTS DATA = data-set;
```

If you omit the DATA= option, then by default SAS will use the most recently created data set.

Example The following DATA step creates a data set so we can run PROC CONTENTS:

```
DATA funnies;
   INPUT Id Name $ Height Weight DoB MMDDYY8.;
   LABEL Id    = 'Identification no.'
      Height = 'Height in inches'
      Weight = 'Weight in pounds'
      DoB    = 'Date of birth';
   INFORMAT DoB MMDDYY8.;
   FORMAT DoB WORDDATE18.;
   DATALINES;
53 Susie    42   41   07-11-81
54 Charlie  46   55   10-26-54
55 Calvin   40   35   01-10-81
56 Lucy     46   52   01-13-55
   ;
* Use PROC CONTENTS to describe data set funnies;
PROC CONTENTS DATA = funnies;
RUN;
```

Note that the DATA step above includes a LABEL statement. For each variable, you can specify a label up to 256 characters long. These optional labels allow you to document your variables in more detail than is possible with just variable names. If you specify a LABEL statement in a DATA step, then the descriptions will be stored in the data set and will be printed by PROC CONTENTS. You can also use LABEL statements in PROC steps to customize your reports, but then the labels apply only for the duration of the PROC step and are not stored in the data set.

INFORMAT and FORMAT statements also appear in this program. You can use these optional statements to associate informats or formats with variables. Just as informats give SAS special instructions for reading a variable, formats give SAS special instructions for writing a variable. If you specify an INFORMAT or FORMAT statement in a DATA step, then the name of that informat or format will be saved in the data set and printed by PROC CONTENTS. FORMAT statements, like LABEL statements, can be used in PROC steps to customize your reports, but then the name of the format is not stored in the data set.[1]

---

[1] Sections 4.5 and 4.6 discuss standard SAS formats more thoroughly.

The output from PROC CONTENTS is like a table of contents for your data set:

```
                     The CONTENTS Procedure

❶ Data Set Name: WORK.FUNNIES        ❷ Observations:          4
   Member Type:   DATA               ❸ Variables:             5
   Engine:        V7                    Indexes:              0
❹ Created:        13:32 Friday, May 15, 1998   Observation Length:   40
   Last Modified: 13:32 Friday, May 15, 1998   Deleted Observations: 0
   Protection:                          Compressed:           NO
   Data Set Type:                       Sorted:               NO
   Label:


               -----Engine/Host Dependent Information-----
   Data Set Page Size:        4096
   Number of Data Set Pages:  1
   First Data Page:           1
   Max Obs per Page:          101
   Obs in First Data Page:    4
   Number of Data Set Repairs: 0
   File Name:                 C:\windows\TEMP\SAS Temporary
                              Files\#TD72977\funnies.sas7bdat
   Release Created:           7.00.00B
   Host Created:              WIN_95


             -----Alphabetic List of Variables and Attributes-----
     #   Variable ❶Type ❷Len  Pos ❸Format      ❹Informat ❺Label
   ----------------------------------------------------------------------
     5   DoB       Num    8   24   WORDDATE18.  MMDDYY8. Date of birth
     3   Height    Num    8    8                         Height in inches
     1   Id        Num    8    0                         Identification no.
     2   Name      Char   8   32
     4   Weight    Num    8   16                         Weight in pounds
```

The output starts with information about your data set and then describes each variable.

For the data set

❶ Data set name
❷ Number of observations
❸ Number of variables
❹ Date created

For each variable

❶ Type (numeric or character)
❷ Length (storage size in bytes)
❸ Format for printing (if any)
❹ Informat for input (if any)
❺ Label (if any)

2.9 Temporary versus Permanent SAS Data Sets

SAS data sets are available in two varieties: temporary and permanent. A temporary SAS data set is one that exists only during the current job or session and is automatically erased by SAS when you finish. If a SAS data set is permanent, that doesn't mean that it lasts for eternity, just that it remains when the job or session is finished.

Each type of data set has its own advantages. Sometimes you want to keep a data set for later use, and sometimes you don't. In this book, most of our examples use temporary data sets because we don't want to clutter up your disks. But, in general, if you use a data set more than once, it is more efficient to save it as a permanent SAS data set than to create a new temporary SAS data set every time you want to use the data.

Temporary SAS data sets You never explicity tell SAS to make a data set temporary or permanent; it is just implied by the name you give the data set when you create it in either a DATA step or a PROC step. The following program creates and then prints a temporary SAS data set named DISTANCE:

```
DATA distance;
   Miles = 26.22;
   Kilometers = 1.61 * Miles;
PROC PRINT DATA = distance;
RUN;
```

If you run this program, the log will contain this note about the new data set:

```
NOTE: The data set WORK.DISTANCE has 1 observations and 2 variables.
```

Permanent SAS data sets Starting with Version 7, creating and using permanent SAS data sets is a lot easier. You can now directly reference SAS data sets in your programs. Just take your operating environment's name for a SAS data set, enclose it in quotes, and put it in your program. The quotes tell SAS that this is a permanent SAS data set. For example, in the Windows operating environment you could run this:

```
DATA 'c:\MySASLib\distance';
   Miles = 26.22;
   Kilometers = 1.61 * Miles;
PROC PRINT DATA = 'c:\MySASLib\distance';
RUN;
```

This time the log contains this note:

```
NOTE: The data set c:\MySASLib\distance has 1 observations and 2 variables.
```

This is a permanent SAS data set, so SAS will not erase it. If you list the files in the MySASLib directory, you will see one named distance.sas7bdat. Notice that SAS automatically appended a file extension, even though no extension appeared in the SAS program.

Here is the general form of the DATA statement for creating permanent SAS data sets under different operating environments:

Windows, NT, OS/2:	DATA '*drive:\directory\filename*';
UNIX:	DATA '*/home/path/filename*';
OpenVMS, VMS:	DATA '*[userid.directory]filename*';
CMS:	DATA '*filename filetype filemode*';
OS/390:	DATA '*OS.data.set.name*';

For directory-based operating environments, if you leave out the directory or path, then SAS uses the current working directory. For example, this statement would create a permanent SAS data set named DISTANCE in your current working directory.

```
DATA 'distance';
```

Under Windows the name of the current working directory is displayed in the lower-right corner. You can change the directory temporarily by double-clicking on the directory name which will open the Change Folder window.

Understanding SAS data set names
It's not always obvious, but all SAS data sets have a two-level name. The first level is called its libref (short for SAS data library reference), and the second level is the member name that uniquely identifies the data set within that library. A libref is like an arrow pointing to a particular location. On some operating environments a libref refers to a physical location, such as a disk. On other systems it refers to a logical location, such as a directory or file.

Both the libref and member name follow the standard rules for valid SAS names. They must start with a letter or underscore and contain only letters, numerals, or underscores. However, librefs cannot be longer than eight characters while member names can be up to 32 characters long.

Here are some sample DATA statements and the characteristics of the data sets they create:

DATA statement	Libref	Member name	Type
DATA baytobreakers;	WORK	baytobreakers	temporary
DATA 'c:\MySASLib\ironman';	*automatically created*	ironman	permanent
DATA mysaslib.bostonmarathon;	mysaslib	bostonmarathon	permanent

The libref WORK is a special name reserved for temporary SAS data sets. If you don't put quotes around a data set name, and you don't specify a libref of your own (section 2.10 explains how to create librefs), then SAS will put your data set in the default WORK library. All data sets in the WORK library are erased by SAS at the end of the current job or session.

If you put quotes around your data set name, then you are using direct referencing, and SAS will create a permanent SAS data set. Since you haven't specified a libref, SAS will make up a libref for you. You don't need to know the name of the libref that SAS makes up, but it is there and you can see it in the SAS windowing environment by issuing the command LIBNAME which opens the LIBNAME window.

2.10 Using LIBNAME Statements with Permanent SAS Data Sets

A libref is a nickname that corresponds to the location of a SAS data library. When you use a libref as the first level in the name of a SAS data set, SAS knows to look for that data set in that location. You can define a libref using either a LIBNAME statement or, with some computers, operating environment control language.[1] The LIBNAME statement is the most universal (and therefore most portable) method of creating a libref. The basic form of the LIBNAME statement is

```
LIBNAME libref 'your-SAS-data-library';
```

After the keyword LIBNAME, you specify the libref and then the location of your permanent SAS data set in quotes. Librefs must be eight characters or shorter; start with a letter or underscore; and contain only letters, numerals, or underscores. Here is the syntax of LIBNAME statements for individual operating environments:

Windows, NT, OS/2:	`LIBNAME libref 'drive:\directory';`
UNIX:	`LIBNAME libref '/home/path';`
OpenVMS, VMS:	`LIBNAME libref '[userid.directory]';`
CMS:	`LIBNAME libref 'filemode';`
OS/390:	`LIBNAME libref 'OS.data.set.name';`

Creating a permanent SAS data set The following example creates a permanent SAS data set containing information about magnolia trees. For each type of tree the raw data file includes the scientific name, common name, maximum height, age at first blooming when planted from seed, whether evergreen or deciduous, and color of flowers.

```
M. grandiflora Southern Magnolia 80 15 E white
M. campbellii                     80 20 D rose
M. liliiflora  Lily Magnolia      12  4 D purple
M. soulangiana Saucer Magnolia    25  3 D pink
M. stellata    Star Magnolia      10  3 D white
```

This program sets up a libref named PLANTS pointing to the MySASLib directory on the C drive (Windows, OS/2). Then it reads the raw data from a file called Mag.dat, creating a permanent SAS data set named MAGNOLIA.

```
LIBNAME plants 'c:\MySASLib';
DATA plants.magnolia;
   INFILE 'c:\MyRawData\Mag.dat';
   INPUT ScientificName $ 1-14 CommonName $ 16-32 MaximumHeight
      AgeBloom Type $ Color $;
RUN;
```

[1] With batch processing under OS/390, you may use Job Control Language (JCL). The DDname is your libref.

The log contains this note showing the two-level data set name:

```
NOTE: The data set PLANTS.MAGNOLIA has 5 observations and 6 variables.
```

If you print a directory of files on your computer, you will not see a file named PLANTS.MAGNOLIA. That is because operating environments have their own systems for naming files. When run under Windows 95 with Version 7 of the SAS System, this data set will be called `magnolia.sas7bdat`. Under OS/390, the filename would be *OS.data.set.name*. Under CMS, it would be MAGNOLIA PLANTS. In other operating environments, the name will usually be a two-level name that starts with the SAS member name and then has a standard extension.

Reading a permanent SAS data set   To use a permanent SAS data set, you can include a LIBNAME statement in your program and refer to the data set by its two-level name. For instance, if you wanted to go back later and print the permanent data set created in the last example, you could use the following statements:

```
LIBNAME example 'c:\MySASLib';
PROC PRINT DATA = example.magnolia;
   TITLE 'Magnolias';
RUN;
```

This time the libref in the LIBNAME statement is EXAMPLE instead of PLANTS, but it points to the same location as before, the MySASLib directory on the C drive. The libref can change, but the member name, MAGNOLIA, stays the same.

The output looks like this:

```
                          Magnolias                                    1

                                     Maximum   Age
    Obs   ScientificName    CommonName    Height  Bloom  Type  Color

     1    M. grandiflora   Southern Magnolia     80     15    E    white
     2    M. campbellii                          80     20    D    rose
     3    M. liliiflora    Lily Magnolia         12      4    D    purple
     4    M. soulangiana   Saucer Magnolia       25      3    D    pink
     5    M. stellata      Star Magnolia         10      3    D    white
```

2.11   Entering Data with the Viewtable Window

The Viewtable window which is part of base SAS[1] is an easy way to create new data sets, or browse and edit existing data sets. True to its name, the Viewtable window displays tables (another name for data sets) in a tabular format. To open the Viewtable window, select Table Editor from the Tools menu. An empty Viewtable window will appear.

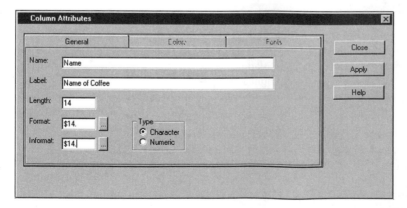

This table contains no data. Instead you see rows (or observations) labeled with numbers and columns (or variables) labeled with letters. You can start typing data into this default table, and SAS will automatically figure out if your columns are numeric or character. However, it's a good idea to tell SAS about your data so each column is set up the way you want. You do this with the Column Attributes window.

Column Attributes window   The letters at the tops of columns are default variable names. By right-clicking on a letter, you can open a Column Attributes window for that column. This window contains default values which you can replace with the values you desire. When you are satisfied with the values, click on Apply. To switch to a new column click on that column in the Viewtable window. When you are finished changing column attributes click on Close.

---

[1] If you are using a non-graphical monitor, then SAS uses FSVIEW to display your tables, so you also need SAS/FSP which is licensed separately.

Entering data Once you have defined your columns you are ready to type in your data. To move the cursor, click on a field, or use tab and arrow keys. Here is a table with column attributes defined and data entered.

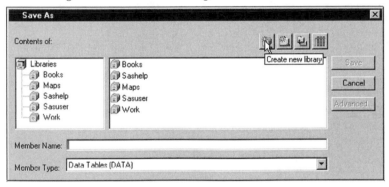

	Name of Coffee	Where Grown	Price
1	A.A.	Kenya	$9.99
2	Antigua	Guatemala	$9.99
3	Blue	Jamaica	$9.99
4	Harrar	Ethiopia	$8.99
5	Kaanapali Moka	Maui USA	$16.99
6	Kona	Hawaii USA	$18.99
7	Malulani	Molokai USA	$15.99
8	Mocha Pure	Yemen	$10.99
9	Santos	Brazil	$9.99
10	Supremo	Columbia	$10.99

Saving your table To save a table, select `Save As…` from the File menu. Select a library, and then specify the member name of your table. The libraries displayed correspond to locations (such as directories) on your computer. If you want to save your table in a different location, you can add another library by clicking on the `New Library` icon. Type in a name for the new library and its path. Then click on `OK`. You can specify the member name either by typing in the `Member Name` field, or by clicking on the library and then clicking on the icon of an existing table.

Opening an existing table To browse or edit an existing table, first select `Table Editor` from the Tools menu to open the Viewtable window. Then select `Open` from the File menu. Click on the library you want and then on the table name. If the table you want to open is not in any of the existing libraries, click on the `New Library` icon. Type in a name for the new library and its path. Then click on `OK`. To switch from browse mode (the default) to edit mode, select `Edit Mode` from the Edit menu.

Other features The Viewtable window has many other features including sorting, printing, adding and deleting rows, and viewing multiple rows (the default, called Table View) or viewing one row at a time (called Form View). You can control these features using either menus or icons.

Using your table in a SAS program Tables that you create in Viewtable can be used in programs just as tables created in programs can be used in Viewtable. For example, if you saved your table in the SASUSER library and named it COFFEE, you could print it with this program:

```
PROC PRINT DATA = Sasuser.coffee;
RUN;
```

2.12   Reading Multiple Lines of Raw Data per Observation

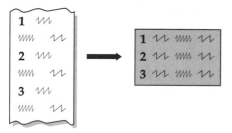

In a typical raw data file each line of data represents one observation, but sometimes the data for each observation are spread out over more than one line. Since SAS will automatically go to the next line if it runs out of data before it has read all the variables in an INPUT statement, you could just let SAS take care of figuring out when to go to a new line. But if you know that your data file has multiple lines of raw data per observation, it is better for you to explicitly tell SAS when to go to the next line than to make SAS figure it out. That way you won't get that suspicious SAS-went-to-a-new-line note in your log. To tell SAS when to skip to a new line, you simply add line pointers to your INPUT statement.

The line pointers, slash (/) and pound-*n* (#*n*), are like road signs telling SAS, "Go this way." To read more than one line of raw data for a single observation, you simply insert a slash into your INPUT statement when you want to skip to the next line of raw data. The #*n* line pointer performs the same action except that you specify the line number. The *n* in #*n* stands for the number of the line of raw data for that observation; so #2 means to go to the second line for that observation, and #4 means go to the fourth line. You can even go backwards using the #*n* line pointer, reading from line 4 and then from line 3, for example. The slash is simpler, but #*n* is more flexible.

Example   A colleague is trying to plan his next summer vacation, but he wants to go someplace where the weather is just right. He obtains data from a meteorology database. Unfortunately, he has not quite figured out how to export from this database and makes a rather odd file.

The file contains information about temperatures for the month of July for Alaska, Florida, and North Carolina. (If your colleague chooses the last state, maybe he can visit SAS Institute headquarters.) The first line contains the city and state, the second line lists the normal high temperature and normal low, and the third line contains the record high and low:

```
Nome AK
55 44
88 29
Miami FL
90 75
97 65
Raleigh NC
88 68
105 50
```

The following program reads the weather data from a file named Temperature.dat:

```
* Create a SAS data set named highlow;
* Read the data file using line pointers;
DATA highlow;
   INFILE 'c:\MyRawData\Temperature.dat';
   INPUT City $ State $
         / NormalHigh NormalLow
         #3 RecordHigh RecordLow;
PROC PRINT DATA = highlow;
   TITLE 'High and Low Temperatures for July';
RUN;
```

The INPUT statement reads the values for City and State from the first line of data. Then the slash tells SAS to move to column 1 of the next line of data before reading NormalHigh and NormalLow. Likewise, the #3 tells SAS to move to column 1 of the third line of data for that observation before reading RecordHigh and RecordLow. As usual, there is more than one way to write this INPUT statement. You could replace the slash with #2 or replace #3 with a slash.

This note appears in the log:

```
NOTE: 9 records were read from the infile 'c:\MyRawData\Temperature.dat'.

      The minimum record length was 5.

      The maximum record length was 10.

NOTE: The data set WORK.HIGHLOW has 3 observations and 6 variables.
```

Notice that while nine records were read from the infile, the SAS data set contains just three observations. Usually this would set off alarms in your mind, but here it confirms that indeed three data lines were read for every observation just as planned. You should always check your log, particularly when using line pointers.

The output looks like this:

```
              High and Low Temperatures for July                 1

                           Normal    Normal    Record    Record
     Obs    City    State    High      Low       High      Low

      1     Nome     AK        55       44        88        29
      2     Miami    FL        90       75        97        65
      3     Raleigh  NC        88       68       105        50
```

2.13   Reading Multiple Observations per Line of Raw Data

There ought to be a Murphy's law of data: whatever form data can take, it will. Normally SAS assumes that each line of raw data represents exactly one observation, no more and no less. When you have multiple observations per line of raw data, you can use double trailing at signs (@@) at the end of your INPUT statement. This line-hold specifier is like a stop sign telling SAS, "Stop, hold that line of raw data." SAS will hold that line of data, continuing to read observations until it either runs out of data or reaches an INPUT statement that does not end with a double trailing @.

Example   Suppose you have a colleague who is planning a vacation and has obtained a file containing data about rainfall for the three cities he is considering. The file contains the name of each city, the state, average rainfall for the month of July, and average number of days with measurable precipitation in July. The raw data look like this:

```
Nome AK 2.5 15 Miami FL 6.75
18 Raleigh NC . 12
```

Notice that in this data file the first line stops in the middle of an observation. The following program reads these data from a file named Precipitation.dat and uses an @@ so SAS does not automatically go to a new line of raw data for each observation:

```
* Input more than one observation from each record;
DATA rainfall;
   INFILE 'c:\MyRawData\Precipitation.dat';
   INPUT City $ State $ NormalRain MeanDaysRain @@;
PROC PRINT DATA = rainfall;
   TITLE 'Normal Total Precipitation and';
   TITLE2 'Mean Days with Precipitation for July';
RUN;
```

These notes will appear in the log:

```
NOTE: 2 records were read from the infile 'c:\MyRawData\Precipitation.dat'
      The minimum record length was 18.
      The maximum record length was 28.

NOTE: SAS went to a new line when INPUT statement reached past the
      end of a line.

NOTE: The data set WORK.RAINFALL has 3 observations and
      4 variables.
```

While only two records were read from the raw data file, the RAINFALL data set contains three observations. The log also includes a note saying SAS went to a new line when the INPUT statement reached past the end of a line. This means that SAS came to the end of a line in the middle of an observation and continued reading with the next line of raw data. Normally these messages would indicate a problem, but in this case they are exactly what you want.

The output looks like this:

```
                   Normal Total Precipitation and              1
               Mean Days with Precipitation for July


                                        Normal      Mean
            Obs     City      State      Rain      DaysRain

             1      Nome       AK        2.50        15
             2      Miami      FL        6.75        18
             3      Raleigh    NC         .          12
```

2.14   Reading Part of a Raw Data File

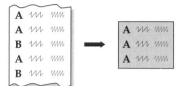

At some time you may find that you need to read a small fraction of the records in a large data file. For example, you might be reading U.S. census data and want only female heads-of-household who have incomes above $125,000 and live in Walla Walla, Washington. You could read all the records in the data file and then throw out the unneeded ones, but that would waste time.

Luckily, you don't have to read all the data before you tell SAS whether to keep an observation. Instead, you can read just enough variables to decide whether to keep the current observation, then end the INPUT statement with an at sign (@), called a trailing at. This tells SAS to hold that line of raw data. While the trailing @ holds that line, you can test the observation with an IF statement to see if it's one you want to keep. If it is, then you can read data for the remaining variables with a second INPUT statement. Without the trailing @, SAS would automatically start reading the next line of raw data with each INPUT statement.

The trailing @ is really a special case of the column pointer, @*n*, introduced in section 2.7. By specifying a number after the @ sign, you tell SAS to move to a particular column. By using an @ without specifying a column, it is as if you are telling SAS, "Stay tuned for more information. Don't touch that dial!" SAS will hold that line of data until it reaches either the end of the DATA step, or an INPUT statement that does not end with a trailing @.

Example   You want to read part of a raw data file containing local traffic data for freeways and surface streets. The data include information about the type of street, name of street, the average number of vehicles per hour traveling that street during the morning, and the average number of vehicles per hour for the evening. Here are the raw data:

```
freeway 408                            3684 3459
surface Martin Luther King Jr. Blvd.   1590 1234
surface Broadway                       1259 1290
surface Rodeo Dr.                      1890 2067
freeway 608                            4583 3860
freeway 808                            2386 2518
surface Lake Shore Dr.                 1590 1234
surface Pennsylvania Ave.              1259 1290
```

Suppose you want to see only the freeway data at this point so you read the raw data file, Traffic.dat, with this program:

```
* Use a trailing @ to delete surface streets;
DATA freeways;
   INFILE 'c:\MyRawData\Traffic.dat';
   INPUT Type $ @;
   IF Type = 'surface' THEN DELETE;
   INPUT Name $ 9-38 AMTraffic PMTraffic;
PROC PRINT DATA = freeways;
   TITLE 'Traffic for Freeways';
RUN;
```

Notice that there are two INPUT statements. The first reads the character variable Type and then ends with an @. The trailing @ holds each line of data while the IF statement tests it. The second INPUT statement reads Name (in columns 9 through 38), AMTraffic, and PMTraffic. If an observation has a value of surface for the variable Type, then the second INPUT statement never executes. Instead SAS returns to the beginning of the DATA step to process the next observation and does not add the unwanted observation to the FREEWAYS data set. (Do not pass go, do not collect $200.)

When you run this program, the log will contain the following two notes, one saying that eight records were read from the input file and another saying that the new data set contains only three observations:

```
NOTE: 8 records were read from the infile 'c:\MyRawData\Traffic.dat'.
      The minimum record length was 47.
      The maximum record length was 47.

NOTE: The data set WORK.FREEWAYS has 3 observations and 4 variables.
```

The other five observations were dropped because they did not satisfy the IF statement. The output looks like this:

```
                   Traffic for Freeways                        1

      Obs      Type       Name      AMTraffic     PMTraffic
       1      freeway      408         3684          3459
       2      freeway      608         4583          3860
       3      freeway      808         2386          2518
```

The double trailing @, discussed in the previous section, is similar to the trailing @. Both are line-hold specifiers; the difference is how long they hold a line of data for input. The trailing @ holds a line of data for subsequent INPUT statements, but releases that line of data when SAS returns to the top of the DATA step to begin building the next observation. The double trailing @ holds a line of data for subsequent INPUT statements even when SAS starts building a new observation. In both cases, the line of data is released if SAS reaches a subsequent INPUT statement that does not contain a line-hold specifier.

2.15 Controlling Input with Options in the INFILE Statement

So far in this chapter, we have seen ways to use the INPUT statement to read many different types of raw data. When reading raw data files, SAS makes certain assumptions. For example, SAS starts reading with the first data line and, if SAS runs out of data on a line, it automatically goes to the next line to read values for the rest of the variables. Most of the time this is OK, but some data files can't be read using the default assumptions. The options in the INFILE statement change the way SAS reads raw data files. The following options are useful for reading particular types of data files. Place these options after the filename in the INFILE statement.

FIRSTOBS= The FIRSTOBS= option tells SAS at what line to begin reading data. This is useful if you have a data file that contains descriptive text or header information at the beginning, and you want to skip over these lines to begin reading the data. The following data file, for example, has a description of the data in the first two lines:

```
Ice-cream sales data for the summer of 1999
Flavor      Location   Boxes sold
Chocolate   213        123
Vanilla     213        512
Chocolate   415        242
```

The following program uses the FIRSTOBS= option to tell SAS to start reading data on the third line of the file:

```
DATA icecream;
   INFILE 'c:\MyRawData\Sales.dat' FIRSTOBS = 3;
   INPUT Flavor $ 1-9 Location BoxesSold;
RUN;
```

OBS= The OBS= option can be used anytime you want to read only a part of your data file. It tells SAS to stop reading when it gets to that line in the raw data file. Note that it does not necessarily correspond to the number of observations. If, for example, you are reading two raw data lines for each observation, then an OBS=100 would read 100 data lines, and the resulting SAS data set would have 50 observations. The OBS= option can be used with the FIRSTOBS= option to read lines from the middle of the file. For example, suppose the ice-cream sales data had a remark at the end of the file that was not part of the data.

```
Ice-cream sales data for the summer of 1999
Flavor      Location   Boxes sold
Chocolate   213        123
Vanilla     213        512
Chocolate   415        242
Data verified by Blake White
```

With FIRSTOBS=3 and OBS=5, SAS will start reading this file on the third data line and stop reading after the fifth data line.

```
DATA icecream;
   INFILE 'c:\MyRawData\Sales.dat' FIRSTOBS = 3 OBS=5;
   INPUT Flavor $ 1-9 Location BoxesSold;
RUN;
```

MISSOVER By default, SAS will go to the next data line to read more data if SAS has reached the end of the data line and there are still more variables in the INPUT statement that have not been assigned values. The MISSOVER option tells SAS that if it runs out of data, don't go to the next data line. Instead, assign missing values to any remaining variables. The following data file illustrates where this option may be useful. This file contains test scores for a self-paced course. Since not all students complete all the tests, some have more scores than others.

```
Nguyen   89 76 91 82
Ramos    67 72 80 76 86
Robbins  76 65 79
```

The following program reads the data for the five test scores, assigning missing values to tests not completed:

```
DATA class102;
   INFILE 'c:\MyRawData\Scores.dat' MISSOVER;
   INPUT Name $ Test1 Test2 Test3 Test4 Test5;
RUN;
```

TRUNCOVER You need the TRUNCOVER option when you are reading data using column or formatted input and some data lines are shorter than others. If a variable's field extends past the end of the data line, then, by default, SAS will go to the next line to start reading the variable's value. This option tells SAS to read data for the variable until it reaches the end of the data line, or the last column specified in the format or column range, whichever comes first. The next file contains addresses and must be read using column or formatted input because the street names have embedded blanks. Note that the data lines are all different lengths:

```
John Garcia     114   Maple Ave.
Sylvia Chung    1302  Washington Drive
Martha Newton    45   S.E. 14th St.
```

This program uses column input to read the address file. Because some of the addresses stop before the end of the variable Street's field (columns 22 through 37), you need the TRUNCOVER option. Without the TRUNCOVER option, SAS would try to go to the next line to read the data for Street on the first and third records.

```
DATA homeaddress;
   INFILE 'c:\MyRawData\Address.dat' TRUNCOVER;
   INPUT Name $ 1-15 Number 16-19 Street $ 22-37;
RUN;
```

TRUNCOVER is similar to MISSOVER. Both will assign missing values to variables if the data line ends before the variable's field starts. But when the data line ends in the middle of a variable field, TRUNCOVER will take as much as is there, whereas MISSOVER will assign the variable a missing value.

2.16 Reading Delimited Files with the DATA Step

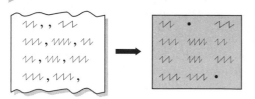

Delimited files are raw data files that have a special character separating data values. Many programs can save data as delimited files, often with commas or tab characters for delimiters. SAS gives you two options for the INFILE statement that make it easy to read delimited data files: the DLM= option and the DSD option.

The DLM= option If you read your data using list input, the DATA step expects your file to have spaces between your data values. The DELIMITER=, or DLM=, option in the INFILE statement allows you to read data files with other delimiters. The comma and tab characters are common delimiters found in data files, but you could read data files with any delimiter character by just enclosing the delimiter character in quotes after the DLM= option (i.e., DLM='&').

Example The following file is comma-delimited where students' names are followed by the number of books they read for each week in a summer reading program:

```
Grace,3,1,5,2,6
Martin,1,2,4,1,3
Scott,9,10,4,8,6
```

This program uses list input to read the student data file specifying the comma as the delimiter:

```
DATA reading;
   INFILE 'c:\MyRawData\Books.dat' DLM = ',';
   INPUT Name $ Week1 Week2 Week3 Week4 Week5;
RUN;
```

If the same data had tab characters between values instead of commas, then you could use the following program to read the file. This program uses the DLM='09'X option. In ASCII, 09 is the hexadecimal equivalent of a tab character, and the notation '09'X means a hexadecimal 09. If your computer uses EBCDIC (IBM mainframes) instead of ASCII, then use DLM='05'X.

```
DATA reading;
   INFILE 'c:\MyRawData\Books.txt' DLM = '09'X;
   INPUT Name $ Week1 Week2 Week3 Week4 Week5;
RUN;
```

By default, SAS interprets two or more delimiters in a row as a single delimiter. If your file has missing values, and two delimiters in a row indicate a missing value, then you will also need the DSD option in the INFILE statement.

The DSD option The DSD (Delimited Separated Data) option for the INFILE statement does three things for you. First, it ignores delimiters in data values enclosed in quotes. Second, it does not read quotes as part of the data value. Third, it treats two delimiters in a row as a missing value. The DSD option assumes that the delimiter is a comma. If your delimiter is not a comma then you can use the DLM= option with the DSD option to specify the delimiter. For example, to read a tab-delimited ASCII file with missing values indicated by two consecutive tab characters use

```
INFILE 'file-specification' DLM='09'X DSD;
```

CSV files Comma Separated Value files, or CSV files, are a common type of file that can be read with the DSD option. Many programs, such as Excel, can save data in CSV format. These files have commas for delimiters and consecutive commas for missing values; if there are commas in any of the data values, then those values are enclosed in quotes.

Example The following example illustrates how to read a CSV file using the DSD option. Jerry's Coffee Shop employs local bands to attract customers. Jerry keeps records of the number of customers for each band, for each night they play in his shop. The band's name is followed by the date and the number of customers present at 8 p.m., 9 p.m., 10 p.m., and 11 p.m.

```
Lupine Lights,5/15/1999,45,63,70,
Awesome Octaves,6/03/1999,17,28,44,12
"Stop, Drop, and Rock-N-Roll",7/10/1999,34,62,77,91
The Silveyville Jazz Quartet,7/19/1999,38,30,42,43
Catalina Converts,8/28/1999,56,,65,34
```

Notice that the name of one group has embedded commas and is enclosed in quotes. Also, the last group has a missing data point for the 9 p.m. hour as indicated by two consecutive commas. Use the DSD option in the INFILE statement to read this data file. It is also prudent, when using the DSD option, to add the MISSOVER option if there is any chance that you have missing data at the end of your data lines (as in the first line of this data file). The MISSOVER option tells SAS that if it runs out of data, don't go to the next data line to continue reading. Here is the program that will read this data file:

```
DATA music;
   INFILE 'c:\MyRawData\Bands.csv' DLM = ',' DSD MISSOVER;
   LENGTH BandName $30;
   INFORMAT GigDate MMDDYY10.;
   INPUT BandName GigDate EightPM NinePM TenPM ElevenPM;
PROC PRINT DATA = music;
   TITLE 'Customers at Each Gig';
RUN;
```

Notice that we also added a LENGTH statement. The LENGTH statement defines the variable BandName as character with a length of 30. Without the LENGTH statement, the data values for BandName would be truncated to the default length of 8 characters. Also, values for the GigDate variable are read using an MMDDYY10. informat. The results of the PROC PRINT follow.

		Customers at Each Gig				1
Obs	BandName	Gig Date[1]	Eight PM	Nine PM	Ten PM	Eleven PM
1	Lupine Lights	14379	45	63	70	.
2	Awesome Octaves	14398	17	28	44	12
3	Stop, Drop, and Rock-N-Roll	14435	34	62	77	91
4	The Silveyville Jazz Quartet	14444	38	30	42	43
5	Catalina Converts	14484	56	.	65	34

---

[1] Notice that these dates are printed as the number of days since January 1, 1960. Section 4.5 discusses how to format these values into readable dates.

2.17 Reading Delimited Files with the IMPORT Procedure

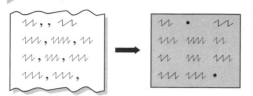

We suspect that by now you have realized that with SAS there is usually more than one way to accomplish the same result. In section 2.16 we showed you how to read delimited data files using the DATA step; now we are going to show you how to read delimited files a different way: using the IMPORT procedure.[1]

There are a few things that PROC IMPORT does for you that make it easy to read certain types of data files. IMPORT will scan your data file and automatically determine the variable types (character or numeric), will assign proper lengths to the character variables, and can recognize some date formats. IMPORT will treat two consecutive delimiters in your data file as a missing value, will read values enclosed by quotes, and assign missing values to variables when it runs out of data on a line. Also, if you want, you can use the first line in your data file for the variable names. The IMPORT procedure actually writes a DATA step for you, and after you submit your program, you can look in the Log window to see the DATA step it produced.

The simplest form of the IMPORT procedure is

```
PROC IMPORT DATAFILE = 'filename' OUT = data-set;
```

where the file you want to read follows the DATAFILE= option, and the name of the SAS data set you want to create follows the OUT= option. SAS will determine the file type by the extension of the file as shown in the following table.

Type of File	Extension	DBMS Identifier
Comma-delimited	.csv	CSV
Tab-delimited	.txt	TAB
Delimiters other than commas or tabs		DLM

If your file does not have the proper extension, or your file is of type DLM, then you must use the DBMS= option in the PROC IMPORT statement. Another option that you might need is REPLACE. If you already have a SAS data set with the name you specified in the OUT= option, then IMPORT will not overwrite it. If you want to overwrite it, then use the REPLACE option. The following code shows both the REPLACE and the DBMS options:

```
PROC IMPORT DATAFILE = 'filename' OUT = data-set
     DBMS = identifier REPLACE;
```

The IMPORT procedure will, by default, get variable names from the first line in your data file. If you do not want this, then add the GETNAMES=NO statement after the PROC IMPORT statement. IMPORT will assign the variables the names VAR1, VAR2, VAR3, and so on. Also if your data file is type DLM, IMPORT assumes that the delimiter is a space. If you have a different delimiter, then specify it in the DELIMITER= statement. The following shows both these statements:

```
PROC IMPORT DATAFILE = 'filename' OUT = data-set
     DBMS = DLM REPLACE;
   GETNAMES = NO;
   DELIMITER = 'delimiter-character';
RUN;
```

---

[1] At the time this book was written, the IMPORT procedure was available on OS/2, UNIX, VMS, and Windows.

Example The following example uses the data from the previous section about Jerry's Coffee Shop, where the band name is followed by the gig date and the number of customers present at 8 p.m., 9 p.m., 10 p.m., and 11 p.m. However, this time the first line of the file contains the variable names.

```
Band Name,Gig Date,Eight PM,Nine PM,Ten PM,Eleven PM
Lupine Lights,5/15/1999,45,63,70,
Awesome Octaves,6/03/1999,17,28,44,12
"Stop, Drop, and Rock-N-Roll",7/10/1999,34,62,77,91
The Silveyville Jazz Quartet,7/19/1999,38,30,42,43
Catalina Converts,8/28/1999,56,,65,34
```

Here is the program that will read this data file:

```
PROC IMPORT DATAFILE ='c:\MyRawData\Bands.csv' OUT = music REPLACE;
 PROC PRINT DATA = music;
   TITLE 'Customers at Each Gig';
RUN;
```

Here are the results of the PROC PRINT. Notice that GigDate is a readable date. This is because IMPORT automatically assigns informats and formats to some forms of dates. (See section 4.5 for a discussion of formats.)

```
                         Customers at Each Gig                         1

     Obs    Band_Name                                Gig_Date    Eight_PM

      1     Lupine Lights                           05/15/1999      45
      2     Awesome Octaves                         06/03/1999      17
      3     Stop, Drop, and Rock-N-Roll             07/10/1999      34
      4     The Silveyville Jazz Quartet            07/19/1999      38
      5     Catalina Converts                       08/28/1999      56

     Obs      Nine_PM        Ten_PM      Eleven_PM

      1          63            70             .
      2          28            44            12
      3          62            77            91
      4          30            42            43
      5           .            65            34
```

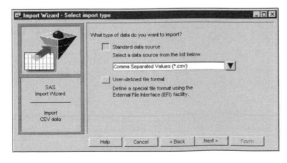

The Import Wizard If you would rather use a Graphical User Interface (GUI) to read your delimited data files, then try the Import wizard. Start the Import wizard by selecting `Import` from the File menu. You can import the same types of delimited files through the Import wizard as you can with the IMPORT procedure. Once you start the wizard, it will guide you through choices and convert your data file into a SAS data set.

2.18   Reading PC Database Files with DDE or the IMPORT Procedure

Two methods for reading PC database files are Dynamic Data Exchange (DDE) and the IMPORT procedure (or the Import wizard). Each has limitations. DDE can be used only in Windows operating environments and when the other PC application is running. The IMPORT procedure requires SAS/ACCESS for PC File Formats to read PC database files. If these limitations do not apply to your situation, then both these methods can be very useful.

DDE For Windows systems only, you can use DDE, or Dynamic Data Exchange, to read other file types. To use DDE you must have the other application running at the same time as SAS.

Example Suppose you have the following Excel spreadsheet up on your computer screen.

	A	B	C	D	E	F	G
1	Visiting Team	C Sales	B Sales	Our Hits	Their Hits	Our Runs	Their Runs
2	Columbia Peaches	35	67	1	10	2	1
3	Plains Peanuts	210		2	5	0	2
4	Gilroy Garlics	15	1035	12	11	7	6
5	Sacramento Tomatoes	124	85	15	4	9	1

Copy the rows and columns you want to read into SAS (A2 to G5) onto the clipboard, then, without closing Excel, submit the following SAS program:

```
* Read an Excel spreadsheet using DDE;
FILENAME baseball DDE 'CLIPBOARD';
DATA sales;
   INFILE baseball NOTAB DLM = '09'x DSD MISSOVER;
   LENGTH VisitingTeam $ 20;
   INPUT VisitingTeam CSales BSales OurHits TheirHits
        OurRuns TheirRuns;
RUN;
```

The FILENAME statement defines a fileref (BASEBALL) as type DDE and specifies that you want to read the contents of the clipboard. If you know the DDE triplet for your data then you can replace the keyword CLIPBOARD with the DDE triplet and then you do not have to copy your data to the clipboard. By default, DDE assumes there are spaces between your data values. So if you have embedded spaces in your data, then you will need the NOTAB and the DLM='09'x options in the INFILE statement. These two options tell SAS to put a tab character (NOTAB) between values and define the tab character as the delimiter (DLM='09'x). In addition, if you have missing values in your data, you will want to add the DSD and MISSOVER options to the INFILE statement. The DSD option treats two delimiters in a row as missing data and the MISSOVER option tells SAS not to go to the next data line to continue reading data if it runs out of data on the current line.

The advantage of using DDE is that you do not need any additional SAS products, and you can read the file directly from another Windows application. The disadvantage is that you must be very careful to define the variables properly and watch out for missing values and embedded spaces in your data.

The IMPORT procedure or the Import wizard If you have SAS/ACCESS for PC File Formats installed on your computer, then you can use the IMPORT procedure or the Import wizard to read data from several popular PC applications. The Import wizard is a Graphical User Interface (GUI) that performs the same function as the IMPORT procedure and can be accessed from the File menu.

The following is the general form of the IMPORT procedure:

```
PROC IMPORT DATAFILE = 'filename' OUT = data-set
    DBMS = identifier REPLACE;
```

where *filename* is the file you want to read and *data-set* is the name of the SAS data set you want to create. The REPLACE option tells SAS to replace the SAS data set named in the OUT= option if it already exists. Except for Excel 97 files, if your data file has the proper extension, as shown in the following table, then you do not need the DBMS= option.

Type of File	Extension	DBMS Identifier[1]
Excel 4 or 5	.xls	EXCEL
Excel 97		EXCEL97
Lotus Files	.wk1, .wk3, .wk4	WK1, WK3, WK4
dBase	.dbf	DBF

Example The following program reads the Excel file used in the previous example using the IMPORT procedure. Excel does not need to be running to use the IMPORT procedure.

```
* Read an Excel spreadsheet using PROC IMPORT;
PROC IMPORT DATAFILE = 'c:\MyExcelFiles\Onions2.xls' OUT = sales2;
PROC PRINT DATA = sales2;
    TITLE 'SAS Data Set Read From Excel File';
RUN;
```

By default, the IMPORT procedure will take the variable names from the first row of the spreadsheet (Excel and Lotus only). If you do not want this, then you can add the GETNAMES=NO statement to the procedure and SAS will name the variables VAR1, VAR2, VAR3, and so on.

Here are the results of the above program:

```
                  SAS Data Set Read From Excel File               1


                                          Their          Their
    Obs VisitingTeam      CSales  BSales OurHits Hits OurRuns  Runs
      1 Columbia Peaches      35      67       1   10       2     1
      2 Plains Peanuts       210       .       2    5       0     2
      3 Gilroy Garlics        15    1035      12   11       7     6
      4 Sacramento Tomatoes  124      85      15    4       9     1
```

---

[1] It is also possible to import Microsoft Access files; see the online documentation for more information.

2.19   Writing Delimited Files with the EXPORT Procedure

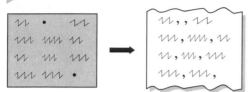

Generally you use SAS to produce a report or analysis, but sometimes your goal might be to create a data file for use with some other software package. SAS can write data files in many different formats including space-, comma-, and tab-delimited files. Many types of software, including spreadsheet and word processing software, can read delimited files of one kind or another. An easy way to create these data files is with PROC EXPORT.[1]

The general form of PROC EXPORT is

```
PROC EXPORT DATA = data-set OUTFILE = 'filename';
```

where *data-set* is the SAS data set you are reading, and *filename* is the name you make up for the output data file. The following statement tells SAS to read a temporary SAS data set named HOTELS and write a comma-delimited file named Hotels.csv in a directory named MyRawData on the C drive (Windows, NT, OS/2).

```
PROC EXPORT DATA = hotels OUTFILE = 'c:\MyRawData\Hotels.csv';
```

SAS uses the last part of the filename, called the file extension, to decide what type of file to create. You can also specify the file type by adding the DBMS= option. The following table shows the filename extensions and DBMS identifiers currently available with base SAS.[2]

Type of file	Extension	DBMS Identifier
Comma-delimited	.csv	CSV
Tab-delimited	.txt	TAB
Space-delimited		DLM

Notice that for space-delimited files, there is no standard extension so you must use the DBMS= option. The REPLACE option tells SAS that it is ok to replace any existing file with the same name. The following statement, containing the DBMS= option, tells SAS to create a space-delimited file named Hotels.spc and to replace any other file with that name.

```
PROC EXPORT DATA = hotels OUTFILE = 'c:\MyRawData\Hotels.spc'
   DBMS = DLM REPLACE;
```

Example   A travel company maintains a SAS database containing information about golf courses. For each golf course the file includes its name, number of holes, par, yardage, and greens fees. Here is a subset of the data:

```
Kapalua Plantation 18 73 7263 125.00
Pukalani            18 72 6945  55.00
Sandlewood          18 72 6469  35.00
Silversword         18 71 6801  57.00
Waiehu Municipal    18 72 6330  25.00
Grand Waikapa       18 72 6122 200.00
```

---

[1] At the time this book was written, the EXPORT procedure was available on OS/2, UNIX, VMS, and Windows.

[2] In addition, if you have SAS/ACCESS for PC File Formats, then you can use PROC EXPORT to write data files in the native format of other software products such as Microsoft Access, dBase, Lotus, and Excel. The syntax is the same as shown here. You just specify different extensions, or DBMS= options similar to those shown for PROC IMPORT in section 2.18.

The following program uses INFILE and INPUT statements to read the data and put them in a permanent SAS data set named GOLF in the MySASLib directory on the C drive (Windows, NT, OS/2). The LIBNAME statement may differ for your operating environment.

```
LIBNAME travel 'c:\MySASLib';
DATA travel.golf;
    INFILE 'c:\MyRawData\Golf.dat';
    INPUT CourseName $18. NumberOfHoles Par Yardage GreenFees;
RUN;
```

Now, suppose you want to write a letter to a potential customer and insert the golf data. The following program writes a file that you can read with a word processor:

```
LIBNAME sports 'c:\MySASLib';
* Create Tab-delimited file;
PROC EXPORT DATA = sports.golf OUTFILE = 'c:\MyRawData\Golf.txt' REPLACE;
RUN;
```

Because the name of the output file ends with .txt, SAS will write a tab-delimited file. If you run this program, your log will contain the following note about the output file:

```
NOTE: 7 records were written to the file 'c:\MyRawData\Golf.txt'.
```

Notice that while the data set contained six observations, SAS wrote seven records. The extra record contains the variable names. If you read this file into a word processor and set the tabs, it will look like this:

```
CourseName          NumberOfHoles  Par  Yardage  GreenFees
Kapalua Plantation  18             73   7263     125
Pukalani            18             72   6945     55
Sandlewood          18             72   6469     35
Silversword         18             71   6801     57
Waiehu Municipal    18             72   6330     25
Grand Waikapa       18             72   6122     200
```

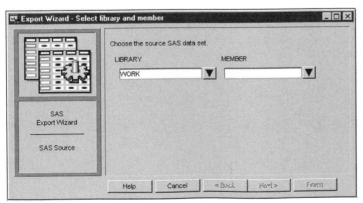

The Export Wizard The Export wizard is a Graphical User Interface (GUI) to the EXPORT procedure. Start the Export wizard by selecting `Export` from the File menu. Once started, the wizard will guide you through a series of screens and then convert your SAS data set into a data file. The Export wizard writes a PROC EXPORT which will appear in your Log window.

2.20 Writing Raw Data Files with the DATA Step

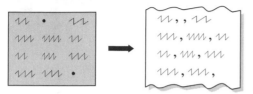

In addition to PROC EXPORT you can also write data files using FILE and PUT statements. This method has, to some extent, been replaced by the easier-to-use PROC EXPORT and Export wizard, but it is included here for three reasons. First, at the time this book was written, PROC EXPORT was not available under all operating environments.[1] Second, you may be asked to maintain or revise older programs that use FILE and PUT statements. Third, if you need total control of the output, exact column specifications, complete sentences, or any other non-standard type of raw data file, this is still the way to do it.

You can write raw data the same way that you read raw data, with just a few changes. Instead of naming your external file in an INFILE statement, you name it in a FILE statement. Instead of reading variables with an INPUT statement, you write them with a PUT statement. To say it another way, you use INFILE and INPUT statements to get raw data into SAS, and FILE and PUT statements to get raw data out.

PUT statements can be in list, column, or formatted style, just like INPUT statements, but since SAS already knows whether a variable is numeric or character, you don't have to put a $ after character variables. If you use list format, SAS will automatically put one space between each variable, creating a space-delimited file. To write files with other delimiters, use a list-style PUT statement and the DSD and DLM= options in your FILE statement.[2]

```
FILE 'filename' DSD DLM = 'delimiter';
```

If you use column or formatted styles of PUT statements, SAS will put the variables wherever you specify. You can control spacing with the same pointer controls that INPUT statements use: @*n* to move to column *n*, +*n* to move *n* columns, / to skip to the next line, #*n* to skip to line *n*, and the trailing @ to hold the current line. In addition to printing variables, you can insert a text string by simply enclosing it in quotes.

Example To show how this differs from PROC EXPORT, this example uses the same data as section 2.19. A travel company maintains a SAS database containing information about golf courses. For each course the file includes the course name, number of holes, par, yardage, and greens fees. Here is a subset of the data:

```
Kapalua Plantation 18 73 7263 125.00
Pukalani           18 72 6945  55.00
Sandlewood         18 72 6469  35.00
Silversword        18 71 6801  57.00
Waiehu Municipal   18 72 6330  25.00
Grand Waikapa      18 72 6122 200.00
```

---

[1] At the time this book was written the EXPORT procedure was available on OS/2, UNIX, OpenVMS, and Windows.

[2] See section 2.16 for a discussion of the DSD and DLM= options.

The following program uses INFILE and INPUT statements to read the data from a file called Golf.dat and put it in a permanent SAS data set named GOLF in the MySASLib directory on the C drive (Windows, NT, OS/2). The LIBNAME statement may differ under your operating environment.

```
LIBNAME travel 'c:\MySASLib';
DATA travel.golf;
    INFILE 'c:\MyRawData\Golf.dat';
    INPUT CourseName $18. NumberOfHoles Par Yardage GreenFees;
RUN;
```

Suppose you want to put the data in a raw data file, but with only three variables, in a new order, and with dollar signs added to the variable GreenFees. The following program reads the SAS data set and writes a raw data file using FILE and PUT statements:

```
LIBNAME activity 'c:\MySASLib';
DATA _NULL_;
    SET activity.golf;
    FILE 'c:\MyRawData\Newfile.dat';
    PUT CourseName 'Golf Course' @32 GreenFees DOLLAR7.2 @40 'Par ' Par;
RUN;
```

The word _NULL_ appears in the DATA statement instead of a SAS data set name. You could put a data set name there, but _NULL_ is a special keyword that tells SAS not to bother making a new SAS data set. By not writing a new SAS data set, you save computer time.

The SET statement simply tells SAS to read the permanent SAS data set GOLF.[3] The FILE statement tells SAS the name of the output file you want to create. Then, the PUT statement tells SAS what to write and where. The PUT statement contains two quoted strings, "Golf Course" and "Par" which SAS inserts in the raw data file.

If you run this program, your log will contain the following note telling how many records were written to the output file:

```
NOTE: 6 records were written to the file 'c:\MyRawData\Newfile.dat'.
```

The output file looks like this:

```
          Kapalua Plantation Golf Course $125.00 Par 73
          Pukalani Golf Course            $55.00 Par 72
          Sandlewood Golf Course          $35.00 Par 72
          Silversword Golf Course         $57.00 Par 71
          Waiehu Municipal Golf Course    $25.00 Par 72
          Grand Waikapa Golf Course      $200.00 Par 72
```

Comparing this output to the previous section, you can see that this is more customized.

---

[3] For more information about this kind of SET statement, see section 5.1.

3

"Contrariwise," continued Tweedledee, "if it was so, it might be; and if it were so, it would be; but as it isn't, it ain't. That's logic."

LEWIS CARROLL

CHAPTER 3

Working with Your Data

3.1   Creating and Redefining Variables

If someone compiled a list of the ten most popular things to do with SAS software, creating and redefining variables would be near the top. Fortunately, SAS is flexible and uses a common sense approach to these tasks. You create and redefine variables with assignment statements using this basic form:

```
variable = expression;
```

On the left side of the equation is a variable name, either new or old. The right side of the equation may be a constant, another variable, or a mathematical expression. Here are examples of these basic types of assignment statements:

Assignment statement	Type of expression
`Qwerty = 10;`	numeric constant
`Qwerty = 'ten';`	character constant
`Qwerty = OldVar;`	a variable
`Qwerty = OldVar + 10;`	addition
`Qwerty = OldVar - 10;`	subtraction
`Qwerty = OldVar * 10;`	multiplication
`Qwerty = OldVar / 10;`	division
`Qwerty = OldVar ** 10;`	exponentiation

Whether the variable Qwerty is numeric or character depends on the expression that defines it. When the expression is numeric, Qwerty will be numeric; when it is character, Qwerty will be character.

When deciding how to execute your equation, SAS follows the standard mathematical rules of precedence: SAS performs exponentiation first, then multiplication and division, followed by addition and subtraction. You can use parentheses to override that order. Here are two similar SAS statements showing that a couple of parentheses can make a big difference:

Assignment statement	Result
`x = 10 * 4 + 3 ** 2;`	`x = 49`
`x = 10 * (4 + 3 ** 2);`	`x = 130`

While SAS can read equations with or without parentheses, people often can't. If you use parentheses, your programs will be a lot easier to read.

Example   The following raw data are from a survey of home gardeners. Gardeners were asked to estimate the number of pounds they harvested for four crops: tomatoes, zucchini, peas, and grapes.

```
Gregor  10   2  40     0
Molly   15   5  10  1000
Luther  50  10  15    50
Susan   20   0   .    20
```

This program reads the data from a file called Garden.dat and then modifies the data:

```
* Modify homegarden data set with assignment statements;
DATA homegarden;
    INFILE 'c:\MyRawData\Garden.dat';
    INPUT Name $ 1-7 Tomato Zucchini Peas Grapes;
    Zone = 14;
    Type = 'home';
    Zucchini = Zucchini * 10;
    Total = Tomato + Zucchini + Peas + Grapes;
    PerTom = (Tomato / Total) * 100;
PROC PRINT DATA = homegarden;
    TITLE 'Home Gardening Survey';
RUN;
```

This program contains five assignment statements. The first creates a new variable, Zone, equal to a numeric constant, 14. The variable Type is set equal to a character constant, home. The variable Zucchini is multiplied by 10 because that just seems natural for zucchini. Total is the sum for all the types of plants. PerTom is not a genetically engineered tomato but the percentage of harvest which were tomatoes. The report from PROC PRINT contains all the variables, old and new:

```
                       Home Gardening Survey                        1


   Obs  Name    Tomato Zucchini Peas Grapes Zone Type  Total  PerTom

    1   Gregor    10      20     40     0    14   home    70   14.2857
    2   Molly     15      50     10   1000   14   home   1075   1.3953
    3   Luther    50     100     15    50    14   home    215  23.2558
    4   Susan     20       0      .    20    14   home     .      .
```

Notice that the variable Zucchini appears only once because the new value replaced the old value. The other four assignment statements each created a new variable. When a variable is new, SAS adds it to the data set you are creating. When a variable already exists, SAS replaces the original value with the new one. Using an existing name has the advantage of not cluttering your data set with a lot of similar variables. However, you don't want to overwrite a variable unless you are really sure you won't need the original value later.

The variable Peas had a missing value for the last observation. Because of this, the variables Total and PerTom, which are calculated from Peas, were also set to missing and this message appeared in the log:

```
NOTE: Missing values were generated as a result of performing an operation on
      missing values.
```

This message is a flag that often indicates an error. However, in this case it is not an error but simply the result of incomplete data collection.[1]

---

[1] If you want to add only non-missing values, you can use the SUM function discussed in section 8.7.

3.2 Using SAS Functions

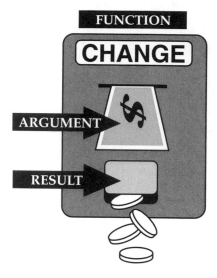

Sometimes a simple equation, using only arithmetic operators, does not give you the new value you are looking for. This is where functions are very handy. Functions simplify your programming task because SAS has already done the programming for you. All you need to do is plug in the right values to the function and out comes the result—like putting a dollar in a change machine and getting back four quarters.

SAS has close to 300 functions in the following general areas:

Array	Probability
Bitwise Logical Operators	Quantile
Character	Random Number
Character String Matching	Sample Statistics
Date and Time	SAS File I/O
Dynamic Link Library	Special Functions
External Files	State and ZIP Code
Financial	Trigonometric
Macro	Truncation
Mathematical	Variable Control
MBCS	Variable Information

Section 3.3 gives a sample of the most common SAS functions.

Functions perform a calculation on, or a transformation of, the arguments given in parentheses following the function name. SAS functions have the following general form:

```
function-name(argument, argument, ...)
```

All functions must have parentheses even if they don't require any arguments. Arguments are separated by commas and can be variable names, constant values such as numbers or characters enclosed in quotes, or expressions. The following statement computes Birthday as a SAS date value using the function MDY and the variables MonthBorn, DayBorn, and YearBorn. The MDY function takes three arguments, one each for the month, day, and year:

```
Birthday = MDY(MonthBorn, DayBorn, YearBorn);
```

Functions can be nested, where one function is the argument of another function. For example, the following statement calculates NewValue using two nested functions, INT and LOG:

```
NewValue = INT(LOG(10));
```

The result for this example is 2, the integer portion of the natural log of the numeric constant 10 (2.3026). Just be careful when nesting functions that each parenthesis has a mate.

Example Data from a pumpkin carving contest illustrate the use of several functions. The contestants' names are followed by their age, type of pumpkin (carved or decorated), date of entry, and the scores from five judges:

```
Alicia Grossman   13 c 10-28-1999 7.8 6.5 7.2 8.0 7.9
Matthew Lee        9 D 10-30-1999 6.5 5.9 6.8 6.0 8.1
Elizabeth Garcia  10 C 10-29-1999 8.9 7.9 8.5 9.0 8.8
Lori Newcombe      6 D 10-30-1999 6.7 5.6 4.9 5.2 6.1
Jose Martinez      7 d 10-31-1999 8.9 9.510.0 9.7 9.0
Brian Williams    11 C 10-29-1999 7.8 8.4 8.5 7.9 8.0
```

The following program reads the data, creates two new variables (AvgScore and DayEntered) and transforms another (Type):

```
DATA contest;
   INFILE 'c:\MyRawData\Pumpkin.dat';
   INPUT Name $16. Age 3. +1 Type $1. +1 Date MMDDYY10.
        (Scr1 Scr2 Scr3 Scr4 Scr5) (4.1);
   AvgScore = MEAN(Scr1, Scr2, Scr3, Scr4, Scr5);
   DayEntered = DAY(Date);
   Type = UPCASE(Type);
PROC PRINT DATA = contest;
   TITLE 'Pumpkin Carving Contest';
RUN;
```

The variable AvgScore is created using the MEAN function, which returns the mean of the non-missing arguments. This differs from simply adding the arguments together and dividing by their number, which would return a missing value if any of the arguments were missing.

The variable DayEntered is created using the DAY function, which returns the day of the month. SAS has all sorts of functions for manipulating dates, and what's great about them is that you don't have to worry about things like leap year—SAS takes care of that for you.

The variable Type is transformed using the UPCASE function. SAS is case sensitive when it comes to variable values; a 'd' is not the same as 'D'. The data file has both lowercase and uppercase letters for the variable Type, so the function UPCASE is used to make all the values uppercase.

Here are the results:

```
                       Pumpkin Carving Contest                              1


                                                            Avg     Day
    Obs      Name        Age Type  Date Scr1 Scr2 Scr3 Scr4 Scr5 Score Entered

     1   Alicia Grossman  13   C   14545  7.8  6.5  7.2  8.0  7.9  7.48    28
     2   Matthew Lee       9   D   14547  6.5  5.9  6.8  6.0  8.1  6.66    30
     3   Elizabeth Garcia 10   C   14546  8.9  7.9  8.5  9.0  8.8  8.62    29
     4   Lori Newcombe     6   D   14547  6.7  5.6  4.9  5.2  6.1  5.70    30
     5   Jose Martinez     7   D   14548  8.9  9.5 10.0  9.7  9.0  9.42    31
     6   Brian Williams   11   C   14546  7.8  8.4  8.5  7.9  8.0  8.12    29
```

3.3 Selected SAS Functions

The following table lists definitions and syntax of commonly used functions.[1]

Function name	Syntax[2]	Definition
Numeric		
INT	INT(*arg*)	Returns the integer portion of argument
LOG	LOG(*arg*)	Natural logarithm
LOG10	LOG10(*arg*)	Logarithm to the base 10
MAX	MAX(*arg,arg,...*)	Largest non-missing value
MIN	MIN(*arg,arg,...*)	Smallest non-missing value
MEAN	MEAN(*arg,arg,...*)	Arithmetic mean of non-missing values
ROUND	ROUND(*arg, round-off-unit*)	Rounds to nearest round-off unit
SUM	SUM(*arg,arg,...*)	Sum of non-missing values
Character		
LEFT	LEFT(*arg*)	Left aligns a SAS character expression
LENGTH	LENGTH(*arg*)	Returns the length of an argument not counting trailing blanks (missing values have a length of 1)
SUBSTR	SUBSTR(*arg,position,n*)	Extracts a substring from an argument starting at *'position'* for *'n'* characters or until end if no *'n'*[3]
TRANSLATE	TRANSLATE(*source,to-1, from-1,...to-n,from-n*)	Replaces *'from'* characters in *'source'* with *'to'* characters (one to one replacement only—you can't replace one character with two, for example)
TRIM	TRIM(*arg*)	Removes trailing blanks from character expression
UPCASE	UPCASE(*arg*)	Converts all letters in argument to uppercase
Date		
DATEJUL	DATEJUL(*julian-date*)	Converts a Julian date to a SAS date value[4]
DAY	DAY(*date*)	Returns the day of the month from a SAS date value
MDY	MDY(*month,day,year*)	Returns a SAS date value from month, day, and year values
MONTH	MONTH(*date*)	Returns the month (1-12) from a SAS date value
QTR	QTR(*date*)	Returns the yearly quarter (1-4) from a SAS date value
TODAY	TODAY()	Returns the current date as a SAS date value

---

[1] Check your online documentation for a complete list of functions.

[2] *arg* is short for argument, which means a literal value, variable name, or expression.

[3] SUBSTR has a different function when on the left side of an equals sign.

[4] A SAS date value is the number of days since January 1, 1960.

Here are examples using the selected functions.

Function name	Example	Result	Example	Result
Numeric				
INT	x=INT(4.32);	x=4	y=INT(5.789);	y=5
LOG	x=LOG(1);	x=0.0	y=LOG(10);	y=2.30259
LOG10	x=LOG10(1);	x=0.0	y=LOG10(10);	y=1.0
MAX	x=MAX(9.3,8,7.5);	x=9.3	y=MAX(-3,.,5);	y=5
MEAN	x=MEAN(1,4,7,2);	x=3.5	y=MEAN(2,.,3);	y=2.5
MIN	x=MIN(9.3,8,7.5);	x=7.5	y=MIN(-3,.,5);	y=-3
ROUND	x=ROUND(12.65);	x=13	y=ROUND(12.65,.1);	y=12.7
SUM	x=SUM(3,5,1);	x=9.0	y=SUM(4,7,.);	y=11
Character				
LEFT	a=' cat'; x=LEFT(a);	x='cat '	a=' my cat'; y=LEFT(a);	y='my cat '
LENGTH	a='my cat'; x=LENGTH(a);	x=6	a=' my cat '; y=LENGTH(a);	y-7
SUBSTR	a='(916)734-6281'; x=SUBSTR(a,2,3);	x='916'	y=SUBSTR('1cat',2);	y='cat'
TRANSLATE	a='6/16/99'; x=TRANSLATE (a,'-','/');	x='6-16-99'	a='my cat can'; y=TRANSLATE (a, 'r','c');	y='my rat ran'
TRIM	a='my '; b='cat'; x=TRIM(a)||b;[5]	x='mycat '	a='my cat '; b='s'; y=TRIM(a)||b;	y='my cats '
UPCASE	a='MyCat'; x=UPCASE(a);	x='MYCAT'	y=UPCASE('Tiger');	y='TIGER'
Date				
DATEJUL	a=60001; x=DATEJUL(a);	x=0	a=60365; y=DATEJUL(a);	y=364
DAY	a=MDY(4,18,99); x=DAY(a);	x=18	a=MDY(9,3,60); y=DAY(a);	y=3
MDY	x=MDY(1,1,60);	x=0	m=2; d=1; y=60; Date=MDY(m,d,y);	Date=31
MONTH	a=MDY(4,18,1999); x=MONTH(a);	x=4	a=MDY(9,3,60); y=MONTH(a);	y=9
QTR	a=MDY(4,18,99); x=QTR(a);	x=2	a=MDY(9,3,60); y=QTR(a);	y=3
TODAY	x=TODAY();	x=*today's date*	x=TODAY()-1;	x=*yesterday's date*

---

[5] The concatenation operator | | concatenates character strings.

3.4 ▶ Using IF-THEN Statements

Frequently, you want an assignment statement to apply to some observations but not all—under some conditions, but not others. This is called conditional logic, and you do it with IF-THEN statements:

```
IF condition THEN action;
```

The *condition* is an expression comparing one thing to another, and the *action* is what SAS should do when the expression is true, often an assignment statement. For example

```
IF Model = 'Mustang' THEN Make = 'Ford';
```

This statement tells SAS to set the variable Make equal to Ford whenever the variable Model equals Mustang. The terms on either side of the comparison may be constants, variables, or expressions. Those terms are separated by a comparison operator, which may be either symbolic or mnemonic. The decision of whether to use symbolic or mnemonic operators depends on your personal preference and the symbols available on your keyboard. Here are the basic comparison operators:

Symbolic	Mnemonic	Meaning
=	EQ	equals
¬ =, ^ =, or ~ =	NE	not equal
>	GT	greater than
<	LT	less than
> =	GE	greater than or equal
< =	LE	less than or equal

The IN operator also makes comparisons, but it works a bit differently. IN compares the value of a variable to a list of values. Here is an example:

```
IF Model IN ('Corvette', 'Camaro') THEN Make = 'Chevrolet';
```

This statement tells SAS to set the variable Make equal to Chevrolet whenever the value of Model is Corvette or Camaro.

A single IF-THEN statement can only have one action. If you add the keywords DO and END, then you can execute more than one action. For example

```
IF condition THEN DO;          IF Model = 'Mustang' THEN DO;
   action;                        Make = 'Ford';
   action;                        Size = 'compact';
END;                           END;
```

The DO statement causes all SAS statements coming after it to be treated as a unit until a matching END statement appears. Together, the DO statement, the END statement, and all the statements in between are called a DO group.

You can also specify multiple conditions with the keywords AND and OR:

```
IF condition AND condition THEN action;
```

For example

```
IF Model = 'Mustang' AND Year < 1975 THEN Status = 'classic';
```

Like the comparison operators, AND and OR may be symbolic or mnemonic:

Symbolic	Mnemonic	Meaning
&	AND	all comparisons must be true
|, ¦, or !	OR	only one comparison must be true

Be careful with long strings of comparisons; they can be a logical maze.

Example The following data about used cars contain values for model, year, make, number of seats, and color:

```
Corvette 1955 .      2 black
XJ6      1985 Jaguar 2 teal
Mustang  1966 Ford   4 red
Miata    1992 .      . silver
CRX      1991 Honda  2 black
Camaro   1990 .      4 red
```

This program reads the data from a file called Cars.dat, uses a series of IF-THEN statements to fill in missing data, and creates a new variable, Status:

```
DATA sportscars;
   INFILE 'c:\MyRawData\Cars.dat';
   INPUT Model $ Year Make $ Seats Color $;
   IF Year < 1975 THEN Status = 'classic';
   IF Model = 'Corvette' OR Model = 'Camaro' THEN Make = 'Chevy';
   IF Model = 'Miata' THEN DO;
      Make = 'Mazda';
      Seats = 2;
   END;
PROC PRINT DATA = sportscars;
   TITLE "Eddy's Excellent Emporium of Used Sports Cars";
RUN;
```

This program contains three IF-THEN statements. The first is a simple IF-THEN that creates the new variable Status based on the value of Year. That is followed by a compound IF-THEN using an OR. The last IF-THEN uses DO and END. The output looks like this:

```
            Eddy's Excellent Emporium of Used Sports Cars          1


     Obs    Model      Year    Make     Seats    Color    Status

      1     Corvette   1955    Chevy      2      black    classic
      2     XJ6        1985    Jaguar     2      teal
      3     Mustang    1966    Ford       4      red      classic
      4     Miata      1992    Mazda      2      silver
      5     CRX        1991    Honda      2      black
      6     Camaro     1990    Chevy      4      red
```

3.5 ▸ Grouping Observations with IF-THEN/ELSE Statements

red ⁗	red warm ⁗
orange ⁗	orange warm ⁗
yellow ⁗	yellow warm ⁗
green ⁗	green cool ⁗
blue ⁗	blue cool ⁗
purple ⁗	purple cool ⁗

➡

One of the most common uses of IF-THEN statements is for grouping observations. Perhaps a variable has too many different values and you want to print a more compact report, or perhaps you are going to run an analysis based on specific groups of interest. There are many possible reasons for grouping data, so sooner or later you'll probably need to do it.

The simplest and most common way to create a grouping variable is with a series of IF-THEN statements.[1] By adding the keyword ELSE to your IF statements, you can tell SAS that these statements are related.

IF-THEN/ELSE logic takes this basic form:

```
IF condition THEN action;
   ELSE IF condition THEN action;
   ELSE IF condition THEN action;
```

Notice that the ELSE statement is simply an IF-THEN statement with an ELSE tacked onto the front. You can have any number of these statements.

IF-THEN/ELSE logic has two advantages when compared to a simple series of IF-THEN statements without any ELSE statements. First, it is more efficient, using less computer time; once an observation satisfies a condition, SAS skips the rest of the series. Second, ELSE logic ensures that your groups are mutually exclusive so you don't accidentally have an observation fitting into more than one group.

Sometimes the last ELSE statement in a series is a little different, containing just an action, with no IF or THEN. Note the final ELSE statement in this series:

```
IF condition THEN action;
   ELSE IF condition THEN action;
   ELSE action;
```

An ELSE of this kind becomes a default which is automatically executed for all observations failing to satisfy any of the previous IF statements. You can only have one of these statements, and it must be the last in the IF-THEN/ELSE series.

Example Here are data from a survey of home improvements. Each record contains three data values: owner's name, description of the work done, and cost of the improvements in dollars:

```
Bob       kitchen cabinet face-lift   1253.00
Shirley   bathroom addition          11350.70
Silvia    paint exterior                   .
Al        backyard gazebo             3098.63
Norm      paint interior               647.77
Kathy     second floor addition      75362.93
```

---

[1] Other ways to create grouping variables include using a SELECT statement, or using a PUT function with a user-defined format from PROC FORMAT.

This program reads the raw data from a file called Home.dat and then assigns a grouping variable called CostGroup. This variable has a value of high, medium, low, or missing, depending on the value of Cost:

```
* Group observations by cost;
DATA homeimprovements;
    INFILE 'c:\MyRawData\Home.dat';
    INPUT Owner $ 1-7 Description $ 9-33 Cost;
    IF Cost = . THEN CostGroup = 'missing';
        ELSE IF Cost < 2000 THEN CostGroup = 'low';
        ELSE IF Cost < 10000 THEN CostGroup = 'medium';
        ELSE CostGroup = 'high';
PROC PRINT DATA = homeimprovements;
    TITLE 'Home Improvement Cost Groups';
RUN;
```

Notice that there are four statements in this IF-THEN/ELSE series, one for each possible value of the variable CostGroup. The first statement deals with observations that have missing data for the variable Cost. Without this first statement, observations with a missing value for Cost would be incorrectly assigned a CostGroup of low. SAS considers missing values to be smaller than non-missing values, smaller than any printable character for character variables, and smaller than negative numbers for numeric variables. Unless you are sure that your data contain no missing values, you should allow for missing values when you write IF-THEN/ELSE statements.

The results look like this:

```
                    Home Improvement Cost Groups                    1

                                                          Cost
     Obs    Owner    Description               Cost       Group

      1     Bob      kitchen cabinet face-lift 1253.00    low
      2     Shirley  bathroom addition         11350.70   high
      3     Silvia   paint exterior               .       missing
      4     Al       backyard gazebo           3098.63    medium
      5     Norm     paint interior            647.77     low
      6     Kathy    second floor addition     75362.93   high
```

3.6 ▸ Subsetting Your Data

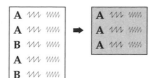

Often programmers find that they want to use some of the observations in a data set and exclude the rest. The most common way to do this is with a subsetting IF statement in a DATA step.[1] The basic form of a subsetting IF is

```
IF expression;
```

Consider this example:

```
IF Sex = 'f';
```

At first subsetting IF statements may seem odd. People naturally ask, "IF Sex = 'f', then what?" The subsetting IF looks incomplete, as if a careless typist pressed the delete key too long. But it is really a special case of the standard IF-THEN statement. In this case the action is merely implied. If the expression is true, then SAS continues with the DATA step. If the expression is false, then no further statements are processed for that observation; that observation is not added to the data set being created; and SAS moves on to the next observation. You can think of the subsetting IF as a kind of on-off switch. If the condition is true, then the switch is on and the observation is processed. If the condition is false, then that observation is turned off.

If you don't like subsetting IFs, there is another alternative, the DELETE statement. DELETE statements do the opposite of subsetting IFs. While the subsetting IF statement tells SAS which observations to include, the DELETE statement tells SAS which observations to exclude:

```
IF expression THEN DELETE;
```

The following two statements are equivalent (assuming there are only two values for the variable Sex, and no missing data):

```
IF Sex = 'f';        IF Sex = 'm' THEN DELETE;
```

Example The members of a local amateur playhouse want to choose a Shakespearean comedy for this spring's play. You volunteer to compile a list of titles using an online encyclopedia. For each play your data file contains title, approximate year of first performance, and type of play:

```
A Midsummer Night's Dream 1595 comedy
Comedy of Errors               1590 comedy
Hamlet                         1600 tragedy
Macbeth                        1606 tragedy
Richard III                    1594 history
Romeo and Juliet               1596 tragedy
Taming of the Shrew            1593 comedy
Tempest                        1611 romance
```

---

[1] Other ways to subset data include using multiple INPUT statements (discussed in section 2.14), and the WHERE statement (discussed in section 4.2 and appendix F).

This program reads the data from a raw data file called Shakespeare.dat and then uses a subsetting IF statement to select only comedies:

```
* Choose only comedies;
DATA comedy;
    INFILE 'c:\MyRawData\Shakespeare.dat';
    INPUT Title $ 1-26 Year Type $;
    IF Type = 'comedy';
PROC PRINT DATA = comedy;
    TITLE 'Shakespearean Comedies';
RUN;
```

The output looks like this:

```
                    Shakespearean Comedies                    1

     Obs    Title                      Year    Type

       1    A Midsummer Night's Dream   1595    comedy
       2    Comedy of Errors            1590    comedy
       3    Taming of the Shrew         1593    comedy
```

These notes appear in the log stating that although eight records were read from the input file, the data set WORK.COMEDY contains only three observations:

```
NOTE: 8 records were read from the infile 'c:\MyRawData\Shakespeare.dat'
NOTE: The data set WORK.COMEDY has 3 observations and 3 variables.
```

It is always a good idea to check the SAS log when you subset observations to make sure that you ended up with what you expected.

In the program above, you could substitute the statement

```
IF Type = 'tragedy' OR Type = 'romance' OR Type = 'history' THEN DELETE;
```

for the statement

```
IF Type = 'comedy';
```

But you would have to do a lot more typing. Generally, you use the subsetting IF when it is easier to specify a condition for including observations, and use the DELETE statement when is easier to specify a condition for excluding observations.

3.7 Working with SAS Dates

Dates can be tricky to work with. Some months have 30 days, some 31, some 28, and don't forget leap year. SAS dates simplify all this. A SAS date is the number of days since January 1, 1960.[1] The table below lists four dates and their values as SAS dates:

Date	SAS date value
January 1, 1959	-365
January 1, 1960	0
January 1, 1961	366
January 1, 2001	14976

SAS has special tools for working with dates: informats for reading dates, functions for manipulating dates, and formats for printing dates.[2] A table of selected date informats, formats, and functions appears in section 3.8.

Informats To read variables that are dates, you use formatted style input. The INPUT statement below tells SAS to read a variable named BirthDate using the MMDDYY10. informat:

```
INPUT BirthDate MMDDYY10.;
```

SAS has a variety of date informats for reading dates in many different forms. All of these informats convert your data to a number equal to the number of days since January 1, 1960.[3]

Setting the default century When SAS sees a date with a two-digit year like 07/04/76, SAS has to decide in which century the year belongs. Is the year 1976, 2076, or perhaps 1776? The system option YEARCUTOFF= specifies the first year of a hundred-year span for SAS to use. The default value for this option is 1920, but you can change this value with the OPTIONS statement. To avoid problems, you may want to specify the YEARCUTOFF= option whenever you have data containing two-digit years. This statement tells SAS to interpret two-digit dates as occurring between 1950 and 2049:

```
OPTIONS YEARCUTOFF = 1950;
```

Dates in SAS expressions Once a variable has been read with a SAS date informat, it can be used in arithmetic expressions like other numeric variables. For example, if a library book is due in three weeks, you could find the due date by adding 21 days to the date it was checked out:

```
DateDue = DateCheck + 21;
```

You can use a date as a constant in a SAS expression by adding quotes and a letter D. The assignment statement below creates a variable named EarthDay05, which is equal to the SAS date value for April 22, 2005:

```
EarthDay05 = '22APR2005'D;
```

---

[1] We don't know why this date was chosen, but since SAS dates are relative, January 1, 1960, is as good as any other date.

[2] SAS also has informats, functions, and formats for working with time values (the number of seconds since midnight), and datetime values (the number of seconds since midnight, you guessed it, January 1, 1960).

[3] For more information about informats, see section 2.5, for functions section 3.2, and for formats section 4.5.

Functions SAS date functions perform a number of handy operations. For example, the TODAY function returns a SAS date value equal to today's date. The statement below uses the TODAY function to compute a person's current age:

```
Age = (TODAY() - BirthDate) / 365.25;
```

The variable Age is equal to today's date minus the variable BirthDate divided by the number of days in a year.

Formats If you print a SAS date value, SAS will by default print the actual value—the number of days since January 1, 1960. Since this is not very meaningful to most people, SAS has a variety of formats for printing dates in different forms. The FORMAT statement below tells SAS to print the variable BirthDate using the WEEKDATE17. format:

```
FORMAT BirthDate WEEKDATE17.;
```

Example A local library has a data file containing details about library cards. Each record contains three data values—the card holder's name, birthdate, and the date that card was issued:

```
A. Jones    1jan60    9-15-95
M. Rincon   05OCT1949 01-24-1997
Z. Grandage 18mar1988 10-10-1999
K. Kaminaka 29may1996 02-29-2000
```

The program below reads the raw data, and then computes the variable ExpireDate (for expiration date) by adding three years (365.25 multiplied by 3) to the variable IssueDate. The variable ExpireQuarter (the quarter the card expires) is computed using the QTR function and the variable ExpireDate. An IF statement uses a date constant to identify cards issued after January 1, 1999:

```
DATA librarycards;
    INFILE 'c:\MyRawData\Dates.dat' TRUNCOVER;
    INPUT Name $11. +1 BirthDate DATE9. +1 IssueDate MMDDYY10.;
    ExpireDate = IssueDate + (365.25 * 3);
    ExpireQuarter = QTR(ExpireDate);
    IF IssueDate > '01jan1999'D THEN NewCard = 'yes';
PROC PRINT DATA = librarycards;
    FORMAT IssueDate MMDDYY8. ExpireDate WEEKDATE17.;
    TITLE 'SAS Dates without and with Formats';
RUN;
```

Here is the output from PROC PRINT. Notice that the variable BirthDate is printed without a date format, while IssueDate and ExpireDate use formats:

```
               SAS Dates without and with Formats                1

               Birth    Issue                       Expire  New
   Obs   Name  Date     Date      ExpireDate        Quarter Card

    1  A. Jones       0  09/15/95  Mon, Sep 14, 1998    3
    2  M. Rincon  -3740  01/24/97  Mon, Jan 24, 2000    1
    3  Z. Grandage 10304 10/10/99  Wed, Oct 9, 2002     4    yes
    4  K. Kaminaka 13298 02/29/00  Fri, Feb 28, 2003    1    yes
```

3.8   Selected Date Informats, Functions, and Formats

Here are definitions for some of the most commonly used date informats, functions, and formats.[1]

Informats	Definition	Width range	Default width
DATE*w*.	Reads dates in form: *ddmmmyy* or *ddmmmyyyy*	7-32	7
DDMMYY*w*.	Reads dates in form: *ddmmyy* or *ddmmyyyy*	6-32	6
JULIAN*w*.	Reads Julian dates in form: *yyddd* or *yyyyddd*	5-32	5
MMDDYY*w*.	Reads dates in form: *mmddyy* or *mmddyyyy*	6-32	6

Functions	Syntax	Definition
DATEJUL	DATEJUL(*julian-date*)	Converts a Julian date to a SAS date value[2]
DAY	DAY(*date*)	Returns the day of the month from a SAS date value
MDY	MDY(*month,day,year*)	Returns a SAS date value from month, day, and year values
MONTH	MONTH(*date*)	Returns the month (1-12) from a SAS date value
QTR	QTR(*date*)	Returns the yearly quarter (1-4) from a SAS date value
TODAY	TODAY()	Returns the current date as a SAS date value

Formats	Definition	Width range	Default width
DATE*w*.	Writes SAS date values in form: *ddmmmyy*	5-9	7
DAY*w*.	Writes the day of the month from a SAS date value	2-32	2
EURDFDD*w*.	Writes SAS date values in form: *dd.mm.yy*	2-10	8
JULIAN*w*.	Writes a Julian date from a SAS date value	5-7	5
MMDDYY*w*.	Writes SAS date values in form: *mmddyy* or *mmddyyyy*	2-10	8
WEEKDATE*w*.	Writes SAS date values in form: *day-of-week, month-name dd, yy or yyyy*	3-37	29
WORDDATE*w*.	Writes SAS date values in form: *month-name dd, yyyy*	3-32	18

---

[1] For a complete list see your online documentation.

[2] A SAS date value is the number of days since January 1, 1960.

Here are examples using the selected date informats, functions, and formats.

Informats	Input data	INPUT statement	Results
DATE*w*.	1jan1961	INPUT Day DATE10.;	366
DDMMYY*w*.	01.01.61 02/01/61	INPUT Day DDMMYY8.;	366 367
JULIAN*w*.	61001	INPUT Day JULIAN7.;	366
MMDDYY*w*.	01-01-61	INPUT Day MMDDYY8.;	366

Functions	Example	Result	Example	Results
DATEJUL	a=60001; x=DATEJUL(a);	x=0	a=60365; y=DATEJUL(a);	y=364
DAY	a=MDY(4,18,99); x=DAY(a);	x=18	a=MDY(9,3,60); y=DAY(a);	y=3
MDY	x=MDY(1,1,60);	x=0	m=2; d=1; y=60; Date=MDY(m,d,y);	Date=31
MONTH	a=MDY(4,18,1999) x=MONTH(a);	x=4	a=MDY(9,3,60); y=MONTH(a);	y=9
QTR	a=MDY(4,18,99); x=QTR(a);	x=2	a=MDY(9,3,60); y=QTR(a);	y=3
TODAY	x=TODAY();	x=*today's date*	x=TODAY()-1;	x=*yesterday's date*

Formats	Input data	PUT statement[3]	Results
DATE*w*.	8966	PUT Birth DATE7.; PUT Birth DATE9.;	19JUL84 19JUL1984
DAY*w*.	8966	PUT Birth DAY2.; PUT Birth DAY7.;	19 19
EURDFDD*w*.	8966	PUT Birth EURDFDD8. PUT Birth EURDFDD10.;	19.07.84 19.07.1984
JULIAN*w*.	8966	PUT Birth JULIAN5.; PUT Birth JULIAN7.;	84201 1984201
MMDDYY*w*.	8966	PUT Birth MMDDYY8.; PUT Birth MMDDYY6.;	07/19/84 071984
WEEKDATE*w*.	8966	PUT Birth WEEKDATE15.; PUT Birth WEEKDATE29.;	Thu, Jul 19, 84 Thursday, July 19, 1984
WORDDATE*w*.	8966	PUT Birth WORDDATE12.; PUT Birth WORDDATE18.;	Jul 19, 1984 July 19, 1984

[3] Formats can be used in PUT statements and PUT functions in DATA steps, and in FORMAT statements in either DATA or PROC steps.

3.9 Using the RETAIN and Sum Statements

When reading raw data, SAS sets the values of all variables equal to missing at the start of each iteration of the DATA step. If a variable is not assigned a new value in either an INPUT statement or an assignment statement, then it will have a missing value in the output data set. The RETAIN and sum statements change this. If a variable appears in a RETAIN statement, then its value will be retained from one iteration of the DATA step to the next. A variable normally has missing values if it is not assigned a value in the DATA step. With the RETAIN statement, though, a variable is assigned its value from the previous iteration of the DATA step. A sum statement is a special SAS statement which also retains values from the previous iteration of the DATA step.

RETAIN statement The RETAIN statement can appear anywhere in the DATA step and has the following form, where all variables to be retained are listed after the RETAIN keyword:

```
RETAIN variables;
```

You can also specify an initial value, other than missing, to the variables. All variables listed before an initial value will start the first iteration of the DATA step with that value:

```
RETAIN variables initial-value;
```

Sum statement A sum statement also retains values from the previous iteration of the DATA step, but you use it for the special cases where you simply want to cumulatively add the value of an expression to a variable. A sum statement, like an assignment statement, contains no keywords. It has the following form:

```
variable + expression;
```

No, there is no typo here and no equals sign either. This statement adds the value of the expression to the variable while retaining the variable's value from one iteration of the DATA step to the next. The variable must be numeric and has the initial value of zero. This statement can be re-written using the RETAIN statement and SUM function as follows:

```
RETAIN variable 0;
variable = SUM(variable, expression);
```

As you can see, a sum statement is really a special case of using RETAIN.

Example This example illustrates the use of both the RETAIN and sum statements. The minor league baseball team, the Walla Walla Sweets, has the following data about their games. The date the game was played and the team played are followed by the number of hits and runs for the game:

```
6-19  Columbia Peaches      8    3
6-20  Columbia Peaches     10    5
6-23  Plains Peanuts        3    4
6-24  Plains Peanuts        7    2
6-25  Plains Peanuts       12    8
6-30  Gilroy Garlics        4    4
7-1   Gilroy Garlics        9    4
7-4   Sacramento Tomatoes  15    9
7-4   Sacramento Tomatoes  10   10
7-5   Sacramento Tomatoes   2    3
```

The team wants two additional variables in their data set. One shows the cumulative number of runs for the season, and one shows the maximum number of runs in a game to date. The following program uses a sum statement to compute the cumulative number of runs, and the RETAIN statement and MAX function to determine the maximum number of runs in a game to date:

```
DATA gamestats;
    INFILE 'c:\MyRawData\Games.dat';
    INPUT Month 1 Day 3-4 Team $ 6-25 Hits 27-28 Runs 30-31;
    RETAIN MaxRuns;
    MaxRuns = MAX(MaxRuns, Runs);
    RunsToDate + Runs;
PROC PRINT DATA = gamestats;
    TITLE "Season's Record to Date";
RUN;
```

The variable MaxRuns is set equal to the maximum of its value from the previous iteration of the DATA step, since it appears in the RETAIN statement, and the value of the variable Runs. The variable RunsToDate adds the number of runs per game, Runs, to itself while retaining its value from one iteration of the DATA step to the next. This produces a cumulative record of the number of runs.

Here are the results:

```
                          Season's Record to Date                              1

                                                            Max     Runs
    Obs   Month   Day        Team          Hits   Runs     Runs    ToDate

     1      6      19    Columbia Peaches     8      3        3        3
     2      6      20    Columbia Peaches    10      5        5        8
     3      6      23    Plains Peanuts       3      4        5       12
     4      6      24    Plains Peanuts       7      2        5       14
     5      6      25    Plains Peanuts      12      8        8       22
     6      6      30    Gilroy Garlics       4      4        8       26
     7      7       1    Gilroy Garlics       9      4        8       30
     8      7       4    Sacramento Tomatoes 15      9        9       39
     9      7       4    Sacramento Tomatoes 10     10       10       49
    10      7       5    Sacramento Tomatoes  2      3       10       52
```

3.10 Simplifying Programs with Arrays

Sometimes you want to do the same thing to many variables. You may want to take the log of every numeric variable or change every occurrence of zero to a missing value. You could write a series of assignment statements or IF statements, but if you have a lot of variables to transform, using arrays will simplify and shorten your program.

An array is an ordered group of similar items. You might think your local mall has a nice array of stores to choose from. In SAS, an array is a group of variables. You can define an array to be any group of variables you like, as long as they are either all numeric or all character. The variables can be ones that already exist in your data set, or they can be new variables that you want to create.

Arrays are defined using the ARRAY statement in the DATA step. The ARRAY statement has the following general form:

```
ARRAY name (n) $ variable-list;
```

In this statement, *name* is a name you give to the array, and *n* is the number of variables in the array. Following the (*n*) is a list of variable names. The number of variables in the list must equal the number given in parentheses. (You may use {} or [ ] instead of parentheses if you like.) This is called an explicit array, where you explicitly state the number of variables in the array. The $ is needed if the variables are character and is only necessary if the variables have not previously been defined.

The array itself is not stored with the data set; it is defined only for the duration of the DATA step. You can give the array any name, as long as it does not match any of the variable names in your data set or any SAS keywords. The rules for naming arrays are the same as those for naming variables (by default, must be 32 characters or fewer and start with a letter or underscore followed by letters, numerals, or underscores).

To reference a variable using the array name, give the array name and the subscript for that variable. The first variable in the variable list has subscript 1, the second has subscript 2, and so forth. So if you have an array defined as

```
ARRAY store (4) Macys Penneys Sears Target;
```

STORE(1) is the variable Macys, STORE(2) is the variable Penneys, STORE(3) is the variable Sears, and STORE(4) is the variable Target. This is all just fine, but simply defining an array doesn't do anything for you. You want to be able to use the array to make things easier for you.

Example The radio station WBRK is conducting a survey asking people to rate ten different songs. Songs are rated on a scale of 1 to 5, where 1 = change the station when it comes on, and 5 = turn up the volume when it comes on. If listeners had not heard the song or didn't care to comment on it, a 9 was entered for that song. The following are the data collected:

```
Albany      54 4 3 5 9 9 2 1 4 4 9
Richmond    33 5 2 4 3 9 2 9 3 3 3
Oakland     27 1 3 2 9 9 9 3 4 2 3
Richmond    41 4 3 5 5 5 2 9 4 5 5
Berkeley    18 3 4 9 1 4 9 3 9 3 2
```

The listener's city of residence, age, and their responses to all ten songs are listed. The following program changes all the 9s to missing values. (The variables are named using the first letters of the words in the song's title.)

```
DATA songs;
    INFILE 'c:\MyRawData\WBRK.dat';
    INPUT City $ 1-15 Age domk wj hwow simbh kt aomm libm tr filp ttr;
    ARRAY song (10) domk wj hwow simbh kt aomm libm tr filp ttr;
    DO i = 1 TO 10;
        IF song(i) = 9 THEN song(i) = .;
    END;
PROC PRINT DATA = songs;
    TITLE 'WBRK Song Survey';
RUN;
```

An array, SONG, is defined as having ten variables, the same ten variables that appear in the INPUT statement representing the ten songs. Next comes an iterative DO statement. All statements between the DO statement and the END statement are executed, in this case, ten times, once for each variable in the array.

The variable I is used as an index variable and is incremented by 1 each time through the DO loop. The first time through the DO loop, the variable I has a value of 1 and the IF statement would read `IF song(1)=9 THEN song(1)=.;`, which is the same as `IF domk=9 THEN domk=.;`. The second time through, I has a value of 2 and the IF statement would read `IF song(2)=9 THEN song(2)=.;`, which is the same as `IF wj=9 THEN wj=.;`. This continues through all 10 variables in the array.

Here are the results:

```
                              WBRK Song Survey                                1

Obs    City      Age domk wj hwow simbh kt aomm libm tr filp ttr  i

 1    Albany      54   4   3   5    .    .  2    1   4   4    . 11
 2    Richmond    33   5   2   4    3    .  2    .   3   3   3  11
 3    Oakland     27   1   3   2    .    .  .    3   4   2   3  11
 4    Richmond    41   4   3   5    5    5  2    .   4   5   5  11
 5    Berkeley    18   3   4   .    1    4  .    3   .   3   2  11
```

Notice that the array members SONG(1) to SONG(10) did not become part of the data set, but the variable I did. You could have written ten IF statements instead of using arrays and accomplished the same result. In this program it would not have made a big difference, but if you had 100 songs in your survey instead of ten, then using arrays would clearly be a better solution.

3.11 Using Shortcuts for Lists of Variable Names

As the title states, this section is about shortcuts, shorthand ways of writing lists of variable names. While writing SAS programs, you will often need to write a list of variable names. When defining ARRAYS, using functions like MEAN or SUM, or using SAS procedures, you must specify which variables to use. Now, if you only have a handful of variables, you might not feel a need for a shortcut. But if, for example, you need to define an array with 100 elements, you might be a little grumpy after typing in the 49th variable name knowing you still have 51 more to go. You might even think, "There must be an easier way." Well, there is.

You can use an abbreviated list of variable names anywhere you can use a regular variable list. In functions, abbreviated lists must be preceded by the keyword OF (for example, SUM(OF Cat8 - Cat12)). Otherwise, you simply replace the regular list of variables with the abbreviated one.

Numbered range lists Variables which start with the same characters and end with consecutive numbers can be part of a numbered range list. The numbers can start and end anywhere as long as the number sequence between is complete. For example, the following INPUT statement shows a variable list and its abbreviated form:

Variable list	**Abbreviated list**
`INPUT Cat8 Cat9 Cat10 Cat11 Cat12;`	`INPUT Cat8 - Cat12;`

Name range lists Name range lists depend on the internal order, or position, of the variables in the SAS data set. This is determined by the order of appearance of the variables in the DATA step. For example, if you had the following DATA step, then the internal variable order would be Y A C H R B:

```
DATA example;
   INPUT y a c h r;
   b = c + r;
RUN;
```

To specify a name range list, put the first variable, then two hyphens, then the last variable. The following PUT statements show the variable list and its abbreviated form using a named range:

Variable list	**Abbreviated list**
`PUT y a c h r b;`	`PUT y -- b;`

If you are not sure of the internal order, you can find out using PROC CONTENTS with the POSITION option. The following program will list the variables in the permanent SAS data set DISTANCE sorted by position.

```
LIBNAME mydir 'c:\MySASLib';
PROC CONTENTS DATA = mydir.distance POSITION;
RUN;
```

Use caution when including name range lists in your programs. Although they can save on typing, they may also make your programs more difficult to understand and debug.

Special SAS name lists The special name lists, _ALL_, _CHARACTER_, and _NUMERIC_ can also be used any place you want either all the variables, all the character variables, or all the numeric variables in a SAS data set. These name lists are useful when you want to do something like compute the mean of all the numeric variables for an observation (MEAN(OF _NUMERIC_)), or list the values of all variables in an observation (PUT _ALL_;).

Example The radio station WBRK wants to modify the program from the previous section, which changes all 9s to missing values. Now, instead of changing the original variables, they use the following program to create new variables (Song1 through Song10) which will have the new missing values:

```
DATA songs;
   INFILE 'c:\MyRawData\WBRK.dat';
   INPUT City $ 1-15 Age domk wj hwow simbh kt aomm libm tr filp ttr;
   ARRAY new (10) Song1 - Song10;
   ARRAY old (10) domk -- ttr;
   DO i = 1 TO 10;
      IF old(i) = 9 THEN new(i) = .;
         ELSE new(i) = old(i);
   END;
   AvgScore = MEAN(OF Song1 - Song10);
PROC PRINT DATA = songs;
   TITLE 'WBRK Song Survey';
RUN;
```

Note that both ARRAY statements use abbreviated variable lists; array NEW uses a numbered range list and array OLD uses a name range list. Inside the iterative DO loop, the Song variables (array NEW) are set equal to missing if the original variable (array OLD) had a value of 9. Otherwise, they are set equal to the original values. After the DO loop, a new variable, AvgScore, is created using an abbreviated variable list in the function MEAN. The output includes variables from both the OLD array (domk, wj, ... ttr) and NEW array (Song1 - Song10):

```
                        WBRK Song Survey                              1

                                                                A
                                                                v
                                                       S        g
                        s             S S S S S S S S o        S
        C           d   h   a l   f   o o o o o o o o n        c
   O    i       A o   w m   o i   i t n n n n n n n n g        o
   b    t       g m w o b k m b t l t g g g g g g g g 1        r
   s    y       e k j w h t m m r p r 1 2 3 4 5 6 7 8 9 0   i   e

   1 Albany   54 4 3 5 9 9 2 1 4 4 9 4 3 5 . . 2 1 4 4 . 11 3.28571
   2 Richmond 33 5 2 4 3 9 2 9 3 3 3 5 2 4 3 . 2 . 3 3 3 11 3.12500
   3 Oakland  27 1 3 2 9 9 9 3 4 2 3 1 3 2 . . . 3 4 2 3 11 2.57143
   4 Richmond 41 4 3 5 5 5 2 9 4 5 5 4 3 5 5 5 2 . 4 5 5 11 4.22222
   5 Berkeley 18 3 4 9 1 4 9 3 9 3 2 3 4 . 1 4 . 3 . 3 2 11 2.85714
```

4

"Once in a while the simple things work right off."

PHIL GALLAGHER, SAS® USER SINCE 1975

From the SAS L listserv, 1994. Reprinted by permission of the author.

CHAPTER 4

Sorting, Printing, and Summarizing Your Data

4.1   Using SAS Procedures

```
PROC whatever
DATA=     _____
BY        _____
TITLE     _____
FOOTNOTE _____
LABEL     _____
```

Using a procedure, or PROC, is like filling out a form. Someone else designed the form, and all you have to do is fill in the blanks and choose from a list of options. Each PROC has its own unique form with its own list of options. But while each procedure is unique, there are similarities too. This section discusses some of those similarities.

All procedures have required statements, and most have optional statements. PROC PRINT, for example, requires only two words:

```
PROC PRINT;
```

At other times you might use the PRINT procedure and, with optional statements, make it a dozen lines long.

Most procedures write results to your Output window or file (also called the listing). You can customize the appearance of that output (centering, dates, line size, and page size, for example) using the system options discussed in section 1.10. Many procedures can also write results to an output SAS data set using an OUTPUT statement or OUT= option. Starting with Version 7, all procedures that generate output can also write SAS data sets using the Output Delivery System (ODS) as discussed in section 4.16.[1]

PROC statement   All procedures start with the keyword PROC followed by the name of the procedure, such as PRINT or CONTENTS. Options, if there are any, follow the procedure name. The DATA= option tells SAS which data set to use as input for that procedure. In this case, SAS will use a temporary SAS data set named BANANA:

```
PROC CONTENTS DATA = banana;
```

The DATA= option is, of course, optional. If you skip it, then SAS will use the most recently created data set, which is not necessarily the same as the most recently used. Sometimes it is easier to specify the data set you want than to figure out which data set SAS will use by default. To use a permanent SAS data set, refer to it directly by placing your operating environment's name for the permanent SAS data set between quotes, as discussed in section 2.9,

```
PROC CONTENTS DATA = 'c:\MySASLib\banana';
```

or issue a LIBNAME statement to set up a libref pointing to the location of your data set, and put the data set's two-level name in the DATA= option, as discussed in section 2.10.

```
LIBNAME tropical 'c:\MySASLib';
PROC CONTENTS DATA = tropical.banana;
```

---

[1] ODS also provides a powerful way to customize the appearance of your output, using ODS templates. For information about using ODS templates see your online documentation.

BY statement The BY statement is required for only one procedure, PROC SORT. In PROC SORT the BY statement tells SAS how to arrange the observations. In all other procedures, the BY statement is optional, and tells SAS to perform a separate analysis for each combination of values of the BY variables rather than treating all observations as one group. For example, this statement tells SAS to run a separate analysis for each state:

```
BY State;
```

All procedures, except PROC SORT, assume that your data are already sorted by the variables in your BY statement. If your observations are not already sorted, then use PROC SORT to do the job.

TITLE and FOOTNOTE statements You have seen TITLE statements many times in this book. FOOTNOTE works the same way, but prints at the bottom of the page. These global statements are not technically part of any step. You can put them anywhere in your program, but since they apply to the procedure output it generally makes sense to put them with the procedure. The most basic TITLE statement consists of the keyword TITLE followed by your title enclosed in quotes. SAS doesn't care if the two quotation marks are single or double as long as they are the same:

```
TITLE 'This is a title';
```

If you find that your title contains an apostrophe, use double quotes around the title, or replace the single apostrophe with two:

```
TITLE "Here's another title";
TITLE 'Here''s another title';
```

You can specify up to ten titles or footnotes by adding numbers to the keywords TITLE and FOOTNOTE:

```
FOOTNOTE3 'This is the third footnote';
```

Titles and footnotes stay in effect until you replace them with new ones or cancel them with a null statement. The following null statement would cancel all current titles:

```
TITLE;
```

When you specify a new title or footnote, it replaces the old title or footnote with the same number and cancels those with a higher number. For example, a new TITLE2 cancels an existing TITLE3, if there is one.

LABEL statement By default, SAS uses variable names to label your output, but with the LABEL statement you can create more descriptive labels, up to 256 characters long, for each variable. This statement creates labels for the variables ReceiveDate and ShipDate:

```
LABEL ReceiveDate = 'Date order was received'
      ShipDate = 'Date merchandise was shipped';
```

When a LABEL statement is used in a DATA step, the labels become part of the data set; but when used in a PROC, the labels stay in effect only for the duration of that step.

4.2 Subsetting in Procedures with the WHERE Statement

One optional statement for any PROC that reads a SAS data set is the WHERE statement. The WHERE statement tells a procedure to use a subset of the data. There are other ways to subset data, as you probably remember, so you could get by without ever using the WHERE statement.[1] However, the WHERE statement is a shortcut. While the other methods of subsetting work only in DATA steps, the WHERE statement works in PROC steps too.

Unlike subsetting in a DATA step, using a WHERE statement in a procedure does not create a new data set. That is one of the reasons why WHERE statements are sometimes more efficient than other ways of subsetting.

The basic form of a WHERE statement is

```
WHERE condition;
```

Only observations satisfying the condition will be used by the PROC. This may look familiar since it is similar to a subsetting IF. The left side of that condition is a variable name, and the right side is a variable name, a constant, or a mathematical equation. Mathematical equations can contain the standard arithmetic symbols for addition (+), subtraction (-), multiplication (*), division (/), and exponentiation (**). Between the two sides of the expression, you can use comparison and logical operators; those operators may be symbolic or mnemonic. Here are the most frequently used operators:

Symbolic	Mnemonic	Example
=	EQ	WHERE Region = 'Spain';
¬=, ~=, ^=	NE	WHERE Region ~= 'Spain';
>	GT	WHERE Rainfall > 20;
<	LT	WHERE Rainfall < AvgRain;
>=	GE	WHERE Rainfall >= AvgRain + 5;
<=	LE	WHERE Rainfall <= AvgRain / 1.25;
&	AND	WHERE Rainfall > 20 AND Temp < 90;
|,¦,!	OR	WHERE Rainfall > 20 OR Temp < 90;
	IS NOT MISSING	WHERE Region IS NOT MISSING;
	BETWEEN AND	WHERE Region BETWEEN 'Plain' AND 'Spain';
	CONTAINS	WHERE Region CONTAINS 'ain';
	IN (*list*)	WHERE Region IN ('Rain', 'Spain', 'Plain');

---

[1] Subsetting while reading a raw data file is discussed in section 2.14, and the subsetting IF statement is discussed in section 3.6.

Example You have a database containing information about well-known painters. A subset of the data appears below. For each artist, the data include the painter's name, primary style, and nation of origin:

```
Mary Cassatt          Impressionism      U
Paul Cezanne          Post-impressionism F
Edgar Degas           Impressionism      F
Paul Gauguin          Post-impressionism F
Claude Monet          Impressionism      F
Pierre Auguste Renoir Impressionism      F
Vincent van Gogh      Post-impressionism N
```

To make this example more realistic, it has two steps: one to create a permanent SAS data set, the other to subset the data. The first DATA step reads the data from a file named Artists.dat, and uses direct referencing to create a permanent SAS data set named STYLE in a directory named MySASLib (Windows or OS/2).

```
DATA 'c:\MySASLib\style';
   INFILE 'c:\MyRawData\Artists.dat';
   INPUT Name $ 1-21 Genre $ 23-40 Origin $ 42;
RUN;
```

Suppose a day later you wanted to print a list of just the impressionist painters. The quick-and-easy way to do this is with a WHERE statement and PROC PRINT. The quotation marks around the data set name tell SAS that this is a permanent SAS data set.

```
PROC PRINT DATA = 'c:\MySASLib\style';
   WHERE Genre = 'Impressionism';
   TITLE 'Major Impressionist Painters';
   FOOTNOTE 'F = France N = Netherlands U = US';
RUN;
```

The output looks like this:

```
              Major Impressionist Painters            1

      Obs   Name                  Genre          Origin
       1    Mary Cassatt          Impressionism  U
       3    Edgar Degas           Impressionism  F
       5    Claude Monet          Impressionism  F
       6    Pierre Auguste Renoir Impressionism  F

             F = France N = Netherlands U = US
```

4.3 Sorting Your Data with PROC SORT

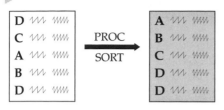

There are many reasons for sorting your data: to organize data for a report, before combining data sets, or before using a BY statement in another PROC or DATA step. Fortunately, PROC SORT is quite simple. The basic form of this procedure is

```
PROC SORT;
    BY variable-1 ... variable-n;
```

The variables named in the BY statement are called BY variables. You can specify as many BY variables as you wish. With one BY variable, SAS sorts the data based on the values of that variable. With more than one variable, SAS sorts observations by the first variable, then by the second variable within categories of the first, and so on. A BY group is all the observations that have the same values of BY variables. If, for example, your BY variable is State then all the observations for North Dakota form one BY group.

The DATA= and OUT= options specify the input and output data sets. If you don't specify the DATA= option, then SAS will use the most recently created data set. If you don't specify the OUT= option, then SAS will replace the original data set with the newly sorted version. This sample statement tells SAS to sort the data set named MESSY, and then put the sorted data into a data set named NEAT:

```
PROC SORT DATA = messy OUT = neat;
```

The NODUPKEY option tells SAS to eliminate any duplicate observations that have the same values for the BY variables. To use this option, just add NODUPKEY to the PROC SORT statement:

```
PROC SORT DATA = messy OUT = neat NODUPKEY;
```

By default SAS sorts data in ascending order, from lowest to highest or from A to Z. To have your data sorted from highest to lowest, add the keyword DESCENDING to the BY statement before each variable that should be sorted from highest to lowest. This statement tells SAS to sort first by State (from A to Z) and then by City (from Z to A) within State:

```
BY State DESCENDING City;
```

Example   The following data show the average length in feet of selected whales and sharks:

```
beluga    whale 15
whale     shark 40
basking   shark 30
gray      whale 50
mako      shark 12
sperm     whale 60
dwarf     shark .5
whale     shark 40
humpback   .    50
blue      whale 100
killer    whale 30
```

This program reads and sorts the data:

```
DATA marine;
    INFILE 'c:\MyRawData\Sealife.dat';
    INPUT Name $ Family $ Length;
* Sort the data;
PROC SORT DATA = marine OUT = seasort NODUPKEY;
    BY Family DESCENDING Length;
PROC PRINT DATA = seasort;
    TITLE 'Whales and Sharks';
RUN;
```

The DATA step reads the raw data from a file called Sealife.dat and creates a SAS data set named MARINE. Then PROC SORT rearranges the observations by family in ascending order, and by length in descending order. The NODUPKEY option of PROC SORT eliminates any duplicates, while the OUT= option writes the sorted data into a new data set named SEASORT. The output from PROC PRINT looks like this:

```
                      Whales and Sharks              1


              Obs    Name        Family    Length
               1     humpback              50.0
               2     whale       shark     40.0
               3     basking     shark     30.0
               4     mako        shark     12.0
               5     dwarf       shark      0.5
               6     blue        whale    100.0
               7     sperm       whale     60.0
               8     gray        whale     50.0
               9     killer      whale     30.0
              10     beluga      whale     15.0
```

Notice that the humpback with a missing value for Family became observation one. That is because missing values are always low for both numeric and character variables. Also, the NODUPKEY option eliminated a duplicate observation for the whale shark. The log contains these notes showing that the sorted data set has one fewer observation than the original data set.

```
NOTE: The data set WORK.MARINE has 11 observations and 3 variables.

NOTE: 1 observations with duplicate key values were deleted.
NOTE: The data set WORK.SEASORT has 10 observations and 3 variables.
```

4.4   Printing Your Data with PROC PRINT

The PRINT procedure is perhaps the most widely used SAS procedure. You have seen this procedure used many times in this book to print the contents of a SAS data set. In its simplest form, PROC PRINT prints all variables for all observations in the SAS data set. SAS decides the best way to format the output, so you don't have to worry about things like how many variables will fit on a page. But there are a few more features of PROC PRINT that you might want to use.

The general form of the PRINT procedure requires just one statement:

```
PROC PRINT;
```

By default, SAS uses the SAS data set created most recently. If you do not want to print the most recent data set, then use the DATA= option to specify the data set. We recommend always using the DATA= option for clarity in your programs as it is not always easy to quickly determine which data set was created last.

```
PROC PRINT DATA = data-set;
```

Also, SAS prints the observation numbers along with the variables' values. If you don't want observation numbers, use the NOOBS option in the PROC PRINT statement. If you define variable labels with a LABEL statement, and you want to print the labels instead of the variable names, then add the LABEL option as well. The following statement shows both of these options together:

```
PROC PRINT DATA = data-set NOOBS LABEL;
```

The following are some optional statements that sometimes come in handy:

BY *variable-list*;	The BY statement starts a new section in the output for each new value of the BY variables and prints the values of the BY variables at the top of each section. The data must be presorted by the BY variables.
ID *variable-list*;	When you use the ID statement, the observation numbers are not printed. Instead, the variables in the ID variable list appear on the left-hand side of the page.
SUM *variable-list*;	The SUM statement prints sums for the variables in the list.[1]
VAR *variable-list*;	The VAR statement specifies which variables to print and the order. Without a VAR statement, all variables in the SAS data set are printed in the order that they occur in the data set.

Example Students from two fourth-grade classes are selling candy to earn money for a special field trip. The class earning more money gets a free box of candy. The following are the data for the results of the candy sale. The students' names are followed by their classroom number, the date they turned in their money, the type of candy: mint patties or chocolate dinosaurs, and the number of boxes sold:

---

[1] You can also use the MEANS procedure to calculate sums along with other summary statistics. The MEANS procedure, however, will not print the individual observations as PROC PRINT does. PROC MEANS is covered in sections 4.9 and 7.2.

```
Adriana     21  3/21/2000 MP   7
Nathan      14  3/21/2000 CD  19
Matthew     14  3/21/2000 CD  14
Claire      14  3/22/2000 CD  11
Caitlin     21  3/24/2000 CD   9
Ian         21  3/24/2000 MP  18
Chris       14  3/25/2000 CD   6
Anthony     21  3/25/2000 MP  13
Stephen     14  3/25/2000 CD  10
Erika       21  3/25/2000 MP  17
```

The class earns $1.25 for each box of candy sold. The teachers want a report giving the money earned for each classroom, the money earned by each student, the type of candy sold, and the date the students returned their money. The following program reads the data, computes money earned (Profit), and sorts the data by classroom using PROC SORT. Then, the PROC PRINT step uses a BY statement to print the data by Class and a SUM statement to give the totals for Profit. The VAR statement lists the variables to be printed:

```
DATA sales;
   INFILE 'c:\MyRawData\Candy.dat';
   INPUT Name $ 1-11 Class @15 DateReturned MMDDYY10. CandyType $
      Quantity;
   Profit = Quantity * 1.25;
PROC SORT DATA = sales;
   BY Class;
PROC PRINT DATA = sales;
   BY Class;
   SUM Profit;
   VAR Name DateReturned CandyType Profit;
   TITLE 'Candy Sales for Field Trip by Class';
RUN;
```

Here are the results. Notice that the values for the variable DateReturned are printed as their SAS date values. You can use formats, covered in section 4.5, to print dates in readable forms.

```
              Candy Sales for Field Trip by Class                    1
---------------------------------- Class=14 ----------------------------------
                          Date      Candy
         Obs    Name    Returned    Type      Profit

           1    Nathan    14690      CD        23.75
           2    Matthew   14690      CD        17.50
           3    Claire    14691      CD        13.75
           4    Chris     14694      CD         7.50
           5    Stephen   14694      CD        12.50
         -----                                ------
         Class                                 75.00
---------------------------------- Class=21 ----------------------------------
                          Date      Candy
         Obs    Name    Returned    Type      Profit

           6    Adriana   14690      MP         8.75
           7    Caitlin   14693      CD        11.25
           8    Ian       14693      MP        22.50
           9    Anthony   14694      MP        16.25
          10    Erika     14694      MP        21.25
         -----                                ------
         Class                                 80.00
                                             ======
                                             155.00
```

4.5 ▸ Changing the Appearance of Printed Values with Formats

0	1002
2	2012
31	4336

Obs	Date	Sales
1	01/01/60	1,002
2	01/03/60	2,012
3	02/01/60	4,336

When SAS prints your data, it decides which format is best—how many decimal places to print, how much space to allow for each value, and so on. This is very convenient and makes your job much easier, but SAS doesn't always do what you want. Fortunately you're not stuck with the format SAS thinks is best. You can change the appearance of printed values using SAS formats.

SAS has many formats for numeric, character, and date values. For example, you can use the COMMA*w.d* format to print numbers with embedded commas, the $*w.* format to control the number of characters printed, and the MMDDYY*w.* format to print SAS date values (the number of days since January 1, 1960) in a readable form like 12/03/99. You can even print your data in more obscure formats like hexadecimal, zoned decimal, and packed decimal, if you like.[1]

The general forms of a SAS format are

Character	**Numeric**	**Date**
`$formatw.`	`formatw.d`	`formatw.`

where the $ indicates character formats, *format* is the name of the format, *w* is the total width including any decimal point, and *d* is the number of decimal places. The period in the format is very important because it distinguishes a format from a variable name, which cannot, by default, contain any special characters except the underscore.

FORMAT statement   You can associate formats with variables in a FORMAT statement. The FORMAT statement starts with the keyword FORMAT, followed by the variable name (or names if more than one variable is to be associated with the same format), followed by the format. For example the following FORMAT statement associates the DOLLAR8.2 format with the variables Profit and Loss and associates the MMDDYY8. format with the variable SaleDate:

```
FORMAT Profit Loss DOLLAR8.2 SaleDate MMDDYY8.;
```

FORMAT statements can go in either DATA steps or PROC steps. If the FORMAT statement is in a DATA step, then the format association is permanent and is stored with the SAS data set. If the FORMAT statement is in a PROC step, then it is temporary—affecting only the results from that procedure.

PUT statement   You can also use formats in PUT statements when writing raw data files or reports. Place a format after each variable name, as in the following example:

```
PUT Profit DOLLAR8.2 Loss DOLLAR8.2 SaleDate MMDDYY8.;
```

Example   In section 4.4, results from the fourth-grade candy sale were printed using the PRINT procedure. The names of the students were printed along with the date they turned in their money, the type of candy sold, and the profit. You may have noticed that the dates printed

---

[1] You can also create your own formats using the FORMAT procedure covered in section 4.7.

were numbers like 14690 and 14694. Using the FORMAT statement in the PRINT procedure, we can print the dates in a readable form. At the same time, we can print the variable Profit using the DOLLAR6.2 format so dollar signs appear before the numbers.

Here are the data, where the students' names are followed by their classroom, the date they turned in their money, the type of candy sold: mint patties or chocolate dinosaurs, and the number of boxes sold:

```
Adriana   21  3/21/2000 MP   7
Nathan    14  3/21/2000 CD  19
Matthew   14  3/21/2000 CD  14
Claire    14  3/22/2000 CD  11
Caitlin   21  3/24/2000 CD   9
Ian       21  3/24/2000 MP  18
Chris     14  3/25/2000 CD   6
Anthony   21  3/25/2000 MP  13
Stephen   14  3/25/2000 CD  10
Erika     21  3/25/2000 MP  17
```

The following program reads the raw data and computes Profit. The FORMAT statement in the PRINT procedure associates the DATE9. format with the variable DateReturned and the DOLLAR6.2 format with the variable Profit:

```
DATA sales;
    INFILE 'c:\MyRawData\Candy.dat';
    INPUT Name $ 1-11 Class @15 DateReturned MMDDYY10. CandyType $
          Quantity;
    Profit = Quantity * 1.25;
PROC PRINT DATA = sales;
    VAR Name DateReturned CandyType Profit;
    FORMAT DateReturned DATE9. Profit DOLLAR6.2;
    TITLE 'Candy Sale Data Using Formats';
RUN;
```

Here are the results:

```
                    Candy Sale Data Using Formats                  1

                            Date     Candy
        Obs    Name       Returned    Type      Profit

         1     Adriana    21MAR2000    MP        $8.75
         2     Nathan     21MAR2000    CD       $23.75
         3     Matthew    21MAR2000    CD       $17.50
         4     Claire     22MAR2000    CD       $13.75
         5     Caitlin    24MAR2000    CD       $11.25
         6     Ian        24MAR2000    MP       $22.50
         7     Chris      25MAR2000    CD        $7.50
         8     Anthony    25MAR2000    MP       $16.25
         9     Stephen    25MAR2000    CD       $12.50
        10     Erika      25MAR2000    MP       $21.25
```

4.6   Selected Standard Formats

Here are definitions of commonly used formats[1] along with the width range and default width.

Format	Definition	Width range	Default width
Character			
$HEX*w*.	Converts character data to hexidecimal (specify *w* twice the length of the variable)	1-32767	4
$*w*.	Writes standard character data—does not trim leading blanks (same as $CHAR*w*.)	1-32767	Length of variable or 1
Date, Time, and Datetime[2]			
DATE*w*.	Writes SAS date values in form *ddmmmyy* or *ddmmmyyyy*	5-9	7
DATETIME*w.d*	Writes SAS datetime values in form *ddmmmyy:hh:mm:ss.ss*	7-40	16
DAY*w*.	Writes day of month from a SAS date value	2-32	2
EURDFDD*w*.	Writes a SAS date value in form: *dd.mm.yy*	2-10	8
JULIAN*w*.	Writes a Julian date from a SAS date value in form *yyddd* or *yyyyddd*	5-7	5
MMDDYY*w*.	Writes SAS date values in form *mmddyy* or *mmddyyyy*	2-10	8
TIME*w.d*	Writes SAS time values in form *hh:mm:ss.ss*	2-20	8
WEEKDATE*w*.	Writes SAS date values in form *day-of-week, month-name dd, yy* or *yyyy*	3-37	29
WORDDATE*w*.	Writes SAS date values in form *month-name dd, yyyy*	3-32	18
Numeric			
BEST*w*.	SAS System chooses best format—this is the default format for writing numeric data	1-32	12
COMMA*w.d*	Writes numbers with commas separating every three digits	2-32	6
DOLLAR*w.d*	Writes numbers with a leading $ and commas separating every three digits	2-32	6
E*w*.	Writes numbers in scientific notation	7-32	12
PD*w.d*	Writes numbers in packed decimal—*w* specifies the number of bytes	1-16	1
w.d	Writes standard numeric data	1-32	none

[1] Check your online documentation for a complete list of formats.

[2] SAS date values are the number of days since January 1, 1960. SAS time values are the number of seconds past midnight, and datetime values are the number of seconds since midnight January 1, 1960.

Here are examples using the selected formats.

Format	Input data	PUT statement	Results
Character			
$HEX*w*.	AB	PUT Name $HEX4.;	C1C2 (EBCDIC)[3] 4142 (ASCII)
$*w*.	my cat my snake	PUT Animal $8. '*';	my cat * my snak*
Date, Time, and Datetime			
DATE*w*.	8966	PUT Birth DATE7.; PUT Birth DATE9.;	19JUL84 19JUL1984
DATETIME*w*.	12182	PUT Start DATETIME13.; PUT Start DATETIME18.1;	01JAN60:03:23 01JAN60:03:23:02.0
DAY*w*.	8966	PUT Birth DAY2.; PUT Birth DAY7.;	19 19
EURDFDD*w*.	8966	PUT Birth EURDFDD8.;	19.07.84
JULIAN*w*.	8966	PUT Birth JULIAN5.; PUT Birth JULIAN7.;	84201 1984201
MMDDYY*w*.	8966	PUT Birth MMDDYY8.; PUT Birth MMDDYY6.;	7/19/84 071984
TIME*w.d*	12182	PUT Start TIME8.; PUT Start TIME11.2;	3:23:02 3:23:02.00
WEEKDATE*w*.	8966	PUT Birth WEEKDATE15.; PUT Birth WEEKDATE29.;	Thu, Jul 19, 84 Thursday, July 19, 1984
WORDDATE*w*.	8966	PUT Birth WORDDATE12.; PUT Birth WORDDATE18.;	Jul 19, 1984 July 19, 1984
Numeric			
BEST*w*.	1200001	PUT Value BEST6.; PUT Value BEST8.;	1.20E6 1200001
COMMA*w.d*	1200001	PUT Value COMMA9.; PUT Value COMMA12.2;	1,200,001 1,200,001.00
DOLLAR*w.d*	1200001	PUT Value DOLLAR10.; PUT Value DOLLAR13.2;	$1,200,001 $1,200,001.00
E*w*.	1200001	PUT Value E7.;	1.2E+06
PD*w.d*	128	PUT Value PD4.;	[4]
w.d	23.635	PUT Value 6.3; PUT Value 5.2;	23.635 23.64

[3] The EBCDIC character set is used on most IBM mainframe computers while the ASCII character set is used on most other computers. So, depending on the computer you are using, you will get one or the other.

[4] These values cannot be printed.

4.7 Creating Your Own Formats Using PROC FORMAT

m	2
f	1
m	3

Obs	Sex	AgeGroup
1	Male	Adult
2	Female	Teen
3	Male	Senior

At some time you will probably want to create your own custom formats—especially if you use a lot of coded data. Imagine that you have just completed a survey for your company and to save disk space and time, all the responses to the survey questions are coded. For example, the age categories teen, adult, and senior are coded as numbers 1, 2, and 3. This is convenient for data entry and analysis but bothersome when it comes time to interpret the results. You could present your results along with a code book, and your company directors could look up the codes as they read the results. But this will probably not get you that promotion you've been looking for. A better solution is to create user-defined formats using PROC FORMAT and print the formatted values instead of the coded values.

The FORMAT procedure creates formats that will later be associated with variables in a FORMAT statement. The procedure starts with the statement PROC FORMAT and continues with one or more VALUE statements (other optional statements are available):

```
PROC FORMAT;
     VALUE name range-1 = 'formatted-text-1'
                 range-2 = 'formatted-text-2'
                         .
                         .
                         .
                 range-n = 'formatted-text-n';
```

The *name* in the VALUE statement is the name of the format you are creating, which can't be longer than eight characters, must not start or end with a number, and cannot contain any special characters except the underscore. The *name* can't be the name of an existing format, and if the format is for character data, it must start with a $. Each *range* is the value of a variable that is assigned to the text given in quotes on the right side of the equals sign. The text can be as long as 200 characters, but some procedures may not print all 200 characters. The following are examples of valid range specifications:

```
            'R' = 'Republican'
 1, 3, 5, 7, 9 = 'Odd'
500000 - HIGH = 'Not Affordable'
       13 -< 20 = 'Teenager'
    0 <- HIGH = 'Positive Non Zero'
         OTHER = 'Bad Data'
```

Character values must be enclosed in quotes ('R' for example). If there is more than one value in the range, then separate the values with a comma or use the hyphen (-) for a continuous range. The keywords LOW and HIGH can be used in ranges to indicate the lowest and the highest non-missing value for the variable. You can also use the less than symbol (<) in ranges to exclude either end point of the range. The OTHER keyword can be used to assign a format to any values not listed in the VALUE statement.

Example Universe Cars is surveying its customers as to their preferences for car colors. They have information about the customer's age, sex (coded as 1 for male and 2 for female), annual income, and preferred car color (yellow, gray, blue, or white). Here are the data:

```
19 1 14000 Y
45 1 65000 G
72 2 35000 B
31 1 44000 Y
58 2 83000 W
```

The following program reads the data; creates formats for age, sex, and car color using the FORMAT procedure; then prints the data using the new formats:

```
DATA carsurvey;
    INFILE 'c:\MyRawData\Cars.dat';
    INPUT Age Sex Income Color $;
PROC FORMAT;
    VALUE gender 1 = 'Male'
                 2 = 'Female';
    VALUE agegroup 13 -< 20 = 'Teen'
                   20 -< 65 = 'Adult'
                   65 - HIGH = 'Senior';
    VALUE $col  'W' = 'Moon White'
                'B' = 'Sky Blue'
                'Y' = 'Sunburst Yellow'
                'G' = 'Rain Cloud Gray';
* Print data using user-defined and standard (DOLLAR8.) formats;
PROC PRINT DATA = carsurvey;
    FORMAT Sex gender. Age agegroup. Color $col. Income DOLLAR8.;
    TITLE 'Survey Results Printed with User-Defined Formats';
RUN;
```

This program creates two numeric formats: GENDER for the variable Sex and AGEGROUP for the variable Age. The program creates a character format, $COL, for the variable Color. Notice that the format names do not end with periods in the VALUE statement, but they do in the FORMAT statement.

Here is the output:

```
         Survey Results Printed with User-Defined Formats          1

   Obs     Age      Sex       Income     Color

    1      Teen     Male      $14,000    Sunburst Yellow
    2      Adult    Male      $65,000    Rain Cloud Gray
    3      Senior   Female    $35,000    Sky Blue
    4      Adult    Male      $44,000    Sunburst Yellow
    5      Adult    Female    $83,000    Moon White
```

This example creates a temporary format that exists only for the current job or session. Creating and using permanent formats is discussed under the FORMAT Procedure in the SAS online documentation.

4.8   Writing Simple Custom Reports

PROC PRINT is flexible and easy to use. Still, there are times when PROC PRINT just won't do. One of the great features of PROC PRINT is that you don't have to worry about trivia such as spacing and page breaks; SAS takes care of that. But there may be times when you are forced to worry about these details: when your report to a state agency has to be spaced just like their fill-in-the-blank form, or when your client insists that the report contain complete sentences, or when you want one page per observation. Whenever you have to be picky about the format of a report, chances are that PROC PRINT won't do.

At those times you can use the flexibility of the DATA step to produce your report.[1] This is really an extension of section 2.20 on using FILE and PUT statements to write a raw data file. The difference is that this time you will write to a file for the purpose of printing. To do that, add the PRINT option after the file name in your FILE statement. This way, SAS knows to include those special printing instructions such as carriage returns and page breaks.

Example   To show how this differs from PROC PRINT, we'll use the candy sales data again. Two fourth-grade classes have sold candy to raise money for a field trip. Here are the data with each student's name, classroom number, the date they turned in their money, the type of candy: mint patties or chocolate dinosaurs, and the number of boxes sold:

```
Adriana    21 3/21/2000 MP  7
Nathan     14 3/21/2000 CD 19
Matthew    14 3/21/2000 CD 14
Claire     14 3/22/2000 CD 11
Caitlin    21 3/24/2000 CD  9
Ian        21 3/24/2000 MP 18
Chris      14 3/25/2000 CD  6
Anthony    21 3/25/2000 MP 13
Stephen    14 3/25/2000 CD 10
Erika      21 3/25/2000 MP 17
```

The teachers want a report for each student showing how much money that student earned. They want each student's report on a separate page so it is easy to hand out. Lastly, they want it to be easy for fourth graders to understand, with complete sentences. Here is the program:

```
* Write a report with FILE and PUT statements;
DATA _NULL_;
   INFILE 'c:\MyRawData\Candy.dat';
   INPUT Name $ 1-11 Class @15 DateReturned MMDDYY10.
      CandyType $ Quantity;
   Profit = Quantity * 1.25;
   FILE 'c:\MyRawData\Student.rep' PRINT;
   TITLE;
   PUT @5 'Candy sales report for ' Name 'from classroom ' Class
      // @5 'Congratulations!  You sold ' Quantity 'boxes of candy'
      / @5 'and earned ' Profit DOLLAR6.2 ' for our field trip.';
   PUT _PAGE_;
RUN;
```

---

[1] Other ways to create reports include PROC TABULATE for reports in rows and columns (see sections 4.12 and 4.13), PROC REPORT for interactive or batch reports, and PROC FORMS for reports with a regular pattern such as mailing labels.

Notice that the keyword _NULL_ appears in the DATA statement instead of a data set name. _NULL_ tells SAS not to bother writing a SAS data set (since our goal is to create a report not a data set), and makes the program run slightly faster. The FILE statement creates the output file for the report, and the PRINT option tells SAS to include carriage returns and page breaks. The null TITLE statement tells SAS to eliminate all automatic titles.

A PUT statement tells SAS exactly what to write and where, like an INPUT statement in reverse. Like INPUT statements, PUT statements can use column and line pointers, as well as list, column, and formatted styles of output. In addition to printing your data, you can print any literal by enclosing it in quotes. The first PUT statement in this program starts with a pointer, @5, telling SAS to go to column 5. Then it tells SAS to print the words `Candy sales report for` followed by the current value of the variable Name. The variables Name, Class, and Quantity are printed in list style whereas Profit is printed using formatted style and the DOLLAR6.2 format. A slash line pointer tells SAS to skip to the next line; two slashes skips two lines. You could use multiple PUT statements instead of slashes to skip lines because SAS goes to a new line every time there is a new PUT statement. The statement PUT _PAGE_ inserts a page break after each student's report. When the program is run, the log will contain these notes:

```
NOTE: 10 records were read from the infile 'c:\MyRawData\Candy.dat'.

NOTE: 30 records were written to the file 'c:\MyRawData\Student.rep'.
```

The first three pages of the report look like this:

```
    Candy sales report for Adriana from classroom 21

    Congratulations!  You sold 7 boxes of candy
    and earned  $8.75 for our field trip.
```

```
    Candy sales report for Nathan from classroom 14

    Congratulations!  You sold 19 boxes of candy
    and earned $23.75 for our field trip.
```

```
    Candy sales report for Matthew from classroom 14

    Congratulations!  You sold 14 boxes of candy
    and earned $17.50 for our field trip.
```

4.9   Summarizing Your Data Using PROC MEANS

One of the first things people usually want to do with their data, after reading it and making sure it is correct, is look at some simple statistics. Statistics such as the mean value, standard deviation, and minimum and maximum values give you a feel for your data. These types of information can also alert you to errors in your data (98 runs scored in a baseball game, for example, is suspect). The MEANS procedure provides simple statistics on numeric variables.

The MEANS procedure starts with the keywords PROC MEANS, followed by options listing the statistics you want printed:

```
PROC MEANS options;
```

If you do not specify any options, MEANS will print the number of non-missing values, the mean, the standard deviation, and the minimum and maximum values for each variable. There are over 30 different statistics you can request with the MEANS procedure. The following is a list of some of the simple statistics. More options for the MEANS procedure are discussed in section 7.2.

N	number of non-missing values
NMISS	number of missing values
MIN	the minimum value
MAX	the maximum value
RANGE	the range
SUM	the sum
MEAN	the mean
MEDIAN	the median
STDDEV	the standard deviation

If you use the PROC MEANS statement with no other statements, then you will get statistics for all observations and all numeric variables in your data set. Here are some of the optional statements you may want to use:

BY *variable-list*;	The BY statement performs separate analyses for each level of the variables in the list. The data must first be sorted in the same order as the *variable-list*. (You can use PROC SORT to do this.)
CLASS *variable-list*;	The CLASS statement performs separate analyses for each level of the variables in the list, but its output is more compact than with the BY statement, and the data do not have to be sorted first.
VAR *variable-list*;	The VAR statement specifies which numeric variables to use in the analysis. If it is absent then SAS uses all numeric variables.

Example A wholesale nursery is selling garden flowers, and they want to summarize their sales figures by month. The data file which follows contains the customer ID, date of sale, and number of petunias, snapdragons, and marigolds sold:

```
756-01   05/04/2001 120   80 110
834-01   05/12/2001  90 160  60
901-02   05/18/2001  50 100  75
834-01   06/01/2001  80   60 100
756-01   06/11/2001 100 160  75
901-02   06/19/2001  60   60  60
756-01   06/25/2001  85 110 100
```

The following program reads the data; computes a new variable, Month, which is the month of the sale; sorts the data by Month using PROC SORT; then summarizes the data by Month using PROC MEANS with a BY statement:

```
DATA sales;
   INFILE 'c:\MyRawData\Flowers.dat';
   INPUT CustomerID $ @9 SaleDate MMDDYY10. Petunia SnapDragon
         Marigold;
   Month = MONTH(SaleDate);
PROC SORT DATA = sales;
   BY Month;
* Calculate means by Month for flower sales;
PROC MEANS DATA = sales;
   BY Month;
   VAR Petunia SnapDragon Marigold;
   TITLE 'Summary of Flower Sales by Month';
RUN;
```

Here are the results of the PROC MEANS:

```
                    Summary of Flower Sales by Month                          1


---------------------------------- Month=5 ------------------------------------
                            The MEANS Procedure
Variable      N          Mean          Std Dev      Minimum         Maximum

Petunia       3     86.6666667      35.1188458    50.0000000     120.0000000
SnapDragon    3    113.3333333      41.6333200    80.0000000     160.0000000
Marigold      3     81.6666667      25.6580072    60.0000000     110.0000000


---------------------------------- Month=6 ------------------------------------
Variable      N          Mean          Std Dev      Minimum         Maximum

Petunia       4     81.2500000      16.5201897    60.0000000     100.0000000
SnapDragon    4     97.5000000      47.8713554    60.0000000     160.0000000
Marigold      4     83.7500000      19.7378655    60.0000000     100.0000000
```

4.10   Writing Summary Statistics to a SAS Data Set

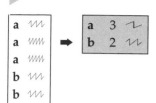 Sometimes you want to save summary statistics to a SAS data set for further analysis, or to merge with other data. For example, you might want to plot the hourly temperature in your office to show how it heats up every afternoon, causing you to fall asleep. But the instrument you have records data for every minute. The MEANS procedure can condense the data by computing the mean temperature for each hour and then writing the results to a SAS data set so it can be plotted using PROC PLOT.

Now, with Version 7 of the SAS System, you have two methods for saving summary statistics to a SAS data set. You can use the Output Delivery System (ODS), which is covered in section 4.16, or you can use the OUTPUT statement in PROC MEANS. The OUTPUT statement has the following form:

```
OUTPUT OUT = data-set output-statistic-list;
```

Here, *data-set* is the name of the SAS data set which will contain the results (this can be either temporary or permanent), and *output-statistic-list* defines which statistics you want and the associated variable names. You can have more than one OUTPUT statement and multiple output statistic lists. The following is one of the possible forms for *output-statistic-list*:

```
statistic(variable-list) = name-list
```

Here, *statistic* can be any of the statistics available in PROC MEANS (SUM, N, MEAN, for example), *variable-list* defines which of the variables in the VAR statement you want to output, and *name-list* defines the new variable names for the statistics. The new variable names must be in the same order as their corresponding variables in *variable-list*. For example, the following PROC MEANS statements produce a new data set called ZOOSUM, which contains one observation with the variables LionWeight, the mean of the lions' weights, and BearWeight, the mean of the bears' weights:

```
PROC MEANS DATA = zoo NOPRINT;
   VAR Lions Tigers Bears;
   OUTPUT OUT = zoosum MEAN(Lions Bears) = LionWeight BearWeight;
RUN;
```

The NOPRINT option in the PROC MEANS statement tells SAS there is no need to produce any printed results since we are saving the results to a SAS data set.

The SAS data set created in the OUTPUT statement will contain all the variables defined in the *output statistic list*; any variables listed in a BY or CLASS statement; plus two new variables, _TYPE_ and _FREQ_. If there is no BY or CLASS statement, then the data set will have just one observation. If there is a BY statement, then the data set will have one observation for each level of the BY group. CLASS statements produce one observation for each level of interaction of the class variables. The value of the _TYPE_ variable depends on the level of interaction. The observation where _TYPE_ has a value of zero is the grand total.[1]

---

[1] For an explanation of the _TYPE_ variable, see your online documentation.

Example The following are sales data for a wholesale nursery with the customer ID; date of sale; and the number of petunias, snapdragons, and marigolds sold:

```
756-01   05/04/2001  120   80  110
834-01   05/12/2001   90  160   60
901-02   05/18/2001   50  100   75
834-01   06/01/2001   80   60  100
756-01   06/11/2001  100  160   75
901-02   06/19/2001   60   60   60
756-01   06/25/2001   85  110  100
```

You want to summarize the data so that you have only one observation per customer containing the sum and mean of the number of plant sets sold, and you want to save the results in a SAS data set for further analysis. The following program reads the data from the file; sorts by the variable, CustomerID; and then uses the MEANS procedure with the NOPRINT option to calculate the sums and means by CustomerID. The results are saved in a SAS data set named TOTALS in the OUTPUT statement. The sums are given the original variable names Petunia, SnapDragon, and Marigold, and the means are given new variable names MeanPetunia, MeanSnapDragon, and MeanMarigold. A PROC PRINT is used to show the TOTALS data set:

```
DATA sales;
   INFILE 'c:\MyRawData\Flowers.dat';
   INPUT CustomerID $ @9 SaleDate MMDDYY10. Petunia SnapDragon Marigold;
PROC SORT DATA = sales;
   BY CustomerID;
* Calculate means by CustomerID, output sum and mean to new data set;
PROC MEANS NOPRINT DATA = sales;
   BY CustomerID;
   VAR Petunia SnapDragon Marigold;
   OUTPUT OUT = totals  MEAN(Petunia SnapDragon Marigold) =
         MeanPetunia MeanSnapDragon MeanMarigold
      SUM(Petunia SnapDragon Marigold) = Petunia SnapDragon Marigold;
PROC PRINT DATA = totals;
   TITLE 'Sum of Flower Data over Customer ID';
   FORMAT MeanPetunia MeanSnapDragon MeanMarigold 3.;
RUN;
```

Here are the results:

```
              Sum of Flower Data over Customer ID                      1


                                     Mean
        Customer              Mean   Snap   Mean           Snap
  Obs     ID    _TYPE_ _FREQ_ Petunia Dragon Marigold Petunia Dragon Marigold

   1    756-01    0      3     102    117     95      305    350     285
   2    834-01    0      2      85    110     80      170    220     160
   3    901-02    0      2      55     80     68      110    160     135
```

4.11   Counting Your Data with PROC FREQ

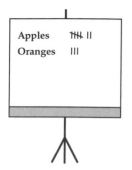

A frequency table is a simple list of counts answering the question "How many?" When you have counts for one variable, they are called one-way frequencies. When you combine two or more variables, the counts are called two-way, three-way, and so on up to *n*-way frequencies; or simply cross-tabulations.

The most obvious reason for using PROC FREQ is to create tables showing the distribution of categorical data values, but PROC FREQ can also reveal irregularities in your data. You could get dizzy proofreading a large data set, but data entry errors are often glaringly obvious in a frequency table. The basic form of PROC FREQ is

```
PROC FREQ;
    TABLES variable-combinations;
```

To produce a one-way frequency table, just list the variable name. This statement produces a frequency table listing the number of observations for each value of YearsEducation:

```
TABLES YearsEducation;
```

To produce a cross-tabulation, list the variables separated by an asterisk. This statement produces a cross-tabulation showing the number of observations for each combination of Sex by YearsEducation:

```
TABLES Sex * YearsEducation;
```

You can specify any number of table requests in a single TABLES statement, and you can have as many TABLES statements as you wish. Be careful though; reading cross-tabulations of three or more levels is like playing three-dimensional tic-tac-toe without the benefit of a three-dimensional board.

Options, if any, appear after a slash in the TABLES statement. For a list of statistical options for PROC FREQ see section 7.3. Options for controlling the output of PROC FREQ include

LIST	prints cross-tabulations in list format rather than grid
MISSING	includes missing values in frequency statistics
NOCOL	suppresses printing of column percentages in cross-tabulations
NOROW	suppresses printing of row percentages in cross-tabulations
OUT = *data-set*	writes a data set containing frequencies

The statement below, for instance, tells SAS to include missing values in the frequencies:

```
TABLES Sex * YearsEducation / MISSING;
```

Example   The proprietor of a local coffee shop, Cathy's Coffee Cup, keeps a record of all sales. For each drink sold, she records the type of coffee (cappuccino, espresso, kona, or iced coffee), and whether the customer walked in or came to the drive-up window. Here are the data with ten observations per line of raw data:

```
esp w cap d cap w kon w ice w kon d esp d kon w ice d esp d
cap w esp d cap d Kon d .   d kon w esp d cap w ice w kon w
kon w kon w ice d esp d kon w esp d esp w kon w cap w kon w
```

The following program reads the data and produces one-way and two-way frequencies:

```
DATA orders;
   INFILE 'c:\MyRawData\Coffee.dat';
   INPUT Coffee $ Window $ @@;
* Print tables for Window and Window by Coffee;
PROC FREQ DATA = orders;
   TABLES Window  Window * Coffee;
   RUN;
```

The output contains two tables. The first is a one-way frequency table for the variable Window. You can see that 13 customers came to the drive-up window while 17 walked into the restaurant.

```
                            The FREQ Procedure

                                          Cumulative    Cumulative
       Window     Frequency      Percent    Frequency      Percent

       d                 13        43.33           13        43.33
       w                 17        56.67           30       100.00

                        Table of Window by Coffee

       Window     Coffee

       Frequency
       Percent
       Row Pct
       Col Pct    Kon      cap      esp      ice      kon       Total

       d               1        2        6        2        1        12
                    3.45     6.90    20.69     6.90     3.45     41.38
                    8.33    16.67    50.00    16.67     8.33
                  100.00    33.33    75.00    50.00    10.00

       w               0        4        2        2        9        17
                    0.00    13.79     6.90     6.90    31.03     58.62
                    0.00    23.53    11.76    11.76    52.94
                    0.00    66.67    25.00    50.00    90.00

       Total           1        6        8        4       10        29
                    3.45    20.69    27.59    13.79    34.48    100.00
                        Frequency Missing = 1
```

The second table is a two-way cross-tabulation of Window by Coffee. Inside each cell, SAS prints the frequency, percentage, percentage for that row, and percentage for that column; while cumulative frequencies and percents appear along the right side and bottom. Notice that the missing value is mentioned but not included in the statistics. (Use the MISSING option if you want missing values to be included in the table.) Also, there is one observation with a value of Kon for Coffee. This data entry error should be kon.

4.12   Producing Tabular Reports with PROC TABULATE

Every summary statistic the TABULATE procedure computes can also be produced by other procedures such as PRINT, MEANS, and FREQ, but PROC TABULATE is poplular because its reports are pretty. If TABULATE were a box, it would be gift-wrapped.

PROC TABULATE is so powerful that it has its own manual, *SAS Guide to TABULATE Processing,* but it is also so concise that you may feel like you're reading hieroglyphics. If you find the syntax of PROC TABULATE a little hard to get used to, that may be because it has roots outside the SAS System. PROC TABULATE is based in part on the Table Producing Language, a complex and sophisticated language developed by the U.S. Department of Labor.

The general form of PROC TABULATE is

```
PROC TABULATE;
   CLASS classification-variable-list;
   TABLE page-dimension, row-dimension, column-dimension;
```

The CLASS statement tells SAS which variables contain categorical data to be used for dividing observations into groups. The TABLE statement tells SAS how to organize your table and what numbers to compute. Each TABLE statement defines only one table, but you may have multiple TABLE statements. By default, PROC TABULATE produces simple counts of the number of observations falling into each category. Section 4.13 describes how to request the many other statistics offered by PROC TABULATE.

Dimensions   Each TABLE statement can specify up to three dimensions. Those dimensions, separated by commas, tell SAS which variables to use for the pages, rows, and columns in the report. If you specify only one dimension, then that becomes, by default, the column dimension. If you specify two dimensions, then you get rows and columns, but no page dimension.

When you write a TABLE statement, start with the column dimension. Once you have that debugged, add the rows. Once you are happy with your rows and columns, then you are ready to add a page dimension, if you need one. Notice that the order of dimensions in the TABLE statement is page, then row, then column. So, to avoid scrambling your table when you add dimensions, insert the page and row specifications in front of the column dimension.

Example   Here are data about pleasure boats including the name of each boat, its length in feet, whether it is a sailing or power vessel, and the type of boat (schooner, catamaran, or yacht).

```
Silent Lady    64 sail   schooner
America II     65 sail   yacht
Ocean Spirit   65 power  catamaran
Lavengro       52 sail   schooner
Pride of Maui 110 power  catamaran
Leilani        45 power  yacht
Kalakaua       70 power  catamaran
Blue Dolphin   65 sail   catamaran
```

Suppose you want a report showing the number of boats of each type that are sailing or power vessels. The following DATA step reads the data from a raw data file named Boats.dat, adding a variable named Port. Then PROC TABULATE creates a three-dimensional report with the values of Port for the pages, Locomotion for the rows, and Type for the columns.

```
DATA boats;
    INFILE 'c:\MyRawData\Boats.dat' TRUNCOVER;
    INPUT Name $13. Length Locomotion $ @25 Type $9.;
    Port = 'Maalea';

* Tabulations with three dimensions;
PROC TABULATE DATA = boats;
    CLASS Port Locomotion Type;
    TABLE Port, Locomotion, Type;
    TITLE 'Number of Boats by Port, Locomotion, and Type';
RUN;
```

Here is the output:

```
       Number of Boats by Port, Locomotion, and Type              1

    Port Maalea

    ┌──────────────┬──────────────────────────────────────┐
    │              │                 Type                 │
    │              ├────────────┬────────────┬────────────┤
    │              │ catamaran  │  schooner  │   yacht    │
    │              ├────────────┼────────────┼────────────┤
    │              │     N      │     N      │     N      │
    ├──────────────┼────────────┼────────────┼────────────┤
    │ Locomotion   │            │            │            │
    ├──────────────┤            │            │            │
    │ power        │      3.00  │       .    │      1.00  │
    ├──────────────┼────────────┼────────────┼────────────┤
    │ sail         │      1.00  │      2.00  │      1.00  │
    └──────────────┴────────────┴────────────┴────────────┘
```

The value of the page dimension, in this case the variable Port, appears in the top, left corner of the output. Since Port had only one value, there is only one page in this report. The Ns in this table tell you that the numbers in this table represent the number of observations in each group.

4.13 Adding Statistics to Tabular Reports

By default, PROC TABULATE produces simple counts, but you can request many other statistics in your TABLE statements. You can also concatenate or cross variables within dimensions. In fact, you can write TABLE statements so complicated that even *you* won't know what the report is going to look like until you run it.

For most statistics you will want to add a VAR statement. Here is the general form:

```
PROC TABULATE;
   VAR analysis-variable-list;
   CLASS classification-variable-list;
   TABLE page-dimension, row-dimension, column-dimension;
```

While the CLASS statement tells SAS which variables contain categorical data, the VAR statement lists continuous variables. You may have both a CLASS statement and a VAR statement, or just one, but all variables listed in a TABLE statement must also appear in either a CLASS or a VAR statement.

Keywords In addition to variable names, each dimension can contain keywords. These are a few of the values TABULATE can compute.

ALL	adds a row, column, or page showing the total
MEAN	the arithmetic mean
MEDIAN	the median
N	number of non-missing values
P90	the 90th percentile
PCTN	the percentage of observations for that group
PCTSUM	the percentage of a total sum represented by that group
SUM	the sum

Concatenating, crossing, and grouping Within a dimension, variables and keywords can be concatenated, crossed, or grouped. To concatenate variables or keywords simply list them separated by a space, to cross variables or keywords separate then with an asterisk (*), and to group them enclose the variables or keywords in parentheses. The keyword ALL is generally concatenated. To request other statistics, however, cross that keyword with the variable name.

Concatenating:	`TABLE Locomotion Type ALL;`
Crossing:	`TABLE MEAN * Length;`
Crossing, grouping, and concatenating:	`TABLE MEAN *(Length Type);`

Example Here again are the boat data containing the name of each boat, its length in feet, whether it is a sailing or power vessel, and the type of boat (schooner, catamaran, or yacht).

```
Silent Lady    64 sail   schooner
America II      65 sail   yacht
Ocean Spirit    65 power  catamaran
Lavengro        52 sail   schooner
```

```
Pride of Maui 110 power catamaran
Leilani        45 power yacht
Kalakaua       70 power catamaran
Blue Dolphin   65 sail  catamaran
```

The following program is similar to the one in section 4.12. However, this PROC TABULATE adds a VAR statement. The TABLE statement in this program contains only two dimensions; but it also concatentates, crosses, and groups variables; and requests statistics.

```
DATA boats;
    INFILE 'c:\MyRawData\Boats.dat' TRUNCOVER;
    INPUT Name $13. Length Locomotion $ @25 Type $9.;
* Tabulations with two dimensions and statistics;
PROC TABULATE DATA = boats;
    CLASS Locomotion Type;
    VAR Length;
    TABLE Locomotion ALL, MEAN*Length*(Type ALL);
    TITLE 'Mean Length of Boat by Locomotion, and Type';
RUN;
```

The row dimension of this table concatenates the classification variable Locomotion with the ALL keyword to get totals. The column dimension, on the other hand, crosses MEAN with the analysis variable Length and with the classification variable Type (which happens to be concatenated and grouped with ALL).

Mean Length of Boat by Locomotion, and Type   1

	Mean			
	Length			
	Type			All
	catamaran	schooner	yacht	All
Locomotion				
power	81.67	.	45.00	72.50
sail	65.00	58.00	65.00	61.50
All	77.50	58.00	55.00	67.00

4.14   Visualizing Your Data with PROC PLOT

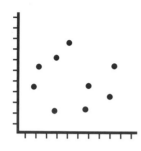

If a picture is worth a thousand words, then PROC PLOT is worth volumes. There are times when trying to see relationships in a table full of abstract numbers can leave you scratching your head. That is when you need to visualize your data.

The scatter plots produced by this procedure provide an easy, intuitive way to get a feel for your data. They also can be displayed on any monitor and printed on any printer, but because of that the plots are rather simple. To get more sophisticated plots, use PROC GPLOT, which is part of SAS/GRAPH software and is licensed separately from base SAS. PROC GPLOT uses the same statements and options as PROC PLOT plus a whole lot more.

The basic form of PROC PLOT is

```
PROC PLOT;
    PLOT vertical-variable * horizontal-variable;
```

The PLOT statement tells SAS which variables to plot and how. SAS plots the first variable on the vertical axis and the second on the horizontal. You can have any number of PLOT statements and any number of plot requests in a single PLOT statement. The statement below requests two plots: one for Height by Weight and another for Height by Age:

```
PLOT Height * Weight  Height * Age;
```

By default, SAS uses letters to mark the points on your plots: A for a single observation, B for two observations at the same point, C for three, and so on. To substitute a different character, such as an asterisk, specify it this way:

```
PLOT Height * Weight = '*';
```

You can also use a third variable as the plot character, making a convenient label for each point. This statement tells SAS to use the first letter from the variable Name to mark each point:

```
PLOT Height * Weight = Name;
```

Example To help visualize the value of PROC PLOT, here are data about the Walla Walla Sweets, a local minor league baseball team. For each home game, the data contain the name of the visiting team, onion ring sales at concession stands and in the bleachers, number of hits for the home team, hits for the visiting team, runs for the home team, and runs for the visiting team:

```
Columbia Peaches     102   67  1 10 2 1
Plains Peanuts       210   54  2  5 0 1
Gilroy Garlics        15  335 12 11 7 6
Sacramento Tomatoes  124  185 15  4 9 1
Boise Spuds          162   75  5  6 2 3
Orlando Tangelos     144   86  9  3 4 2
Des Moines Corncobs   73  210 10  5 9 3
```

The ballpark owners suspect that in games with a lot of hits and runs, more onion rings are sold in the bleachers. To investigate this, the DATA step below reads the raw data and adds together all the runs and hits to create a variable named Action. Then PROC PLOT plots sales in the bleachers by Action:

```
DATA onionrings;
    INFILE 'c:\MyRawData\Onions.dat';
    INPUT VisTeam $ 1-20 CSales BSales OurHits VisHits OurRuns VisRuns;
    Action = OurHits + VisHits + OurRuns + VisRuns;

* Plot Action by BSales;
PROC PLOT DATA = onionrings;
    PLOT BSales * Action = VisTeam;
    TITLE 'Onion Ring Sales';
RUN;
```

The output looks like this:

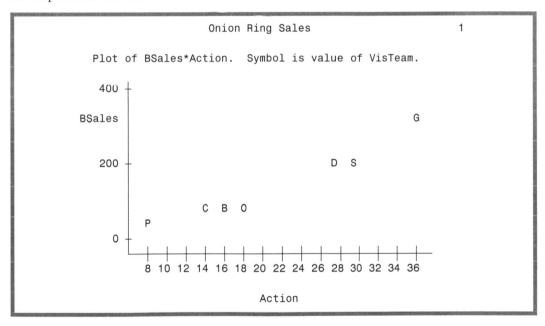

Looking at this plot, it appears that the ballpark owners are right. As Action increases, BSales do tend to increase.

You can plot more than one variable on the vertical axis by using the OVERLAY option. For example, in the preceding program you could rewrite the PLOT statement as shown below. Notice that the plot character is no longer VisTeam because you need to distinguish the points for CSales from the points for BSales:

```
PLOT   CSales * Action = 'C'  BSales * Action = 'B' / OVERLAY;
```

If you add a BY statement, SAS will produce a separate plot for each value of the BY variable. Remember, though, that your data must already be sorted by the variables in the BY statement.

4.15   Formatting Procedure Output for Display on the Internet

The SAS System makes it easy for you to create output that can be displayed with a Web browser such as Netscape or Internet Explorer. With the explosion of Internet use, more and more documents are being stored in Hypertext Markup Language (HTML), a standard file format for Web browsers. Using this standard, you can produce reports that everyone feels comfortable with: your colleague down the hall, the company CEO, your children, or the world.

Output Delivery System   Now, with Version 7 of the SAS System, all your procedure output is routed through the Output Delivery System (ODS). ODS determines where your procedure output will go and what it will look like when it gets there. At the time this book was written, there were two output destinations available: the standard listing that goes in the output window, and HTML. Your release of SAS may have additional output destinations available (such as Rich Text Format or RTF).

The ODS statement   To create HTML files containing your procedure output, you can use the ODS statement. There are four types of HTML files that you can create.

BODY	The body file contains the results of your procedures.
CONTENTS	The contents file is a table of contents with links to the body file. The contents file will list each part of your output, and when you click on an entry in the table of contents, that part of the output will appear.
PAGE	This file is similar to the contents file, except instead of labeling the different parts of the output, it lists the output by page number.
FRAME	The frame file allows you to view the body file and the contents or the page file at the same time in different areas, or frames, of the browser window. If you do not want either the contents or the page file, then there is no need to create a frame file.

You need two ODS statements to make HTML files. The first opens the HTML files, and the second one closes the files. The general form of the ODS statement to open HTML files is

```
ODS HTML    BODY='BodyFile.html'
            CONTENTS='ContentsFile.html'
            PAGE='PageFile.html'
            FRAME='FrameFile.html';
```

You always want to create a body file, but the other files are optional. If, for example, you don't want a page file, then just leave the PAGE= specification out of the ODS statement. The ODS statement does not belong to either a DATA step or a PROC step. It is possible to put the ODS statement almost anywhere in your program, but it makes the most sense to put it at the beginning.

Here is the second ODS statement which closes the HTML files. This statement generally goes at the end of your program.

```
ODS HTML CLOSE;
```

Example This example uses data about average lengths, in feet, of selected whales and sharks.

```
beluga    whale 15   dwarf    shark .5
basking   shark 30   whale    shark 40
gray      whale 50   blue     whale 100
mako      shark 12   killer   whale 30
sperm     whale 60
```

The following program produces two pieces of output: one from the FREQ procedure and one from the MEANS procedure. There are two ODS statements in the program. The first ODS statement creates four HTML files: the body, contents, page, and frame. The last ODS statement closes the HTML files.

```
* Create the HTML files;
ODS HTML BODY = 'c:\MyHTMLFiles\MarineBody.html'
         CONTENTS = 'c:\MyHTMLFiles\MarineTOC.html'
         PAGE = 'c:\MyHTMLFiles\MarinePage.html'
         FRAME = 'c:\MyHTMLFiles\MarineFrame.html';
* Read the data and produce FREQ and MEANS output;
DATA marine;
   INFILE 'c:\MyRawData\Sealife2.dat';
   INPUT Name $ Family $ Length @;
PROC FREQ DATA = marine;
   TABLES Family;
   TITLE 'Whales and Sharks';
PROC SORT DATA = marine;
   BY Family;
PROC MEANS DATA = marine;
   BY Family;
RUN;
* Close the HTML files;
ODS HTML CLOSE;
```

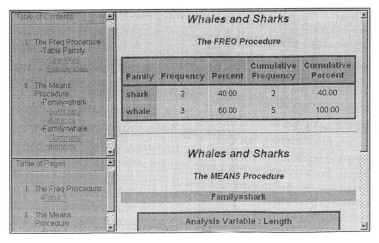

Here is what the MarineFrame.html file looks like when viewed with a browser.

4.16 Creating SAS Data Sets from Procedure Output

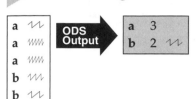

Sometimes you want to put the results from procedures into SAS data sets. Once the results are in a data set, you can merge them with the original data, create new variables based on the results, or use the results in other procedures such as PLOT. Some procedures have OUTPUT statements, or OUT= options, that allow you to save parts of the results to a SAS data set. But now, with Version 7, you can save any part of any procedure output in a SAS data set.

The Output Delivery System With the Output Delivery System (ODS), every result produced by a procedure has a name. This gives you a handle, a way to access, each piece of information generated by the procedure. Once you know the name of the piece of output you want, you can save it.

The ODS TRACE statement An easy way to determine the names for the different parts of the output is to use the ODS TRACE statement in your program. There are two ODS TRACE statements: one to turn on the trace (ODS TRACE ON), and one to turn it off (ODS TRACE OFF). When the trace is turned on, information about your procedure output, including the names of the output parts, is written to the SAS log. Here is how to use these statements in a program:

```
ODS TRACE ON;
your program statements here;
ODS TRACE OFF;
```

Example This program starts with the ODS TRACE ON statement to turn on the trace. Then it reads the data from a file, the same data about pleasure boats used in section 4.12, and runs PROC TABULATE. The program ends with the ODS TRACE OFF statement to close the trace. Notice that there is no RUN statement after the ODS TRACE OFF statement. Unlike most other SAS statements, the ODS statement executes immediately—without waiting for a RUN, PROC, or DATA statement. If you put the ODS TRACE OFF statement before the RUN statement in this program, then you would not get the trace from the TABULATE procedure. This is because the trace would be turned off before the TABULATE procedure completes.

```
* Trace ODS for TABULATE procedure;
ODS TRACE ON;
DATA boats;
   INFILE 'c:\MyRawData\Boats.dat' TRUNCOVER;
   INPUT Name $13. Length Locomotion $ @25 Type $9.;
   Port = 'Maalea';
PROC TABULATE DATA = boats;
   CLASS Port Locomotion Type;
   TABLE Port, Locomotion, Type;
   TITLE 'Number of Boats by Port, Locomotion, and Type';
RUN;
ODS TRACE OFF;
```

Here is an excerpt from the SAS log showing the results of the ODS trace. The TABULATE procedure produces one output part: Report. Some procedures produce several pieces of output, each with a different name.

```
Output Added:
-------------
Name:       Report
Label:      Cross-tabular summary report
Data Name:  Summary
Data Label: Summary descriptive statistics
Path:       Tabulate.Report
-------------
```

The ODS OUTPUT statement Once you have determined the name of the piece of output that you want, use the ODS OUTPUT statement to save the result to a SAS data set. Here is the ODS OUTPUT statement in its simplest form:

```
ODS OUTPUT name = data-set;
```

where *name* is the name of the output you want to save, and *data-set* is the name of the SAS data set you want to create. The ODS OUTPUT statement does not belong in either a DATA or PROC step, but you need to be careful where you put it in your program. The ODS OUTPUT statement opens a SAS data set and waits for the correct procedure output. The data set remains open until the next encounter with an end of a PROC step. Because the ODS statement executes immediately, it will apply to whatever PROC is currently being processed, or the next PROC if there is not a current PROC. To ensure that you get the correct output, we recommend that you put the ODS OUTPUT statement after your PROC statement, and before the next PROC, DATA, or RUN statement.

Example From the previous example, we have determined that the name of the TABULATE output is REPORT. The following program uses the ODS OUTPUT statement in the PROC TABULATE step to create a SAS data set named TABULATEOUTPUT.

```
* Create an output data set from TABULATE procedure;
PROC TABULATE DATA = boats;
   CLASS Port Locomotion Type;
   TABLE Port, Locomotion, Type;
ODS OUTPUT REPORT = tabulateoutput;

PROC PRINT DATA = tabulateoutput;
   TITLE 'Output Data Set from Tabulate';
RUN;
```

Here is the output showing the data set created by the ODS statement:

```
                   Output Data Set from Tabulate                    1
   Obs    Port     Locomotion    Type       _TYPE_    _PAGE_    _TABLE_    N

    1    Maalea     power      catamaran     111        1         1       3
    2    Maalea     power      yacht         111        1         1       1
    3    Maalea     sail       catamaran     111        1         1       1
    4    Maalea     sail       schooner      111        1         1       2
    5    Maalea     sail       yacht         111        1         1       1
```

5

" I usually say, 'The computer is the dumbest thing on campus. It does exactly what you tell it to; not necessarily what you want. Logic is up to you.' "

NECIA A. BLACK, R.N., PH.D., SAS® USER SINCE 1987

From the SAS L listserv, May 6, 1994. Reprinted by permission of the author.

CHAPTER 5

Modifying and Combining SAS® Data Sets

5.1 Modifying a Data Set Using the SET Statement

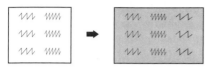

The SET statement in the DATA step allows you to read a SAS data set so you can add new variables, create a subset, or otherwise modify the data set. If you were short on disk space, for example, you might not want to store your calculated variables in a permanent SAS data set. Instead, you might want to calculate them as needed for analysis. Likewise, to save processing time, you might want to create a subset of a SAS data set when you only want to look at a small portion of a large data set. The SET statement brings a SAS data set, one observation at a time, into the DATA step for processing.[1]

To read a SAS data set, start with the DATA statement specifying the name of the new SAS data set. Then follow with the SET statement specifying the name of the old SAS data set you want to read. If you don't want to create a new SAS data set, you can specify the same name in the DATA and SET statements. Then the results of the DATA step will overwrite the old data set named in the SET statement.[2] The following shows the general form of the DATA and SET statements:

```
DATA new-data-set;
   SET data-set;
```

Any assignment, subsetting IF, or other DATA step statements usually follow the SET statement. For example, the following creates a new data set, FRIDAY, which is a replica of the SALES data set, except FRIDAY has only the observations for Fridays, and it has an additional variable, Total:

```
DATA friday;
   SET sales;
   IF Day = 'F';
   Total = Popcorn + Peanuts;
RUN;
```

Example The Fun Times Amusement Park is collecting data about their train ride. They can add more cars on the train during peak hours to shorten the wait, or take them off when they're not needed to save fuel costs. The raw data file contains data for the time of day, the number of cars on the train, and the total number of people on the train:

```
10:10   6 21
12:15  10 56
15:30  10 25
11:30   8 34
13:15   8 12
10:45   6 13
20:30   6 32
23:15   6 12
```

---

[1] The MODIFY statement also allows you to modify a single data set. See the online documentation for more information.

[2] By default, SAS will not overwrite a data set in a DATA step that has errors.

The data are read into a permanent SAS data set, TRAINS, stored in the MySASLib directory on the park's central computer by means of the following program:

```
* Create permanent SAS data set trains;
DATA 'c:\MySASLib\trains';
   INFILE 'c:\MyRawData\Train.dat';
   INPUT Time TIME5. Cars People;
RUN;
```

Each train car holds a maximum of six people. After collecting the data, the Fun Times management decides they want to know the average number of people per car on each ride. This number was not calculated in the original DATA step which created the permanent SAS data set, but can be calculated by the following program:

```
* Read the SAS data set trains with a SET statement;
DATA averagetrain;
   SET 'c:\MySASLib\trains';
   PeoplePerCar = People / Cars;
PROC PRINT DATA = averagetrain;
   TITLE 'Average Number of People per Train Car';
   FORMAT Time TIME5.;
RUN;
```

The DATA statement defines the new SAS data set AVERAGETRAIN. The SET statement reads the permanent SAS data set TRAINS creating a copy of the data in the temporary data set AVERAGETRAIN. An assignment statement follows the SET statement, creating the new variable PeoplePerCar. Here are the results of the PROC PRINT:

```
            Average Number of People per Train Car                1

                                              People
           Obs     Time    Cars    People     PerCar

            1     10:10      6       21       3.50000
            2     12:15     10       56       5.60000
            3     15:30     10       25       2.50000
            4     11:30      8       34       4.25000
            5     13:15      8       12       1.50000
            6     10:45      6       13       2.16667
            7     20:30      6       32       5.33333
            8     23:15      6       12       2.00000
```

5.2 Stacking Data Sets Using the SET Statement

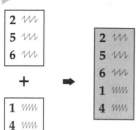

The SET statement with one SAS data set allows you to read and modify the data. With two or more data sets, in addition to reading and modifying the data, the SET statement concatenates or stacks the data sets one on top of the other. This is useful when you want to combine data sets with all or most of the same variables but different observations. You might, for example, have data from two different locations or data taken at two separate times, but you need the data together for analysis.

In a DATA step, first specify the name of the new SAS data set in the DATA statement, then list the names of the old data sets you want to combine in the SET statement:

```
DATA new-data-set;
   SET data-set-1 data-set-n;
```

The number of observations in the new data set will equal the sum of the number of observations in the old data sets. The order of observations is determined by the order of the list of old data sets. If one of the data sets has a variable not contained in the other data sets, then the observations from the other data sets will have missing values for that variable.

Example The Fun Times Amusement Park has two entrances where they collect data about their customers. The data file for the south entrance has an S (for south) followed by the customers' Fun Times pass numbers, the sizes of their parties, and their ages. The file for the north entrance has an N (for north), the same data as the south entrance, plus one more column for the parking lot where they left their cars (the south entrance has only one lot). The following shows samples of the two data files:

Data for South Entrance	Data for North Entrance
S 43 3 27	N 21 5 41 1
S 44 3 24	N 87 4 33 3
S 45 3 2	N 65 2 67 1
	N 66 2 7 1

The first two parts of the following program read the raw data for the south and north entrances into SAS data sets and print them to make sure they are correct. The third part combines the two SAS data sets using a SET statement. The same DATA step creates a new variable, AmountPaid, which tells how much each customer paid based on their age. This final data set is printed using PROC PRINT:

```
DATA southentrance;
   INFILE 'c:\MyRawData\South.dat';
   INPUT Entrance $ PassNumber PartySize Age;
PROC PRINT DATA = southentrance;
   TITLE 'South Entrance Data';

DATA northentrance;
   INFILE 'c:\MyRawData\North.dat';
   INPUT Entrance $ PassNumber PartySize Age Lot;
PROC PRINT DATA = northentrance;
   TITLE 'North Entrance Data';
```

```
* Create a data set, both, combining northentrance and southentrance;
* Create a variable, AmountPaid, based on value of variable Age;
DATA both;
   SET southentrance northentrance;
   IF Age = . THEN AmountPaid = .;
      ELSE IF Age < 3  THEN AmountPaid = 0;
      ELSE IF Age < 65 THEN AmountPaid = 17;
      ELSE AmountPaid = 12;
PROC PRINT DATA = both;
   TITLE 'Both Entrances';
RUN;
```

The following are the results of the three PRINT procedures in the program. Notice that the final data set has missing values for the variable Lot for all the observations which came from the south entrance. This is because the variable Lot was not in the SOUTHENTRANCE data set. SAS assigns missing values to those observations.

```
                      South Entrance Data                        1

                         Pass      Party
            Obs    Entrance   Number    Size     Age

             1       S        43         3       27
             2       S        44         2       24
             3       S        45         3        2
                      North Entrance Data                        2

                      Pass     Party
            Obs   Entrance   Number   Size    Age    Lot

             1      N         21        5      41     1
             2      N         87        4      33     3
             3      N         65        2      67     1
             4      N         66        2       7     1
                       Both Entrances                            3

                      Pass     Party                   Amount
            Obs   Entrance   Number   Size   Age   Lot   Paid

             1      S         43        3     27     .     17
             2      S         44        2     24     .     17
             3      S         45        3      2     .      0
             4      N         21        5     41     1     17
             5      N         87        4     33     3     17
             6      N         65        2     67     1     12
             7      N         66        2      7     1     17
```

5.3 Interleaving Data Sets Using the SET Statement

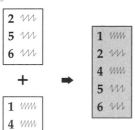

The previous section explained how to stack data sets that have all or most of the same variables but different observations. However, if you have data sets that are already sorted by some important variable, then simply stacking the data sets may unsort the data sets. You could stack the two data sets and then re-sort them using PROC SORT. But if your data sets are already sorted, it is more efficient to preserve that order, than to stack and re-sort. All you need to do is use a BY statement with your SET statement. Here's the general form:

```
DATA new-data-set;
   SET data-set-1 data-set-n;
   BY variable-list;
```

In a DATA statement, you specify the name of the new SAS data set you want to create. In a SET statement, you list the data sets to be interleaved. Then in a BY statement, you list one or more variables that SAS should use for ordering the observations. The number of observations in the new data set will be equal to the sum of the number of observations in the old data sets. If one of the data sets has a variable not contained in the other data sets, then values of that variable will be set to missing for observations from the other data sets.

Before you can interleave observations, the data sets must be sorted by the BY variables. If one or the other of your data sets is not already sorted, then use PROC SORT to do the job.

Example To show how this is different from stacking data sets, we'll use the amusement park data again. There are two data sets, one for the south entrance and one for the north. For every customer, the park collects the following data: the entrance (S or N), the customer's Fun Times pass number, size of that customer's party, and age. For customers entering from the north, the data set also includes parking lot number. Here is a sample of the data:

Data for South Entrance	Data for North Entrance
S 43 3 27	N 21 5 41 1
S 44 3 24	N 87 4 33 3
S 45 3 2	N 65 2 67 1
	N 66 2 7 1

Notice that the data for the south entrance are already sorted by pass number, but the data for the north entrance are not.

Instead of stacking the two data sets, this program interleaves the data sets by pass number. This program first reads the data for the south entrance and prints them to make sure they are correct. Then the program reads the data for the north entrance, sorts them, and prints them. Then in the final DATA step, SAS combines the two data sets, NORHTENTRANCE and SOUTHENTRANCE, creating a new data set named INTERLEAVE. The BY statement tells SAS to combine the data sets by PassNumber:

```
DATA southentrance;
   INFILE 'c:\MyRawData\South.dat';
   INPUT Entrance $ PassNumber PartySize Age;
PROC PRINT DATA = southentrance;
   TITLE 'South Entrance Data';
```

```
DATA northentrance;
    INFILE 'c:\MyRawData\North.dat';
    INPUT Entrance $ PassNumber PartySize Age Lot;
PROC SORT DATA = northentrance;
    BY PassNumber;
PROC PRINT DATA = northentrance;
    TITLE 'North Entrance Data';

* Interleave observations by PassNumber;
DATA interleave;
    SET northentrance southentrance;
    BY PassNumber;
PROC PRINT DATA = interleave;
    TITLE 'Both Entrances, By Pass Number';
RUN;
```

Here are the results of the three PRINT procedures. Notice how the observations have been interleaved so that the new data set is sorted by PassNumber:

```
                        South Entrance Data                          1


                          Pass      Party
            Obs    Entrance   Number    Size    Age

             1        S        43       3       27
             2        S        44       2       24
             3        S        45       3        2


                        North Entrance Data                          2


                       Pass      Party
        Obs    Entrance   Number    Size    Age    Lot

         1        N        21       5      41      1
         2        N        65       2      67      1
         3        N        66       2       7      1
         4        N        87       4      33      3


                   Both Entrances, By Pass Number                    3


                       Pass      Party
        Obs    Entrance   Number    Size    Age    Lot

         1        N        21       5      41      1
         2        S        43       3      27      .
         3        S        44       2      24      .
         4        S        45       3       2      .
         5        N        65       2      67      1
         6        N        66       2       7      1
         7        N        87       4      33      3
```

5.4   Combining Data Sets Using a One-to-One Match Merge

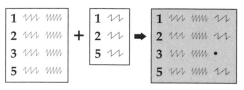

When you have two SAS data sets with related data and you want to combine them, use the MERGE statement in the DATA step. If you know the two data sets are in EXACTLY the same order you don't have to have any common variables between the data sets. Typically, however, you will want to have, for matching purposes, a common variable or several variables which taken together uniquely identify each observation. This is important. Having a common variable to merge by ensures that the observations in the data sets are properly matched. For example, to merge patient data with billing data, you would use the patient ID as a matching variable. Otherwise you risk getting Mary Smith's visit to the obstetrician mixed up with Matthew Smith's visit to the optometrist.

Merging SAS data sets is a simple process. First, if the data are not already sorted, use the SORT procedure to sort all data sets by the common variables. Then, in the DATA statement, name the new SAS data set to hold the results and follow with a MERGE statement listing the data sets to be combined. Use a BY statement to indicate the common variables:

```
DATA new-data-set;
   MERGE data-set-1 data-set-2;
   BY variable-list;
```

If you merge two data sets, and they have variables with the same names—besides the BY variables—then variables from the second data set will overwrite any variables having the same name in the first data set.

Example A Belgian chocolatier keeps track of the number of each type of chocolate sold each day. The code number for each chocolate and the number of pieces sold that day are kept in a file. In a separate file she keeps the names and descriptions of each chocolate as well as the code number. In order to print the day's sales along with the descriptions of the chocolates, the two files must be merged together using the code number as the common variable. Here is a sample of the data:

Sales data

```
C865 15
K086  9
A536 21
S163 34
K014  1
A206 12
B713 29
```

Descriptions

```
A206 Mokka     Coffee buttercream in dark chocolate
A536 Walnoot   Walnut halves in bed of dark chocolate
B713 Frambozen Raspberry marzipan covered in milk chocolate
C865 Vanille   Vanilla-flavored rolled in ground hazelnuts
K014 Kroon     Milk chocolate with a mint cream center
K086 Koning    Hazelnut paste in dark chocolate
M315 Pyramide  White with dark chocolate trimming
S163 Orbais    Chocolate cream in dark chocolate
```

The first two parts of the following program read the descriptions and sales data. The descriptions data are already sorted by CodeNum, so we don't need to use PROC SORT. The sales data are not sorted, so a PROC SORT follows the DATA step. (If you attempt to merge data which are not sorted, SAS will refuse and give you this error message: ERROR: BY variables are not properly sorted.)

```
DATA descriptions;
    INFILE 'c:\MyRawData\chocolate.dat' TRUNCOVER;
    INPUT CodeNum $ 1-4 Name $ 6-14 Description $ 15-60;
DATA sales;
    INFILE 'c:\MyRawData\chocsales.dat';
    INPUT CodeNum $ 1-4 PiecesSold 6-7;
PROC SORT DATA = sales;
    BY CodeNum;

* Merge data sets by CodeNum;
DATA chocolates;
    MERGE sales descriptions;
    BY CodeNum;
PROC PRINT DATA = chocolates;
    TITLE "Today's Chocolate Sales";
RUN;
```

The final part of the program creates a data set named CHOCOLATES by merging the SALES data set and the DESCRIPTIONS data set. The common variable CodeNum in the BY statement is used for matching purposes. The following output shows the final data set after merging:

```
                         Today's Chocolate Sales                      1

        Code  Pieces
Obs     Num    Sold   Name         Description

  1     A206     12   Mokka        Coffee buttercream in dark chocolate
  2     A536     21   Walnoot      Walnut halves in bed of dark chocolate
  3     B713     29   Frambozen    Raspberry marzipan covered in milk chocolate
  4     C865     15   Vanille      Vanilla-flavored rolled in ground hazelnuts
  5     K014      1   Kroon        Milk chocolate with a mint cream center
  6     K086      9   Koning       Hazelnut paste in dark chocolate
  7     M315      .   Pyramide     White with dark chocolate trimming
  8     S163     34   Orbais       Chocolate cream in dark chocolate
```

Notice that the final data set has a missing value for PiecesSold in the seventh observation. This is because there were no sales for the Pyramide chocolate. All observations from both data sets were included in the final data set whether they had a match or not.

5.5 ▶ Combining Data Sets Using a One-to-Many Match Merge

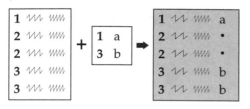

Sometimes you need to combine two data sets by matching one observation from one data set with more than one observation in another. Suppose you had data for every state in the U.S. and wanted to combine it with data for every county. This would be a one-to-many match merge because each state observation matches with many county observations.

The statements for a one-to-many match merge are identical to the statements for a one-to-one match merge:

```
DATA new-data-set;
   MERGE data-set-1 data-set-2;
   BY variable-list;
```

The order of the data sets in the MERGE statement does not matter to SAS. In other words, a one-to-many merge is the same as a many-to-one merge.

Before you merge two data sets, they must be sorted by one or more common variables. If your data sets are not already sorted in the proper order, then use PROC SORT to do the job.

You cannot do a one-to-many merge without a BY statement. SAS uses the variables listed in the BY statement to decide which observations belong together. Without any BY variables for matching, SAS simply joins together the first observation from each data set, then the second observation from each data set, and so on. In other words, SAS performs a one-to-one unmatched merge, which is probably not what you want.

If you merge two data sets, and they have variables with the same names—besides the BY variables—then variables from the second data set will overwrite any variables having the same name in the first data set. For example, if you merge two data sets by a variable named Id, and both data sets contain a variable named Score, then the final data set will contain only one variable named Score. The values for Score will come from the second data set. You can fix this by renaming the variables (perhaps Score1 and Score2) so that they will not overwrite each other.[1]

Example A distributor of exercise video tapes is putting all its tapes on sale at 20 to 30% off the regular price. The distributor has two data files, one with information about each video and one with the discount factors. The first file contains one record for each video with values for

---

[1] The RENAME= data set option is discussed in section 5.9.

title, type of exercise (aerobics, step, or weights), and regular price. The second file contains one record for each type of exercise and its discount. Here are samples from the two raw data files:

Videos data

```
Adorable Abs                        aerobics 12.99
Aerobic Childcare for Parents  aerobics 13.99
Judy Murphy's Fun Fitness        step     12.99
Lavonnes' Low Impact Workout   aerobics 13.99
Muscle Makers                      weights  15.99
Rock N Roll Step Workout         step     12.99
```

Discount data

```
aerobics  .20
step      .30
weights   .25
```

To find the sale price, the following program combines the two data files:

```
DATA videos;
    INFILE 'c:\MyRawData\Vid.dat';
    INPUT Name $ 1-29 ExerciseType $ RegularPrice;
PROC SORT DATA = videos;
    BY ExerciseType;

DATA discount;
    INFILE 'c:\MyRawData\Disc.dat';
    INPUT ExerciseType $ Adjustment;

* Perform many-to-one match merge;
DATA prices;
    MERGE videos discount;
    BY ExerciseType;
    NewPrice = ROUND(RegularPrice - (RegularPrice * Adjustment), .01);
PROC PRINT DATA = prices;
    TITLE 'Price List for May 21-27';
RUN;
```

The first DATA step reads the regular prices, creating a data set named VIDEOS. That data set is then sorted by ExerciseType using PROC SORT. The second DATA step reads the price adjustments, creating a data set named DISCOUNT. This data set is already arranged by ExerciseType, so PROC SORT is not needed. The third DATA step creates a data set named PRICES, merging the first two data sets by ExerciseType, and computes a variable called NewPrice. The output looks like this:

```
                         Price List for May 21-27                     1

                                    Exercise  Regular            New
        Obs  Name                     Type     Price  Adjustment  Price

         1   Adorable Abs            aerobics  12.99     0.20     10.39
         2   Aerobic Childcare for Parents aerobics  13.99     0.20     11.19
         3   Lavonnes' Low Impact Workout  aerobics  13.99     0.20     11.19
         4   Judy Murphy's Fun Fitness     step      12.99     0.30      9.09
         5   Rock N Roll Step Workout      step      12.99     0.30      9.09
         6   Muscle Makers           weights   15.99     0.25     11.99
```

Notice that the values for Adjustment from the DISCOUNT data set are repeated for every observation in the VIDEOS data set with the same value of ExerciseType.

5.6 ▸ Merging Summary Statistics with the Original Data

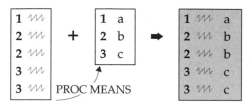

Once in a while you need to combine summary statistics with your data, such as when you want to compare each observation to the group mean, or when you want to calculate a percentage using the group total. To do this, summarize your data using PROC MEANS, and write the results in a new data set. Then merge the summarized data back with the original data using a one-to-many match merge.

Example A distributor of exercise videos is considering doing a special promotion for the top selling titles. The vice-president of marketing has asked you to produce a report. The report should be divided by type of exercise (aerobic, step, or weights) and show the percentage of sales for each title within its type. For each video, the raw data file contains the title, type of exercise, and total sales for the last quarter:

```
Adorable Abs                     aerobics 1930
Aerobic Childcare for Parents aerobics 2250
Judy Murphy's Fun Fitness        step     4150
Lavonnes' Low Impact Workout  aerobics 1130
Muscle Makers                    weights  2230
Rock N Roll Step Workout         step     1190
```

Here is the program:

```
DATA videos;
   INFILE 'c:\MyRawData\Vidsales.dat';
   INPUT Title $ 1-29 ExerciseType $ Sales;
PROC SORT DATA = videos;
   BY ExerciseType;

* Summarize sales by ExerciseType and print;
PROC MEANS NOPRINT DATA = videos;
   VAR Sales;
   BY ExerciseType;
   OUTPUT OUT = summarydata SUM(Sales) = Total;
PROC PRINT DATA = summarydata;
   TITLE 'Summary Data Set';

* Merge totals with the original data set;
DATA videosummary;
   MERGE videos summarydata;
   BY ExerciseType;
   Percent = Sales / Total * 100;
PROC PRINT DATA = videosummary;
   BY ExerciseType;
   ID ExerciseType;
   VAR Title Sales Total Percent;
   TITLE 'Sales Share by Type of Exercise';
RUN;
```

This program is long but straightforward. It starts by reading the raw data in a DATA step and sorting them with PROC SORT. Then it summarizes the data with PROC MEANS by the variable ExerciseType. The OUTPUT statement tells SAS to create a new data set named SUMMARYDATA, containing a variable named Total, which equals the sum of Sales. The NOPRINT option tells SAS not to print the standard PROC MEANS report. Instead, the summary data set is printed by PROC PRINT:

```
                           Summary Data Set                         1

                  Exercise
        Obs         Type        _TYPE_      _FREQ_      Total

         1        aerobics         0           3         5310
         2        step             0           2         5340
         3        weights          0           1         2230
```

In the last part of the program, the original data set, VIDEOS, is merged with SUMMARYDATA to make a new data set, VIDEOSUMMARY. This DATA step computes a new variable called Percent. Then the last PROC PRINT writes the final report with percentage of sales by ExerciseType for each title. Using a BY and an ID statement together gives this report a little different look:

```
                    Sales Share by Type of Exercise                 2

    Exercise
      Type      Title                        Sales    Total    Percent

    aerobics    Adorable Abs                  1930     5310     36.347
                Aerobic Childcare for Parents 2250     5310     42.373
                Lavonnes' Low Impact Workout  1130     5310     21.281

    step        Judy Murphy's Fun Fitness     4150     5340     77.715
                Rock N Roll Step Workout       1190     5340     22.285

    weights     Muscle Makers                 2230     2230    100.000
```

5.7 Combining a Grand Total with the Original Data

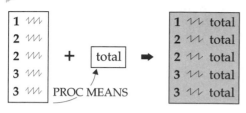

You can use the MEANS procedure to create a data set containing a grand total rather than BY group totals. But you cannot use a MERGE statement to combine a grand total with the original data because there is no common variable to merge by. If you try merging them anyway, SAS will combine the grand total with the first observation of the original data, and then set the variables for the grand total data set to missing for all other observations. Luckily, there is a better way. You can use two SET statements like this:

```
DATA new-data-set;
   IF _N_ = 1 THEN SET summary-data-set;
   SET original-data-set;
```

In this DATA step, *original-data-set* is the data set with more than one observation, the original data, and *summary-data-set* is the data set with a single observation, the grand total. SAS reads *original-data-set* in a normal SET statement, simply reading the observations in a straightforward way. SAS also reads *summary-data-set* with a SET statement but only in the first iteration of the DATA step (when _N_ equals 1).[1] SAS then retains the values of variables from *summary-data-set* for all observations in *new-data-set*.

This works because variables read with a SET statement are automatically retained. Normally you don't notice this because the retained values are overwritten by the next observation. But in this case the variables from *summary-data-set* are read once at the first iteration of the DATA step and then retained for all other observations. The effect is similar to a RETAIN statement. This technique can be used any time you want to combine a single observation with many observations, without a common variable.

Example To show how this is different from merging BY group summary statistics with original data, we'll use the same data as in the previous section. A distributor of exercise videos is considering doing a special promotion for the top-selling titles. The vice-president of marketing asks you to produce a report. The report should show the percentage of total sales for each title. For each video the raw data file contains the title, type of exercise, and sales for the last quarter:

```
Adorable Abs                   aerobics 1930
Aerobic Childcare for Parents  aerobics 2250
Judy Murphy's Fun Fitness      step     4150
Lavonnes' Low Impact Workout   aerobics 1130
Muscle Makers                  weights  2230
Rock N Roll Step Workout       step     1190
```

---

[1] See section 5.14 for an explanation of _N_.

Here is the program:

```
DATA videos;
   INFILE 'c:\MyRawData\Vidsales.dat';
   INPUT Title $ 1-29 ExerciseType $ Sales;

* Output grand total of sales to a data set and print;
PROC MEANS NOPRINT DATA = videos;
   VAR Sales;
   OUTPUT OUT = summarydata SUM(Sales) = GrandTotal;
PROC PRINT DATA = summarydata;
   TITLE 'Summary Data Set';

* Combine the grand total with the original data;
DATA videosummary;
   IF _N_ = 1 THEN SET summarydata;
   SET videos;
   Percent = Sales / GrandTotal * 100;
PROC PRINT DATA = videosummary;
   VAR Title ExerciseType Sales GrandTotal Percent;
   TITLE 'Overall Sales Share';
RUN;
```

This program starts with a DATA step to input the raw data. Then PROC MEANS creates an output data set named SUMMARYDATA with one observation containing a variable named GrandTotal, which is equal to the sum of Sales. This will be a grand total because there is no BY or CLASS statement. The second DATA step combines the original data with the grand total using two SET statements and then computes the variable Percent using the grand total data.

The output looks like this:

```
                    Summary Data Set                          1

                                      Grand
            Obs    _TYPE_    _FREQ_    Total
             1       0         6       12880


                   Overall Sales Share                        2

                                   Exercise         Grand
    Obs   Title                      Type    Sales  Total  Percent
     1    Adorable Abs             aerobics   1930  12880  14.9845
     2    Aerobic Childcare for Parents  aerobics   2250  12880  17.4689
     3    Lavonnes' Low Impact Workout   aerobics   1130  12880   8.7733
     4    Judy Murphy's Fun Fitness      step       4150  12880  32.2205
     5    Rock N Roll Step Workout       step       1190  12880   9.2391
     6    Muscle Makers                  weights    2230  12880  17.3137
```

5.8 Updating a Master Data Set with Transactions

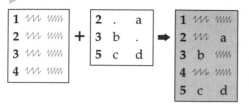

The UPDATE statement is used far less than the MERGE statement, but it is just right for those times when you have a master data set that must be updated with bits of new information. A bank account is a good example of this type of transaction-oriented data, since it is regularly updated with credits and debits.

The UPDATE statement is similar to the MERGE statement, because both combine data sets by matching observations on common variables.[1] However, there are critical differences:

♦   First, with UPDATE the resulting master data set always has just one observation for each unique value of the common variables. That way, you don't get a new observation for your bank account every time you deposit a paycheck.

♦   Second, missing values in the transaction data set do not overwrite existing values in the master data set. That way, you are not obliged to enter your address and tax ID number every time you make a withdrawal.

The basic form of the UPDATE statement is

```
DATA master-data-set;
   UPDATE master-data-set transaction-data-set;
   BY variable-list;
```

Here are a few points to remember about the UPDATE statement. You can specify only two data sets: one master and one transaction. Both data sets must be sorted by their common variables. Also, the values of those BY variables must be unique in the master data set. Using the bank example, you could have many transactions for a single account, but only one observation per account in the master data set.

Example   A hospital maintains a master database with information about patients. A sample appears below. Each record contains the patient's account number, last name, address, date of birth, sex, insurance code, and the date that patient's information was last updated.

```
620135 Smith    234 Aspen St.     12-21-1975 m CBC 02-16-1998
645722 Miyamoto 65 3rd Ave.       04-03-1936 f MCR 05-30-1999
645739 Jensvold 505 Glendale Ave. 06-15-1960 f HLT 09-23-1993
874329 Kazoyan  76-C La Vista     .          . MCD 01-15-2001
```

Whenever a patient is admitted to the hospital, the admissions staff check the data for that patient. They create a transaction record for every new patient and for any returning patients whose status has changed. Here are three transactions:

```
620135 .                  .          . HLT 06-15-2001
874329 .                  04-24-1954 m .   06-15-2001
235777 Harman   5656 Land Way     01-18-1960 f MCD 06-15-2001
```

---

[1] The MODIFY statement is another way to update a master data set. See the online documentation for more information.

The first transaction is for a returning patient whose insurance has changed. The second transaction fills in missing information for a returning patient. The last transaction is for a new patient who must be added to the database.

Since master data sets are updated frequently, they are usually saved as permanent SAS data sets. To make this example more realistic, this program puts the master data into a permanent data set named PATIENTMASTER in the MySASLib directory on the C drive (Windows, OS/2).

```
DATA 'c:\MySASLib\patientmaster';
   INFILE 'c:\MyRawData\Admit.dat';
   INPUT Account LastName $ 8-16 Address $ 17-34
      BirthDate MMDDYY10. Sex $ InsCode $ 48-50 @52 LastUpdate MMDDYY10.;
RUN;
```

The next program reads the transaction data and sorts them with PROC SORT. Then it adds the transactions to PATIENTMASTER with an UPDATE statement. The master data set is already sorted by Account and, therefore, doesn't need to be sorted again:

```
DATA transactions;
   INFILE 'c:\MyRawData\NewAdmit.dat';
   INPUT Account LastName $ 8-16 Address $ 17-34 BirthDate MMDDYY10.
      Sex $ InsCode $ 48-50 @52 LastUpdate MMDDYY10.;
PROC SORT DATA = transactions;
   BY Account;

* Update patient data with transactions;
DATA 'c:\MySASLib\patientmaster';
   UPDATE 'c:\MySASLib\patientmaster' transactions;
   BY Account;
PROC PRINT DATA = 'c:\MySASLib\patientmaster';
   FORMAT BirthDate LastUpdate MMDDYY10.;
   TITLE 'Admissions Data';
RUN;
```

The output of PROC PRINT looks like this:

```
                          Admissions Data                              1

                                                      Ins
     Obs Account LastName Address          BirthDate Sex Code LastUpdate

      1   235777 Harman   5656 Land Way     01/18/1960  f  MCD  06/15/2001
      2   620135 Smith    234 Aspen St.     12/21/1975  m  HLT  06/15/2001
      3   645722 Miyamoto 65 3rd Ave.       04/03/1936  f  MCR  05/30/1999
      4   645739 Jensvold 505 Glendale Ave. 06/15/1960  f  HLT  09/23/1993
      5   874329 Kazoyan  76-C La Vista     04/24/1954  m  MCD  06/15/2001
```

5.9 ## Using SAS Data Set Options

In this book, you have already seen a lot of options. It may help you to keep them straight if you realize that the SAS language has three basic types of options: system options, statement options, and data set options. System options have the most global influence, followed by statement options, with data set options having the most limited effect.

System options are those that stay in effect for the duration of your job or session. These options affect how SAS operates. Options are usually issued when you invoke SAS or when you use the OPTIONS statement. System options include the CENTER option, which tells SAS to center all output, and the LINESIZE= option setting the maximum line length for output.[1]

Statement options appear in individual statements and influence how SAS runs that particular DATA or PROC step. DATA=, for example, is a statement option that tells SAS which data set to use for a procedure. You can use DATA= in any procedure that reads a SAS data set. Without it, SAS defaults to the most recently created data set.

In contrast, data set options affect only how SAS reads or writes an individual data set. You can use data set options in DATA steps (in DATA, SET, MERGE, or UPDATE statements) or in PROC steps (with a DATA= statement option). To use a data set option, you simply put it between parentheses directly following the data set name. These are the most frequently used data set options:

KEEP = *variable-list*   tells SAS which variables to keep.

DROP = *variable-list*   tells SAS which variables to drop.

RENAME = (*oldvar* = *newvar*)   tells SAS to rename certain variables.

FIRSTOBS = *n*   tells SAS to start reading at observation *n*.

OBS = *n*   tells SAS to stop reading at observation *n*.

IN = *new-var-name*   creates a temporary variable for tracking whether that data set contributed to the current observation.

Selecting and renaming variables Here are examples of the KEEP=, DROP=, and RENAME= data set options:

```
DATA small;
   SET animals (KEEP = Cat Mouse Rabbit);

DATA big (DROP = Cat Mouse Rabbit);
   SET animals;

DATA animals (RENAME = (Cat = Feline Dog = Canine));
   SET animals;
```

---

[1] Other system options are discussed in section 1.10.

You could probably get by without these options, but they play an important role in fine tuning SAS programs. Data sets, for example, have a way of accumulating unwanted variables. Dropping unwanted variables will make your program run faster and use less disk space. Often when you read a large data set you need only a few variables. By using the KEEP= option, you can avoid reading a lot of variables you don't intend to use.

The DROP=, KEEP=, and RENAME= options are similar to the DROP, KEEP, and RENAME statements. However, the statements apply to all data sets named in the DATA statement while the options apply only to the particular data set whose name they follow. Also, the statements are more limited than the options since they can be used only in DATA steps, and apply only to the data set being created. In contrast, the data set options can be used in DATA or PROC steps and can apply to input or output data sets. Please note that these options do not change input data sets; they change only what is read from input data sets.

Selecting observations by observation number
You can use the FIRSTOBS= and OBS= data set options together to tell SAS which observations to read from a data set. The options in this statement tell SAS to read just 20 observations:

```
PROC PRINT DATA = animals (FIRSTOBS = 101 OBS = 120);
```

If you use large data sets, you can save development time by testing your programs with a subset of your data with the FIRSTOBS= and OBS= options.

The FIRSTOBS= and OBS= data set options are similar to statement and system options with the same name. The statement options apply only to raw data files being read with an INFILE statement, whereas the data set options apply only to SAS data sets. The system options apply to all files and data sets. If you use similar system and data set options, the data set option will override the system option for that particular data set.

Tracking observations
The IN= option is somewhat different from other options covered here. While the other options affect existing variables, IN= creates a new variable. That new variable is temporary and has the name you specify in the option. In this example, SAS would create two temporary variables, one named InAnimals and the other named InHabitat:

```
DATA animals;
   MERGE animals (IN = InAnimals) habitat (IN = InHabitat);
   BY Species;
```

These variables exist only for the duration of the current DATA step and are not added to the data set being created. SAS gives IN= variables a value of 0 if that data set did not contribute to the current observation and a value of 1 if it did. You can use the IN= variable to track, select, or eliminate observations based on the data set of origin. The next section explains the IN= option in more detail.

5.10 Tracking and Selecting Observations with the IN= Option

Select matching observations

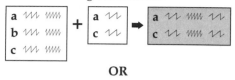

OR

Select non-matching observations

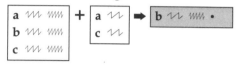

When you combine two data sets, you can use IN= options to track which of the original data sets contributed to each observation in the new data set. You can think of the IN= option as a sort of tag. Instead of saying "Product of Canada," the tag says something like "Product of data set one." Once you have that information, you can use it in many ways including selecting matching or non-matching observations during a merge.

The IN= data set option can be used any time you read a SAS data set in a DATA step—with SET, MERGE, or UPDATE—but is most often used with MERGE. To use the IN= option, you simply put the option in parentheses directly following the data set you want to track, and specify a name for the IN= variable. The names of IN= variables must follow standard SAS naming conventions—start with a letter or underscore; be 32 characters or fewer in length; and contain only letters, numerals, or underscores.

The DATA step below creates a data set named BOTH by merging two data sets named STATE and COUNTY. Then the IN= options create two variables named InState and InCounty:

```
DATA both;
    MERGE state (IN = InState) county (IN = InCounty);
    BY StateName;
```

Unlike most variables, IN= variables are temporary, existing only during the current DATA step. SAS gives the IN= variables a value of 0 or 1. A value of 1 means that data set did contribute to the current observation, and a value of 0 means the data set did not contribute. Suppose the COUNTY data set above contained no data for Louisiana. (Louisiana has parishes, not counties.) In that case, the BOTH data set would contain one observation for Louisiana which would have a value of 1 for the variable InState and a value of 0 for InCounty because the STATE data set contributed to that observation, but the COUNTY data set did not.

You can use this variable like any other variable in the current DATA step, but it is most often used in subsetting IF or IF-THEN statements such as these:

```
Subsetting IF:   IF InState = 1;
                 IF InCounty = 0;
                 IF InState = 1 AND InCounty = 1;
IF-THEN:         IF InCounty = 1 THEN Origin = 1;
                 IF InState = 1 THEN State = 'Idaho';
```

Example A sporting goods manufacturer wants to send a sales rep to contact all customers who did not place any orders during the third quarter of the year. The company has two data files, one that contains all customers and one that contains all orders placed during the third quarter. To compile a list of customers without orders, you merge the two data sets using the IN= option, and then select customers who had no observations in the orders data set. The customer data file contains the customer number, name, and address. The orders data file contains the customer number and total price, with one observation for every order placed during the third quarter. Here are samples of the two raw data files:

Customer data		Orders data
101 Murphy's Sports	115 Main St.	102 562.01
102 Sun N Ski	2106 Newberry Ave.	104 254.98
103 Sports Outfitters	19 Cary Way	104 1642.00
104 Cramer & Johnson	4106 Arlington Blvd.	101 3497.56
105 Sports Savers	2708 Broadway	102 385.30

Here is the program that finds customers who did not place any orders:

```
DATA customer;
    INFILE 'c:\MyRawData\Address.dat' TRUNCOVER;
    INPUT CustomerNumber Name $ 5-21 Address $ 23-42;
DATA orders;
    INFILE 'c:\MyRawData\OrdersQ3.dat';
    INPUT CustomerNumber Total;
PROC SORT DATA = orders;
    BY CustomerNumber;

* Combine the data sets using the IN= option;
DATA noorders;
    MERGE customer orders (IN = Recent);
    BY CustomerNumber;
    IF Recent = 0;
PROC PRINT DATA = noorders;
    TITLE 'Customers with No Orders in the Third Quarter';
RUN;
```

The customer data are already sorted by customer number and so do not need to be sorted with PROC SORT. The orders data, however, are in the order received and must be sorted by customer number before merging. In the final DATA step, the IN= option creates a variable named Recent, which equals 1 if the ORDERS data set contributed to that observation and 0 if it did not. Then a subsetting IF statement keeps only the observations where Recent is equal to 0—those observations with no orders data. Notice that there is no IN= option on the CUSTOMER data set. Only one IN= option was needed to identify customers who did not place any orders. Here is the list that can be given to sales reps:

```
           Customers with No Orders in the Third Quarter              1

           Customer
    Obs     Number           Name              Address          Total

     1        103       Sports Outfitters   19 Cary Way           .
     2        105       Sports Savers       2708 Broadway         .
```

The values for the variable Total are missing because these customers did not have observations in the ORDERS data set. The variable Recent does not appear in the output because, as a temporary variable, it was not added to the NOORDERS data set.

5.11 Writing Multiple Data Sets Using the OUTPUT Statement

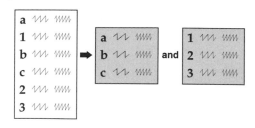

Up to this point, all the DATA steps in this book have created a single data set, except for DATA _NULL_ statements which produce no data set at all. Normally you want to make only one data set in each DATA step. However, there may be times when it is more efficient or more convenient to create multiple data sets in a single DATA step. You can do this by simply putting more than one data set name in your DATA statement. The statement below tells SAS to create three data sets named LIONS, TIGERS, and BEARS:

```
DATA lions tigers bears;
```

If that is all you do, then SAS will write all the observations to all the data sets, and you will have three identical data sets. Normally, of course, you want to create different data sets. You can do that with an OUTPUT statement.

Every DATA step has an implied OUTPUT statement at the end which tells SAS to write the current observation to the output data set before returning to the beginning of the DATA step to process the next observation. You can override this implicit OUTPUT statement with your own OUTPUT statement. The basic form of the OUTPUT statement is

```
OUTPUT data-set-name;
```

If you leave out the data set name then the observation will be written to all data sets named in the DATA statement. OUTPUT statements can be used alone or in IF-THEN or DO-loop processing.

```
IF family = 'Ursidae' THEN OUTPUT bears;
```

Example A local zoo maintains a data base about the feeding of the animals. A portion of the data appears below. For each group of animals the data include the scientific class, the enclosure those animals live in, and whether they get fed in the morning, afternoon, or both:

```
bears     Mammalia E2 both
elephants Mammalia W3 am
flamingos Aves     W1 pm
frogs     Amphibia S2 pm
kangaroos Mammalia N4 am
lions     Mammalia W6 pm
snakes    Reptilia S1 pm
tigers    Mammalia W9 both
zebras    Mammalia W2 am
```

To help with feeding the animals, the following program creates two lists, one for morning feedings and one for afternoon feedings.

```
DATA morning afternoon;
   INFILE 'c:\MyRawData\Zoo.dat';
   INPUT Animal $ 1-9 Class $ 11-18 Enclosure $ FeedTime $;
   IF FeedTime = 'am' THEN OUTPUT morning;
      ELSE IF FeedTime = 'pm' THEN OUTPUT afternoon;
      ELSE IF FeedTime = 'both' THEN OUTPUT;
PROC PRINT DATA = morning;
   TITLE 'Animals with Morning Feedings';
PROC PRINT DATA = afternoon;
   TITLE 'Animals with Afternoon Feedings';
RUN;
```

This DATA step creates two data sets named MORNING and AFTERNOON. Then the IF-THEN/ELSE statements tell SAS which observations to put in each data set. Because the final OUTPUT statement does not specify a data set, SAS adds those observations to both data sets. The log contains these notes saying that SAS read one input file and wrote two data sets:

```
NOTE: 9 records were read from the infile 'c:\MyRawData\Zoo.dat'.

NOTE: The data set WORK.MORNING has 5 observations and 4 variables.

NOTE: The data set WORK.AFTERNOON has 6 observations and 4 variables.
```

Here are the two reports, one for each data set:

```
                  Animals with Morning Feedings                  1

                                            Feed
   Obs     Animal       Class     Enclosure  Time

    1      bears        Mammalia     E2      both
    2      elephants    Mammalia     W3      am
    3      kangaroos    Mammalia     N4      am
    4      tigers       Mammalia     W9      both
    5      zebras       Mammalia     W2      am


                 Animals with Afternoon Feedings                 2

                                            Feed
   Obs     Animal       Class     Enclosure  Time

    1      bears        Mammalia     E2      both
    2      flamingos    Aves         W1      pm
    3      frogs        Amphibia     S2      pm
    4      lions        Mammalia     W6      pm
    5      snakes       Reptilia     S1      pm
    6      tigers       Mammalia     W9      both
```

OUTPUT statements have other uses besides writing multiple data sets in a single DATA step and can be used any time you want to explicitly control when SAS writes observations to a data set.

5.12   Making Several Observations from One Using the OUTPUT Statement

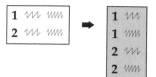

Usually SAS writes an observation to a data set at the end of the DATA step, but you can override this default using the OUTPUT statement. If you want to write several observations for each pass through the DATA step, you can put an OUTPUT statement in a DO loop or just use several OUTPUT statements. The OUTPUT statement gives you control over when an observation is written to a SAS data set. If your DATA step doesn't have an OUTPUT statement, then it is implied at the end of the step. Once you put an OUTPUT statement in your DATA step, it is no longer implied, and SAS writes an observation only when it encounters an OUTPUT statement.

Example   The following program demonstrates how you can use an OUTPUT statement in a DO loop to generate data. Here we have a mathematical equation ($y=x^2$) and we want to generate data points for later plotting:

```
* Create data for variables x and y;
DATA generate;
   DO x = 1 TO 6;
      y = x ** 2;
      OUTPUT;
   END;
PROC PRINT DATA = generate;
   TITLE 'Generated Data';
RUN;
```

This program has no INPUT or SET statement—so there is only one iteration of the entire DATA step—but it has a DO loop with six iterations. Because the OUTPUT statement is inside the DO loop, an observation is created each time through the loop. Without the OUTPUT statement, SAS would have written only one observation at the end of the DATA step when it reached the implied OUTPUT. The following are the results of the PROC PRINT:

```
                         Generated Data                        1

                         Obs    x    y

                          1     1    1
                          2     2    4
                          3     3    9
                          4     4    16
                          5     5    25
                          6     6    36
```

Example   Here's how you can use OUTPUT statements to create several observations from a single pass through the DATA step. The following data are for ticket sales at three movie theaters. After the month are the theaters' names and sales for all three theaters:

```
Jan Varsity 56723 Downtown 69831 Super-6 70025
Feb Varsity 62137 Downtown 43901 Super-6 81534
Mar Varsity 49982 Downtown 55783 Super-6 69800
```

For the analysis you want to do, you need to have the theater name as one variable and the ticket sales as another variable. The month should be repeated three times, once for each theater.

The following program has three INPUT statements all reading from the same raw data file. The first INPUT statement reads values for Month, Location, and Tickets, and then holds the data line using the trailing at sign (@). The OUTPUT statement that follows writes an observation. The next INPUT statement reads the second set of data for Location and Tickets and again holds the data line. Another OUTPUT statement writes another observation. Month still has the same value because it isn't in the second INPUT statement. The last INPUT statement reads the last values for Location and Tickets, this time releasing the data line for the next iteration through the DATA step. The final OUTPUT statement writes the third observation for that iteration of the DATA step. The program has three OUTPUT statements for the three observations created in each iteration of the DATA step:

```
* Create three observations for each data line read
*    using three OUTPUT statements;
DATA theaters;
    INFILE 'c:\MyRawData\Movies.dat';
    INPUT Month $ Location $ Tickets @;
    OUTPUT;
    INPUT Location $ Tickets @;
    OUTPUT;
    INPUT Location $ Tickets;
    OUTPUT;
PROC PRINT DATA = theaters;
    TITLE 'Ticket Sales';
RUN;
```

The following are the results of the PROC PRINT. Notice that there are three observations in the data set for each line in the raw data file and that the value for Month is repeated:

```
                         Ticket Sales                        1

       Obs    Month    Location    Tickets

        1      Jan     Varsity      56723
        2      Jan     Downtown     69831
        3      Jan     Super-6      70025
        4      Feb     Varsity      62137
        5      Feb     Downtown     43901
        6      Feb     Super-6      81534
        7      Mar     Varsity      49982
        8      Mar     Downtown     55783
        9      Mar     Super-6      69800
```

5.13   Changing Observations to Variables Using PROC TRANSPOSE

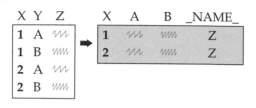

We have already seen ways to combine data sets, create new variables, and sort data. Now, using PROC TRANSPOSE, we will flip data—so get your spatulas ready.

The TRANSPOSE procedure transposes SAS data sets, turning observations into variables or variables into observations. In most cases, to convert observations into variables, you can use the following statements:

```
PROC TRANSPOSE DATA = oldname OUT = newname;
   BY variable-list;
   ID variable;
   VAR variable-list;
```

In the PROC TRANSPOSE statement, *oldname* refers to the SAS data set you want to transpose, and *newname* is the name of the newly transposed data set.

BY statement   You can use the BY statement if you have any grouping variables that you want to keep as variables. These variables are included in the transposed data set, but they are not themselves transposed. The transposed data set will have one observation for each BY level per variable transposed. For example, in the figure above, the variable X is the BY variable. The data set must be sorted by these variables before transposing.

ID statement   The ID statement names the variable whose formatted values will become the new variable names. The ID values must occur only once in the data set; or if a BY statement is present, then the values must be unique within BY-groups. If the ID variable is numeric, then the new variable names have an underscore for a prefix (_1 or _2, for example). If you don't use an ID statement, then the new variables will be named COL1, COL2, and so on. In the figure above, the variable Y is the ID variable. Notice how its values are the new variable's names in the transposed data set.

VAR statement   The VAR statement names the variables whose values you want to transpose. In the figure above, the variable Z is the VAR variable. SAS creates a new variable, _NAME_, which has as values the names of the variables in the VAR statement. If there is more than one VAR variable, then _NAME_ will have more than one value.

Example   Suppose you have the following data about players for minor league baseball teams. You have the team name, player's number, the type of data (salary or batting average), and the entry:

```
Garlics 10 salary 43000
Peaches  8 salary 38000
Garlics 21 salary 51000
Peaches 10 salary 47500
Garlics 10 batavg .281
Peaches  8 batavg .252
Garlics 21 batavg .265
Peaches 10 batavg .301
```

You want to look at the relationship between batting average and salary using PROC PLOT. To do this, salary and batting average must be variables. The following program reads the raw data

into a SAS data set and sorts the data by team and player. Then the data are transposed using
PROC TRANSPOSE

```
DATA baseball;
    INFILE 'c:\MyRawData\Transpos.dat';
    INPUT Team $ Player Type $ Entry;
PROC SORT DATA = baseball;
    BY Team Player;
PROC PRINT DATA = baseball;
    TITLE 'Baseball Data After Sorting and Before Transposing';

* Transpose data so salary and batavg are variables;
PROC TRANSPOSE DATA = baseball OUT = flipped;
    BY Team Player;
    ID Type;
    VAR Entry;
PROC PRINT DATA = flipped;
    TITLE 'Baseball Data After Transposing';
RUN;
```

In the PROC TRANSPOSE step, the BY variables are Team and Player. You want those variables to
remain in the data set, and they define the new observations (you want only one observation for each
team and player combination). The ID variable is Type, whose values (salary and batavg) will be the
new variable names. The variable to be transposed, Entry, is given in the VAR statement. Notice that
its name, Entry, now appears as a value under the variable _NAME_. The TRANSPOSE procedure
automatically generates the _NAME_ variable, but in this application it is not very meaningful and
could be dropped.

Here are the results:

```
            Baseball Data After Sorting and Before Transposing        1

        Obs      Team       Player     Type        Entry

         1      Garlics       10      salary      43000.00
         2      Garlics       10      batavg          0.28
         3      Garlics       21      salary      51000.00
         4      Garlics       21      batavg          0.27
         5      Peaches        8      salary      38000.00
         6      Peaches        8      batavg          0.25
         7      Peaches       10      salary      47500.00
         8      Peaches       10      batavg          0.30


                Baseball Data After Transposing                       2

        Obs      Team       Player     _NAME_     salary     batavg

         1      Garlics       10       Entry       43000      0.281
         2      Garlics       21       Entry       51000      0.265
         3      Peaches        8       Entry       38000      0.252
         4      Peaches       10       Entry       47500      0.301
```

5.14 Using SAS Automatic Variables

In addition to the variables you create in your SAS data set, SAS creates a few more called automatic variables. You don't ordinarily see these variables because they are temporary and are not saved with your data. But they are available in the DATA step, and you can use them just like you use any variable that you create yourself.

_N_ and _ERROR_ The _N_ and _ERROR_ variables are always available to you in the DATA step. _N_ indicates the number of times SAS has looped through the DATA step. This is not necessarily equal to the observation number, since a simple subsetting IF statement can change the relationship between observation number and the number of iterations of the DATA step. The _ERROR_ variable has a value of 1 if there is a data error for that observation and 0 if there isn't. Things that can cause data errors include invalid data (such as characters in a numeric field), conversion errors (like division by zero), and illegal arguments in functions (including log of zero).

FIRST.*variable* and LAST.*variable* Other automatic variables are available only in special circumstances. The FIRST.*variable* and LAST.*variable* automatic variables are available when you are using a BY statement in a DATA step. The FIRST.*variable* will have a value of 1 when SAS is processing an observation with the first occurrence of a new value for that variable and a value of 0 for the other observations. The LAST.*variable* will have a value of 1 for an observation with the last occurrence of a value for that variable and the value 0 for the other observations.

Example Your hometown is having a walk around the town square to raise money for the library. You have the following data: entry number, age group, and finishing time. (Notice that there is more than one observation per line of data.)

```
54 youth  35.5 21 adult   21.6  6 adult   25.8 13 senior 29.0
38 senior 40.3 19 youth   39.6  3 adult   19.0 25 youth  47.3
11 adult  21.9  8 senior  54.3 41 adult   43.0 32 youth  38.6
```

The first thing you want to do is create a new variable for overall finishing place and print the results. The first part of the following program reads the raw data, and sorts the data by finishing time (Time). Then another DATA step creates the new Place variable and gives it the current value of _N_. The PRINT procedure produces the list of finishers:

```
DATA walkers;
   INFILE 'c:\MyRawData\Walk.dat';
   INPUT Entry AgeGroup $ Time @@;
PROC SORT DATA = walkers;
   BY Time;
* Create a new variable, Place;
DATA ordered;
   SET walkers;
   Place = _N_;
PROC PRINT DATA = ordered;
   TITLE 'Results of Walk';
```

```
PROC SORT DATA = ordered;
   BY AgeGroup Time;
* Keep the first observation in each age group;
DATA winners;
   SET ordered;
   BY AgeGroup;
   IF FIRST.AgeGroup = 1;
PROC PRINT DATA = winners;
   TITLE 'Winners in Each Age Group';
RUN;
```

The second part of this program produces a list of the top finishers in each age category. The ORDERED data set containing the new Place variable is sorted by AgeGroup and Time. In the DATA step, the SET statement reads the ORDERED data set. The BY statement in the DATA step generates the FIRST.AgeGroup and LAST.AgeGroup temporary variables. The subsetting IF statement, IF FIRST.AgeGroup = 1, keeps only the first observation in the BY group. Since the Winners data set is sorted by AgeGroup and Time, the first observation in each BY group is the top finisher of that group.

Here are the results of the two PRINT procedures. The first page shows the data after sorting by Time and including the new variable Place. Notice that the _N_ temporary variable does not appear in the printout. The second page shows the results of the second part of the program—the winners for each age category and their overall place:

```
                         Results of Walk                        1


                           Age
        Obs    Entry      Group     Time    Place

          1       3       adult     19.0      1
          2      21       adult     21.6      2
          3      11       adult     21.9      3
          4       6       adult     25.8      4
          5      13       senior    29.0      5
          6      54       youth     35.5      6
          7      32       youth     38.6      7
          8      19       youth     39.6      8
          9      38       senior    40.3      9
         10      41       adult     43.0     10
         11      25       youth     47.3     11
         12       8       senior    54.3     12

                 Winners in Each Age Group                      2
                           Age
        Obs    Entry      Group     Time    Place

          1       3       adult     19.0      1
          2      13       senior    29.0      5
          3      54       youth     35.5      6
```

6 ▶

> " Nobody is too old to learn—but a lot of people keep putting it off. "

WILLIAM O'NEILL

CHAPTER 6

Writing Flexible Code with the SAS© Macro Facility

6.1 ▶ Macro Concepts

Not so long ago the SAS macro facility was considered an advanced topic relevant only to experienced SAS users. Over time, however, macros have become more prevalent so that now even new SAS users would do well to know a little about the SAS macro facility. Fortunately, the basic macro concepts are not difficult to understand.

This chapter introduces the most commonly used features of the SAS macro language. For a complete description, see *SAS Macro Language: Reference.*

Because macros take longer to write and debug than standard SAS code, you generally won't want macros in programs that will be run only a few times. But used properly, macros can make the development and maintenance of production programs much easier. They do this in several ways. First, with macros you can make one small change in your program and have SAS echo that change throughout your program. Second, macros allow you to write a piece of code once and use it over and over, in the same program or in different programs. You can even store programs in a central location—an autocall library—and share them between programs and between programmers. Third, you can make your programs data driven, letting SAS decide what to do based on actual data values.

The macro processor When you submit a standard SAS program, SAS compiles and then immediately executes it. But when you write a macro, there is an additional step. Before SAS can compile and execute your program, SAS must pass your macro statements to the macro processor which "resolves" your macros, generating standard SAS code. Because you are writing a program that writes a program, this is sometimes called meta-programming.

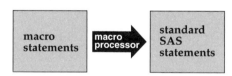

Macros and macro variables SAS macro code consists of two basic parts: macros and macro variables. The names of macro variables are prefixed with an ampersand (&) while the names of macros are prefixed with a percent sign (%).[1] A macro variable is like a standard data variable except that, having only a single value, it does not belong to a data set, and its value is always character. This value could be a variable name, a number, or any text that you want substituted into your program. A macro, on the other hand, is a larger piece of a program that may contain complex logic including complete DATA and PROC steps and macro statements such as %DO, %END, and %IF-%THEN/%ELSE.

When SAS users talk about "macros" they sometimes mean macros, and sometimes mean macro processing in general. Macro variables are usually called *macro variables*.

---

[1] There are exceptions. Macro names prefixed with a % are called name-style macros. Two other types of macros do not start with a %: command-style and statement-style. In general, macros starting with a prefix are superior both because they are more efficient (the macro processor recognizes them more quickly) and because they are less easily confused with SAS keywords.

Also the %INCLUDE, %LIST, and %RUN statements are NOT part of the macro facility despite their % prefix.

Local versus global   Macro variables can have two kinds of "scope"—either local or global. Generally, a macro variable is local if it is defined inside a macro. A macro variable is generally global if it is defined in "open code" which is everything outside a macro. You can use a global macro variable anywhere in your program, but you can use a local macro variable only inside its own macro.[2] If you keep this in mind as you write your programs, you will avoid two common errors: trying to use a local macro variable outside its macro and accidentally creating local and global macro variables with the same name.

Turning on the macro processor   Before you can use macros you must have the MACRO system option turned on. This option is usually turned on by default, but may be turned off, especially on mainframes, because SAS runs slightly faster when it doesn't have to bother with checking for macros. If you are not sure whether the MACRO option is on, you can find out by submitting these statements:

```
PROC OPTIONS OPTION = MACRO; RUN;
```

Check your SAS log. If you see the option MACRO, then the macro processor is turned on, and you can use it. If you see NOMACRO there, you need to specify the MACRO option at invocation or in a configuration file. Specifying this type of option is system dependent. For details about specifying the MACRO option, see your SAS Site Representative or check the Companion for your operating environment.

Avoiding macro errors   There's no question about it, macros can make your head hurt. You can avoid the macro migraine by adding individual statements or features one at a time, and debugging each one before adding another. This modular approach to programming is always a good idea, but it's critical with macros.

---

[2] There are ways to force a local macro variable to become global and vice versa. See *SAS Macro Language: Reference* if you need to change the scope of your macro variables.

6.2 Substituting Text with Macro Variables

Macro variables may be the most straightforward and easy-to-use part of the macro facility, yet if you master only this one feature of macro programming you will have greatly increased your flexibility as a SAS programmer. Suppose you have a SAS program that you run once a week. Each time you run it you have to edit the program so it will select data for the correct range of dates and print the correct dates in the title. This process is time-consuming and prone to errors. (What if you accidentally delete a semicolon?!) Instead, you can use a macro variable to insert the correct date. Then you can have another cup of coffee while someone else, someone who knows very little about SAS, runs this program for you.

When SAS encounters the name of a macro variable, the macro processor simply replaces the name with the value of that macro variable. That value is a character constant that you specify.

Creating a macro variable with %LET The simplest way to assign a value to a macro variable is with the %LET statement. The general form of this statement is

```
%LET macro-variable-name = value;
```

where *macro-variable-name* must follow the rules for SAS variable names (32 characters or fewer in length; start with a letter or underscore; and contain only letters, numerals, and underscores). *Value* is the text to be substituted for the macro variable name, and can be longer than you are ever likely to need—almost 64,000 characters long. The following statements each create a macro variable.

```
%LET iterations = 10;
%LET state = State of Florida;
```

Notice that unlike an ordinary assignment statement, *value* does not require quotation marks even when it contains characters. Except for blanks at the beginning and end, which are trimmed, everything between the equals sign and the semicolon becomes part of the value for that macro variable.

Using a macro variable To use a macro variable you simply add the ampersand prefix (&) and stick the macro variable name wherever you want its value to be substituted. Keep in mind that the macro processor doesn't look for macros inside *single* quotes. To get around this, simply use double quotes. The following statements show possible ways to use the previous macro variables.

```
DO i = 1 to &iterations;
TITLE "Addresses in the &state";
```

After being resolved by the macro processor, these statements would become

```
DO i = 1 to 10;
TITLE "Addresses in the State of Florida";
```

Example A grower of tropical flowers records information about each sale in a raw data file. The data include customer ID, date of sale, variety of flower, and quantity.

```
240W 02-07-2000 Ginger     120
356W 02-08-2000 Heliconia   60
356W 02-08-2000 Anthurium  300
188R 02-11-2000 Ginger      24
188R 02-11-2000 Anthurium   24
240W 02-12-2000 Protea     180
356W 02-12-2000 Ginger     240
```

Periodically, the grower needs a report about sales of a single variety. The macro variable in this program allows the grower to choose one variety without editing the DATA or PROC step. Instead he just types the name of the variety once, in the %LET statement.

```
%LET flowertype = Ginger;

* Read the data and subset with a macro variable;
DATA flowersales;
    INFILE 'c:\MyRawData\TropicalSales.dat';
    INPUT CustomerID $ @6 SaleDate MMDDYY10.
       @17 Variety $9. Quantity;
    IF Variety = "&flowertype";

* Print the report using a macro variable;
PROC PRINT DATA = flowersales;
    FORMAT SaleDate WORDDATE18.;
    TITLE "Sales of &flowertype";
RUN;
```

The program starts with a %LET statement that creates a macro variable named &FLOWERTYPE, assigning to it a value of Ginger. Because the variable &FLOWERTYPE is defined outside a macro, it is a global macro variable and can be used anywhere in this program. In this case, the value Ginger is substituted for &FLOWERTYPE in a subsetting IF statement and a TITLE statement. Here are the results:

```
                       Sales of Ginger                         1

            Customer
    Obs        ID              SaleDate    Variety    Quantity

     1        240W        February 7, 2000   Ginger       120
     2        188R        February 11, 2000  Ginger        24
     3        356W        February 12, 2000  Ginger       240
```

This is a short program, so using a macro variable didn't save much trouble. However, if you had a program 100 or even 1,000 lines long, a macro variable could be a blessing.

6.3 Creating Modular Code with Macros

Anytime you find yourself writing the same or similar SAS statements over and over, you should consider using a macro. A macro lets you package a piece of bug-free code and use it repeatedly within a single SAS program or in many SAS programs.

You can think of a macro as a kind of sandwich. The %MACRO and %MEND statements are like two slices of bread. Between those slices you can put any statements you want. The general form of a macro is

```
%MACRO macro-name;
   macro-text
%MEND macro-name;
```

The %MACRO statement tells SAS that this is the beginning of a macro, while %MEND marks the end. *Macro-name* is a name you make up, and can be up to 32 characters in length, start with a letter or underscore, and contain only letters, numerals, and underscores. The *macro-name* in the MEND statement is optional, but your macros will be easier to debug and maintain if you include it. That way there's no question of which %MACRO statement goes with which %MEND. *Macro-text* (also called a macro definition) is a set of SAS statements.

Invoking a macro   After you have defined a macro you can invoke it by adding the percent sign prefix to its name like this:

```
%macro-name
```

A semicolon is not required when invoking a macro, though adding one generally does no harm.

Example   Using the data from the previous section, this example creates a simple macro. The data include customer ID, date of sale, variety of flower, and quantity.

```
240W 02-07-2000 Ginger     120
356W 02-08-2000 Heliconia   60
356W 02-08-2000 Anthurium  300
188R 02-11-2000 Ginger      24
188R 02-11-2000 Anthurium   24
240W 02-12-2000 Protea     180
356W 02-12-2000 Ginger     240
```

The following program creates a macro named %SAMPLE to sort the data by Quantity and print the five observations with the largest sales. Then the program reads the data in a standard DATA step, and invokes the macro.

```
* Macro to print 5 largest sales;
%MACRO sample;
    PROC SORT DATA = flowersales;
        BY DESCENDING Quantity;
    PROC PRINT DATA = flowersales (OBS = 5);
        FORMAT SaleDate WORDDATE18.;
        TITLE 'Five Largest Sales';
%MEND sample;

* Read the flower sales data;
DATA flowersales;
    INFILE 'c:\MyRawData\TropicalSales.dat';
    INPUT CustomerID $ @6 SaleDate MMDDYY10. @17
        Variety $9. Quantity;
RUN;

* Invoke the macro;
%sample
RUN;
```

Here is the output:

```
                        Five Largest Sales                        1

              Customer
     Obs         ID              SaleDate      Variety      Quantity

      1         356W         February 8, 2000   Anthurium      300
      2         356W         February 12, 2000  Ginger         240
      3         240W         February 12, 2000  Protea         180
      4         240W         February 7, 2000   Ginger         120
      5         356W         February 8, 2000   Heliconia       60
```

This macro is fairly limited because it does the same thing every time. To increase the flexibility of macros, combine them with %LET statements or add parameters as described in section 6.4.

Macro autocall libraries   The macros in this book are defined and invoked inside a single program, but you can also store macros in a central location, called an autocall library. Macros in a library can be shared by programs and programmers. Basically you save your macros as files in a directory or as members of a partitioned data set (depending on your operating environment), and use the MAUTOSOURCE and SASAUTOS= system options to tell SAS where to look for macros. Then you can invoke a macro even though the original macro does not appear in your program. For more information see *SAS Macro Language: Reference* or the Companion for your operating environment.

6.4 Adding Parameters to Macros

Macros can save you a lot of trouble, allowing you to write a set of statements once and then use them over and over. However, you usually don't want to repeat exactly the same statements. You may want the same report, but for a different data set, or product, or patient. Parameters allow you to do this.

Parameters are macro variables whose value you set when you invoke a macro. The simplest macros, like the macro in section 6.3, have no parameters. To add parameters to a macro, you simply list the macro-variable names between parentheses in the %MACRO statement. Here is one of the possible forms of the parameter-list.

```
%MACRO macro-name (parameter-1= ,parameter-2= , . . . parameter-n=);
    macro-text
%MEND macro-name;
```

For example, a macro named %QUARTERLYREPORT might start like this:

```
%MACRO quarterlyreport(quarter=,salesrep=);
```

This macro has two parameters: &QUARTER and &SALESREP. You could invoke the macro with this statement:

```
%quarterlyreport(quarter=3,salesrep=Smith)
```

The SAS macro processor would replace each occurrence of the macro variable &QUARTER with the value 3, and would substitute Smith for &SALESREP.

Example Suppose the grower often needs a report showing sales to an individual customer. The following program defines a macro that lets the grower select sales for a single customer and then sort the results. As before, the data contain the customer ID, date of sale, variety of flower, and quantity.

```
240W 02-07-2000 Ginger     120
356W 02-08-2000 Heliconia   60
356W 02-08-2000 Anthurium  300
188R 02-11-2000 Ginger      24
188R 02-11-2000 Anthurium   24
240W 02-12-2000 Protea     180
356W 02-12-2000 Ginger     240
```

The following program defines a macro named %SELECT and then invokes the macro twice. This macro sorts and prints the FlowerSales data, using parameters to create two macro variables named &CUSTOMER and &SORTVAR.

```
* Macro with parameters;
%MACRO select(customer=,sortvar=);
   PROC SORT DATA = flowersales OUT = salesout;
      BY &sortvar;
      WHERE CustomerID = "&customer";
   PROC PRINT DATA = salesout;
      FORMAT SaleDate WORDDATE18.;
      TITLE "Orders for Customer Number &customer";
%MEND select;

* Read all the flower sales data;
DATA flowersales;
   INFILE 'c:\MyRawData\TropicalSales.dat';
   INPUT CustomerID $ @6 SaleDate MMDDYY10. @17
      Variety $9. Quantity;
RUN;

*Invoke the macro;
%select(customer = 356W, sortvar = Variety)
%select(customer = 240W, sortvar = Quantity)
RUN;
```

Here is the output:

```
                   Orders for Customer Number 356W                    1

           Customer
    Obs      ID                SaleDate     Variety     Quantity

     1      356W          February 8, 2000   Anthurium     300
     2      356W          February 12, 2000  Ginger        240
     3      356W          February 8, 2000   Heliconia      60

                   Orders for Customer Number 240W                    2

           Customer
    Obs      ID                SaleDate     Variety     Quantity

     1      240W          February 7, 2000   Ginger        120
     2      240W          February 12, 2000  Protea        180
```

6.5 ▶ Writing Macros with Conditional Logic

Combining macros and macro variables gives you a lot of flexibility, but you can increase that flexibility even more by adding macro statements such as %IF. Fortunately, many macro statements have parallel statements in standard SAS code so they should feel familiar. Here are the general forms of the statements used for conditional logic in macros:

```
%IF condition %THEN action;
   %ELSE %IF condition %THEN action;
   %ELSE action;

%IF condition %THEN %DO;
   SAS statements
%END;
```

These macro statements can be used only inside a macro.

You may be wondering why anyone needs these statements. Why not just use the standard IF-THEN? You may indeed use standard IF-THEN statements in your macros, but you will use them for different actions. %IF statements can contain actions that standard IF statements can't contain, such as complete DATA or PROC steps and even other macro statements. The %IF-%THEN statements don't appear in the standard SAS code generated by your macro. Remember you are writing a program that writes a program.

Automatic macro variables   Every time you invoke SAS, the macro processor automatically creates certain macro variables. You can use these variables in your programs. The most common automatic macro variables are

Variable name	Example	Description
&SYSDATE	29MAY02	the character value of the date that job or session began
&SYSDAY	Wednesday	the day of the week that job or session began

For example, you could combine conditional logic and an automatic variable like this:

```
%IF &SYSDAY = Tuesday %THEN %LET country = Belgium;
   %ELSE %LET country = France;
```

Example   Using the tropical flower data again, this example shows a macro with conditional logic. The grower wants to print one report on Monday and a different report on Tuesday. You can write one program that will run either report. The raw data contain the customer ID, date of sale, variety of flower, and quantity.

```
240W 02-07-2000 Ginger     120
356W 02-08-2000 Heliconia   60
356W 02-08-2000 Anthurium  300
188R 02-11-2000 Ginger      24
188R 02-11-2000 Anthurium   24
240W 02-12-2000 Protea     180
356W 02-12-2000 Ginger     240
```

Here is the program:

```
%MACRO dailyreports;
   %IF &SYSDAY = Monday %THEN %DO;
      PROC PRINT DATA = flowersales;
         FORMAT SaleDate WORDDATE18.;
         TITLE 'Monday Report: Current Flower Sales';
   %END;
   %ELSE %IF &SYSDAY = Tuesday %THEN %DO;
      PROC MEANS DATA = flowersales;
         CLASS Variety;
         VAR Quantity;
         TITLE 'Tuesday Report: Summary of Flower Sales';
   %END;
%MEND dailyreports;

DATA flowersales;
   INFILE 'c:\MyRawData\TropicalSales.dat';
   INPUT CustomerID $ @6 SaleDate MMDDYY10. @17
      Variety $9. Quantity;
RUN;

%dailyreports
RUN;
```

When the program is submitted on Tuesday, the macro processor will write this program:

```
DATA flowersales;
   INFILE 'c:\MyRawData\TropicalSales.dat';
   INPUT CustomerID $ @6 SaleDate MMDDYY10. @17
      Variety $9. Quantity;
RUN;

PROC MEANS DATA = flowersales;
   CLASS Variety;
   VAR Quantity;
   TITLE 'Tuesday Report: Summary of Flower Sales';
RUN;
```

If you run this program on Tuesday the output will look like this:

```
            Tuesday Report: Summary of Flower Sales          1

                      The MEANS Procedure
                   Analysis Variable : Quantity
                  N
      Variety    Obs       Mean       Minimum       Maximum
      ─────────────────────────────────────────────────────
      Anthurium    2   162.0000000    24.0000000   300.0000000
      Ginger       3   128.0000000    24.0000000   240.0000000
      Heliconia    1    60.0000000    60.0000000    60.0000000
      Protea       1   180.0000000   180.0000000   180.0000000
      ─────────────────────────────────────────────────────
```

6.6 ▶ Writing Data-Driven Programs with CALL SYMPUT

When you submit a SAS program containing macros it goes first to the macro processor which generates standard SAS code from the macro references. Then SAS compiles and executes your program. Not until execution—the final stage—does SAS see any actual data values. This is the tricky part of writing data-driven programs: SAS doesn't know the values of your data until the execution phase, and by that time it is ordinarily too late. However, there is a way to have your digital cake and eat it too—CALL SYMPUT.

CALL SYMPUT takes a value from a DATA step and assigns it to a macro variable. You can then use this macro variable in later steps. To assign a value to a single macro variable, you use CALL SYMPUT with this general form:

```
CALL SYMPUT("macro-variable-name",value);
```

where *macro-variable-name*, enclosed in quotes, is the name of a macro variable, either new or old, and *value* is the value you want to assign to that macro variable. *Value* can be the name of a variable whose value SAS will use, or it can be a constant value (either character or numeric) enclosed in quotes.

CALL SYMPUT is often used in IF-THEN statements such as this:

```
IF Age >= 21 THEN CALL SYMPUT("status", "Adult");
   ELSE CALL SYMPUT("status", "Minor");
```

These statements create a macro variable named &STATUS and assign to it a value of either Adult or Minor depending on the variable Age. The following CALL SYMPUT uses a variable as its *value*:

```
IF TotalSales > 1000000 THEN CALL SYMPUT("bestseller", BookTitle);
```

This statement tells SAS to create a macro variable named &BESTSELLER which is equal to the value of the variable BookTitle when TotalSales exceed 1,000,000.

Caution You cannot create a macro variable with CALL SYMPUT and use it in the same DATA step because SAS does not assign a value to the macro variable until the DATA step executes. DATA steps execute when SAS encounters a step boundary such as a subsequent DATA, PROC, or RUN statement.

Example Here are the flower sales data consisting of customer ID, date of sale, variety of flower, and quantity.

```
240W 02-07-2000 Ginger     120
356W 02-08-2000 Heliconia   60
356W 02-08-2000 Anthurium  300
188R 02-11-2000 Ginger      24
188R 02-11-2000 Anthurium   24
240W 02-12-2000 Protea     180
356W 02-12-2000 Ginger     240
```

In this example, the grower wants a program that will find the customer with the single largest order, and print all the orders for that customer.

```
* Read the raw data;
DATA flowersales;
    INFILE 'c:\MySASLib\TropicalSales.dat';
    INPUT CustomerID $4. @6 SaleDate MMDDYY10. @17
        Variety $9. Quantity;
PROC SORT DATA = flowersales;
    BY DESCENDING Quantity;

* Find biggest order and pass the customer id to a macro variable;
DATA _NULL_;
    SET flowersales;
    IF _N_ = 1 THEN CALL SYMPUT("selectedcustomer",CustomerID);
    ELSE STOP;

PROC PRINT DATA = flowersales;
    WHERE CustomerID = "&selectedcustomer";
    TITLE "Customer &selectedcustomer Had the Single Largest Order";
RUN;
```

This program has a lot of steps, but each step is fairly simple. The first DATA step reads the data from the raw data file. Then PROC SORT sorts the data by descending Quantity. That way, the largest single order will be the first observation in the newly sorted data set.

The second DATA step then uses CALL SYMPUT to assign the value of the variable CustomerID to the macro variable &SELECTEDCUSTOMER when _N_ equals 1 (the first iteration of the DATA step). Since that is all we need from this DATA step, we can use the STOP statement to tell SAS to end this DATA step. The STOP statement is not necessary, but it is efficient because it prevents SAS from reading the remaining observations for no reason.

When SAS reaches the PROC PRINT statement, SAS knows that the DATA step has ended so SAS executes the DATA step. At this point the macro variable &SELECTEDCUSTOMER has the value 356W (the customer ID with the largest single order) and can be used in the PROC PRINT. The output looks like this:

```
      Customer 356W Had the Single Largest Order            1

              Customer    Sale
      Obs        ID       Date    Variety     Quantity

       1        356W      14648   Anthurium      300
       2        356W      14652   Ginger         240
       5        356W      14648   Heliconia       60
```

For more information on CALL routines, see your online documentation.

6.7 Debugging Macro Errors

Many people find that writing macros is not that hard. Debugging them, however, is another matter. This section covers techniques to ease the debugging process.

Avoiding macro errors   As much as possible, develop your program in standard SAS code first. Then, when it is bug-free, add the macro logic one feature at a time. Add your %MACRO and %MEND statements. When that's working, add your macro variables, one at a time, and so on, until your macro is complete and bug-free.

Quoting problems   The macro processor doesn't resolve macros inside single quotes. To get around this, use double quotes whenever you refer to a macro or macro variable and you want SAS to resolve it. For example, below are two TITLE statements containing a macro variable named &MONTH. If the value of &MONTH is January, then SAS will substitute January in the title with the double quotes, but not the title with single quotes.

Original statement	Statement after resolution
`TITLE 'Report for &month';`	`TITLE 'Report for &month';`
`TITLE "Report for &month";`	`TITLE "Report for January";`

System options for debugging macros   These five system options affect the kinds of messages SAS writes in your log. The default settings appear in bold.

MERROR | NOMERROR	when this option is on, SAS will issue a warning if you invoke a macro that SAS cannot find.
SERROR | NOSERROR	when this option is on, SAS will issue a warning if you use a macro variable that SAS cannot find.
MLOGIC | **NOMLOGIC**	when this option is on, SAS prints in your log details about the execution of macros.
MPRINT | **NOMPRINT**	when this option is on, SAS prints in your log the standard SAS code generated by macros.
SYMBOLGEN | **NOSYMBOLGEN**	when this option is on, SAS prints in your log the values of macro variables.

While you want, the MERROR and SERROR options to be on at all times, you will probably want to turn on MLOGIC, MPRINT, and SYMBOLGEN one at a time and only while you are debugging since they tend to make your log hard to read. To turn them on (or off), use the OPTIONS statement, for example:

```
OPTIONS MPRINT NOSYMBOLGEN NOMLOGIC;
```

MERROR message If SAS has trouble finding a macro, and the MERROR option is on, then SAS will print this message:

```
WARNING: Apparent invocation of macro SAMPL not resolved.
```

Check for a misspelled macro name.

SERROR message If SAS has trouble resolving a macro variable in open code, and the SERROR option is on, then SAS will print this message:

```
WARNING: Apparent symbolic reference FLOWER not resolved.
```

Check for a misspelled macro variable name. If the name is spelled right, then the scope may be wrong. Check to see if you are using a local variable outside of its macro. See section 6.1 for definitions of local and global macro variables.

MLOGIC messages When the MLOGIC option is on, SAS prints messages in your log describing the actions of the macro processor. Here is a macro named %SAMPLE:

```
%MACRO sample(flowertype=);
   PROC PRINT DATA = flowersales;
      WHERE Variety = "&flowertype";
   RUN;
%MEND sample;
```

If you run %SAMPLE with the MLOGIC option, your log will look like this:

```
24    OPTIONS MLOGIC;
25    %sample(flowertype=Anthurium)
MLOGIC(SAMPLE):  Beginning execution.
MLOGIC(SAMPLE):  Parameter FLOWERTYPE has value Anthurium
MLOGIC(SAMPLE):  Ending execution.
```

MPRINT messages When the MPRINT option is on, SAS prints messages in your log showing the SAS statements generated by your macro. If you run %SAMPLE with the MPRINT option, your log will look like this:

```
36    OPTIONS MPRINT;
37    %sample(flowertype=Anthurium)
MPRINT(SAMPLE):    PROC PRINT DATA = flowersales;
MPRINT(SAMPLE):    WHERE Variety = "Anthurium";
MPRINT(SAMPLE):    RUN;
```

SYMBOLGEN messages When the SYMBOLGEN option is on, SAS prints messages in your log showing the values of each macro variable after resolution. If you run %SAMPLE with the SYMBOLGEN option, your log will look like this:

```
30    OPTIONS SYMBOLGEN;
31    %sample(flowertype=Anthurium)
SYMBOLGEN:  Macro variable FLOWERTYPE resolves to Anthurium
```

"33⅓ % of the mice used in the experiment were cured by the test drug; 33⅓ % of the test population were unaffected by the drug and remained in a moribund condition; the third mouse got away."

ERWIN NETER

From "How to Write a Scientific Paper" by Robert A. Day, *ASM News*, vol. 41, no. 7, pp 486–494, July 1975. Reprinted by permission of publisher and author. Also appears in *How to Write and Publish a Scientific Paper* 4th edition by Robert A. Day, copyright 1994 by Oryx Press.

CHAPTER 7

Using Basic Statistical Procedures

7.1 Examining the Distribution of Data with PROC UNIVARIATE

When you are doing statistical analysis, you usually have a goal in mind, a question you are trying to answer, hypotheses you want to test. But before you jump into statistical tests, it is a good idea to pause and do a little exploration. A good procedure to use at this point is PROC UNIVARIATE.

PROC UNIVARIATE, which is part of base SAS software, produces statistics describing the distribution of a single variable. These statistics include the mean, median, mode, standard deviation, skewness, and kurtosis.

Using PROC UNIVARIATE is fairly simple. After the PROC statement, you specify one or more numeric variables in a VAR statement:

```
PROC UNIVARIATE;
    VAR variable-list;
```

Without a VAR statement, SAS will calculate statistics for all numeric variables in your data set. You can specify other options in the PROC statement, if you wish, such as PLOT or NORMAL:

```
PROC UNIVARIATE  PLOT  NORMAL;
```

The NORMAL option produces tests of normality while the PLOT option produces three plots of your data (stem-and-leaf plot, box plot, and normal probability plot). You can use a BY statement to obtain separate analyses for BY groups. (Just remember to use PROC SORT first if your data are not already sorted by your BY variables.)

Example The following data consist of test scores from a statistics class. Each line contains scores for 10 students.

```
56 78 84 73 90 44 76 87 92 75
85 67 90 84 74 64 73 78 69 56
87 73 100 54 81 78 69 64 73 65
```

This program reads the data from a file called Scores.dat and then runs PROC UNIVARIATE:

```
DATA class;
    INFILE 'c:\MyRawData\Scores.dat';
    INPUT Score @@;
PROC UNIVARIATE DATA = class;
    VAR Score;
    TITLE;
RUN;
```

Here is the output:

```
                    The UNIVARIATE Procedure                    1

                        Variable:  Score

                             Moments

N                       30     Sum Weights               30
Mean              74.633333    Sum Observations        2239
Std Deviation     12.584839    Variance            158.37816
Skewness          -0.349506    Kurtosis            0.1038576
Uncorrected SS       171697    Corrected SS        4592.9667
Coeff Variation   16.862222    Std Error Mean      2.2976666

                    Basic Statistical Measures

           Location                    Variability

      Mean      74.63333     Std Deviation        12.58484
      Median       74.5      Variance             158.3782
      Mode           73      Range                      56
                             Interquartile Range        17

             Tests for Location: Mu0=0.00
        Test Statistic       Value           p-value

        Student's t   t    32.48223     Pr > |t|    <.0001
        Sign          M          15     Pr >= |M|   <.0001
        Signed Rank   S       232.5     Pr >= |S|   <.0001

                    Quantiles (Definition 5)
                    Quantile     Estimate

                    100% Max        100
                    99%            100
                    95%             92
                    90%             90
                    75% Q3          84
                    50% Med       74.5
                    25% Q1          67
                    10%             56
                    5%              54
                    1%              44
                    0% Min          44

                    Extreme Observations

          ------Lowest-----        -----Highest-----

          Value       Obs          Value       Obs

             44         6             87         21
             54        24             90          5
             56        20             90         13
             56         1             92          9
             64        28            100         23
```

The output starts with basic information about your distribution: number of observations (N), mean, and standard deviation. Skewness indicates how symmetrical the distribution is (whether it is more spread out on one side) while kurtosis indicates how flat or peaked the distribution is. The normal distribution has values of zero for both skewness and kurtosis. Other sections of the output contain the three averages: mean, median, and mode; tests of the hypothesis that the average is zero; quantiles; and extreme observations (in case you have outliers).

7.2 Producing Statistics with PROC MEANS

Most of the descriptive statistics that you produce with PROC UNIVARIATE you can also produce with PROC MEANS, but you have to ask for them. UNIVARIATE is useful when you know you want all the summary statistics: mean, variance, skewness, quantiles, extremes, *t* tests, standard error— to name a few. UNIVARIATE prints out all these things by default. But if you know you want only a few of these statistics then MEANS is a better way to go. With MEANS you can ask for just the statistics you want, and you don't have to wade through all the other output to find the result you want.

The MEANS procedure requires only one statement:

```
PROC MEANS statistic-keywords;
```

If you do not include any statistic keywords, then MEANS will produce the mean, the number of non-missing values, the standard deviation, the minimum value, and the maximum value for each numeric variable. The following table shows statistics you can request. (Some statistics have two names; the alternate name is shown in parentheses.) If you add any statistic keywords in the PROC MEANS statement, then MEANS will no longer produce the default statistics—you must request them.

CLM	two-sided confidence limits	RANGE	the range
CSS	corrected sum of squares	SKEWNESS	skewness
CV	coefficient of variation	STDDEV	standard deviation
KURTOSIS	kurtosis	STDERR	standard error of the mean
LCLM	lower confidence limit	SUM	the sum
MAX	maximum value	SUMWGT	sum of weight variables
MEAN	mean	UCLM	upper confidence limit
MIN	minimum value	USS	uncorrected sum of squares
N	number of non-missing values	VAR	variance
NMISS	number of missing values	PROBT	probability for Student's *t*
MEDIAN (P50)	median	T	Student's *t*
Q1 (P25)	25% quantile	Q3 (P75)	75% quantile
P1	1% quantile	P5	5% quantile
P10	10% quantile	P90	90% quantile
P95	95% quantile	P99	99% quantile

Confidence Limits The default confidence level for the confidence limits is .05 or 95%. If you want a different confidence level, then request it with the ALPHA= option in the PROC MEANS statement. For example, if you want 90% confidence limits, then specify ALPHA=.10 along with the CLM option. Then the PROC MEANS statement would look like this:

```
PROC MEANS ALPHA=.10 CLM;
```

The VAR statement By default MEANS will produce statistics for all numeric variables in your data set. If you do not want all the variables, then specify the ones you want in the VAR statement. Here is the general form of the MEANS procedure with the VAR statement:

```
PROC MEANS options;
   VAR variable-names;
```

Example   Your friend is an aspiring author of children's books. To increase her chances of getting her books published, she wants to know how many pages her books should have. At the local library, she counts the number of pages in a random selection of children's picture books. Here are the data:

```
34 30 29 32 52 25 24 27 31 29
24 26 30 30 30 29 21 30 25 28
28 28 29 38 28 29 24 24 29 31
30 27 45 30 22 16 29 14 16 29
32 20 20 15 28 28 29 31 29 36
```

To determine the average number of pages in children's picture books, use the MEANS procedure. MEANS can also produce the median number of pages as well as the 90% confidence limits. Here is the program that will read the data and produce the desired statistics.

```
DATA booklengths;
    INFILE 'c:\MyRawData\Picbooks.dat';
    INPUT NumberOfPages @@;
*Produce summary statistics;
PROC MEANS DATA=booklengths N MEAN MEDIAN CLM ALPHA=.10;
    TITLE 'Summary of Picture Book Lengths';
RUN;
```

Here are the results of the MEANS procedure:

```
                     Summary of Picture Book Lengths                      1

                            The MEANS Procedure

                     Analysis Variable : NumberOfPages

                                        Lower 90.0%     Upper 90.0%
       N        Mean        Median      CL for Mean     CL for Mean
      ─────────────────────────────────────────────────────────────
      50     28.0000000   29.0000000    26.4419136      29.5580864
      ─────────────────────────────────────────────────────────────
```

The average number of pages in the children's books sampled was 28. The median value of 29 says that half the books sampled had 29 pages or fewer. The confidence limits tell us that we are 90% certain that the true population mean (all children's picture books) falls between 26.44 and 29.56 pages. From this analysis your friend concludes that she should make her books between 26 and 30 pages long to maximize her chances of getting published (of course subject matter, and writing style might also help).

7.3   Testing Categorical Data with PROC FREQ

PROC FREQ, which is part of base SAS software, produces many statistics for categorical data. The best known of these is chi-square, but all the tests examine the same null hypothesis, the hypothesis of no association between the variables. All the measures of association indicate the strength of the relationship between the variables. The basic form of PROC FREQ is

```
PROC FREQ;
   TABLES variable-combinations / options;
```

Options   Here are a few of the statistical options available:

AGREE	requests tests and measures of classification agreement including McNemar's test, Bowker's test, Cochran's Q test, and kappa statistics
CHISQ	requests chi-square tests of homogeneity and measures of association
CL	requests confidence limits for measures of association
CMH	requests Cochran-Mantel-Haenszel statistics
EXACT	requests Fisher's exact test for tables larger than 2X2
MEASURES	requests measures of association including Pearson and Spearman correlation coefficients, gamma, Kendall's tau-b, Stuart's tau-c, Somer's D, lambda, odds ratios, risk ratios, and confidence intervals
PLCORR	requests polychoric correlation coefficient
RELRISK	requests relative risk measures for 2X2 tables
TREND	requests the Cochran-Armitage test for trend

Example   One day your neighbor, who rides the bus to work, complains that the regular bus is usually late. He says the express bus is usually on time. Realizing that this is categorical data, you decide to test whether there really is a relationship between type of bus and arriving on time. You collect two variables: type of bus (E for express or R for regular) and promptness (L for late or O for on time).

```
E O E L E L R O E O E O E O R L R O R L   L
R O E O R L E O R L R O E O E O R L E L
E O R L E O R L E O R L E O R O E L E O
E O E O E O E L E O E O R L R L R O R L
E L E O R L R O E O E O E O E L R O R L
```

The following program reads the raw data and runs PROC FREQ with the CHISQ option:

```
DATA bus;
   INFILE 'c:\MyRawData\Bus.dat';
   INPUT BusType $  OnTimeOrLate $ @@;
PROC FREQ DATA = bus;
   TABLES BusType * OnTimeOrLate / CHISQ;
   TITLE;
RUN;
```

Here is the output:

```
                        The FREQ Procedure                    1

              Table of BusType by OnTimeOrLate

         BusType      OnTimeOrLate
         Frequency
         Percent
         Row Pct
         Col Pct    L        0          Total

         E                7       22         29
                      14.00    44.00     58.00
                      24.14    75.86
                      35.00    73.33


         R               13        8         21
                      26.00    16.00     42.00
                      61.90    38.10
                      65.00    26.67


         Total           20       30         50
                      40.00    60.00    100.00


              Statistics for Table of BusType by OnTimeOrLate

         Statistic                    DF      Value      Prob

         Chi-Square                    1      7.2386    0.0071
         Likelihood Ratio Chi-Square   1      7.3364    0.0068
         Continuity Adj. Chi-Square    1      5.7505    0.0165
         Mantel-Haenszel Chi-Square    1      7.0939    0.0077
         Fisher's Exact Test (Left)                     0.0081
                            (Right)                     0.9987
                            (2-Tail)                    0.0097
         Phi Coefficient                     -0.3805
         Contingency Coefficient              0.3556
         Cramer's V                          -0.3805

                        Sample Size = 50
```

The probability of obtaining a chi-square this large or larger by chance alone is 0.0071 so the data do support the idea that there is a relationship between type of bus and arrival time.

7.4 Examining Correlations with PROC CORR

The CORR procedure, which is included with base SAS, computes correlations. A correlation coefficient measures the relationship between two variables, or how co-related they are. If two variables were completely unrelated they would have a correlation of zero. If they were perfectly correlated they would have a correlation of 1.0 or –1.0. In real life, correlations fall somewhere between these numbers. The basic statement for PROC CORR is rather simple:

```
PROC CORR;
```

These two words tell SAS to compute correlations between all the numeric variables in the most recently created data set. You can add the VAR and WITH statements to specify variables:

```
VAR variable-list;
WITH variable-list;
```

Variables listed in the VAR statement appear across the top of the table of correlations, while variables listed in the WITH statement appear down the side of the table. If you use a VAR statement but no WITH statement, then the variables appear both along the top and the side.

By default, PROC CORR computes Pearson product-moment correlation coefficients. You can add options to the PROC statement to request non-parametric correlation coefficients. The SPEARMAN option in the statement below tells SAS to compute Spearman's rank correlations instead of Pearson's correlations:

```
PROC CORR  SPEARMAN;
```

Other options include HOEFFDING (for Hoeffding's D statistic) and KENDALL (for Kendall's tau-b coefficients). Many other options are available with PROC CORR including options for saving statistics in an output data set.

Example Each student in a statistics class recorded three values: test score, the number of hours spent watching television in the week prior to the test, and the number of hours spent exercising during the same week. Here are the raw data:

```
56 6 2    78 7 4    84 5 5    73 4 0    90 3 4
44 9 0    76 5 1    87 3 3    92 2 7    75 8 3
85 1 6    67 4 2    90 5 5    84 6 5    74 5 2
64 4 1    73 0 5    78 5 2    69 6 1    56 7 1
87 8 4    73 8 3   100 0 6    54 8 0    81 5 4
78 5 2    69 4 1    64 7 1    73 7 3    65 6 2
```

Notice that each line contains data for five students. The following program reads the raw data from a file called Exercise.dat and then uses PROC CORR to compute the correlations:

```
DATA class;
   INFILE 'c:\MyRawData\Exercise.dat';
   INPUT Score Television Exercise @@;
```

```
PROC CORR DATA = class;
   VAR Television Exercise;
   WITH Score;
      TITLE 'Correlations for Test Scores';
      TITLE2 'With Hours of Television and Exercise';
RUN;
```

Here is the report from PROC CORR:

```
                   Correlations for Test Scores              1
              With Hours of Television and Exercise

                        The CORR Procedure

           1 'WITH' Variables:  Score
           2 'VAR'  Variables:  Television Exercise


                        Simple Statistics

     Variable       N      Mean    Std Dev      Sum   Minimum    Maximum

     Score         30   74.6333   12.5848    2239.0   44.0000      100.0
     Television    30    5.1000    2.3393     153.0         0     9.0000
     Exercise      30    2.8333    1.9491   85.0000         0     7.0000


              ❶ Pearson Correlation Coefficients, N = 30
                   ❷ Prob > |R| under Ho: Rho=0


                        Television          Exercise

              Score     ❶ -0.55390        ❶ 0.79733
                        ❷  0.0015         ❷ 0.0001
```

This report starts with descriptive statistics for each variable and then lists the correlation matrix which contains: ❶ correlation coefficients (in this case, Pearson), and ❷ the probability of getting a larger absolute value for each correlation.

In this example, both hours of television and hours of exercise are correlated with test score, but exercise is positively correlated while television is negatively correlated. This means students who watched more television tended to have lower scores, while the students who spent more time exercising tended to have higher scores.

7.5 Using PROC REG for Simple Regression Analysis

The REG procedure fits linear regression models by least-squares and is one of several SAS procedures which perform regression analysis. PROC REG is part of the SAS/STAT product, which is licensed separately from base SAS. We will show an example of a simple regression analysis using continuous numeric variables with only one regressor variable. However, PROC REG is capable of analyzing models with many regressor variables using a variety of model-selection methods including stepwise regression, forward selection, and backward elimination. Other procedures in SAS/STAT will perform non-linear, mixed linear, and logistic regression. In SAS/ETS software you will find procedures for time-series analysis. If you are unsure about what type of analysis you need, or are unfamiliar with basic statistical principles, we recommend that you seek advice from a trained statistician, or consult a good statistical textbook.

The REG procedure has only two required statements. It must start with the PROC REG statement and have a MODEL statement specifying the analysis model. The following shows the general form of the REG procedure:

```
PROC REG;
   MODEL dependent = independent;
```

In the MODEL statement, the dependent variable is listed on the left side of the equals sign and the independent, or regressor, variable on the right.

The PLOT statement is one of many optional statements in the REG procedure. You can use the PLOT statement to generate scatter plots of your data, including some of the statistics generated by the regression analysis. If you have SAS/GRAPH installed on your computer, then REG will use SAS/GRAPH software's capabilities to produce nice quality plots. To produce a simple scatter plot of your data, along with the regression line, use the following PLOT statement if you have SAS/GRAPH.

```
PLOT dependent * independent;
```

If you do not have SAS/GRAPH, then you will need the LINEPRINTER option in the PROC REG statement to produce plots. Because you cannot produce lines without SAS/GRAPH, you will need to simulate the regression line by plotting the predicted values overlaid on the observed values. The following shows the general form of the REG procedure to produce a simple scatter plot of your data, along with the predicted values:

```
PROC REG LINEPRINTER;
   MODEL dependent = independent;
   PLOT dependent * independent = 'symbol' P. * independent = 'symbol'/
      OVERLAY;
```

The value for *symbol* specifies what symbol to use to represent the data points for lineprinter plots. If you don't specify a symbol, SAS will use numbers indicating how many observations fall in that location on the plot. When you overlay two plots, it is best to choose two different symbols for the plots. The P. is the keyword for the predicted values.

We have shown you how to produce one type of plot with PROC REG. There are many options available to you for plotting the results of your regression analysis. For example, you can plot residual values, studentized residuals, Cook's D influence statistics, and confidence intervals. If you have SAS/GRAPH software, then you have a lot of control over the apperance of your plot, and your plots will be higher quality. Check your online documentation for a complete list of options available to you for plotting with PROC REG.

Example   At your young neighbor's T-ball game (that's where the players hit the ball from the top of a tee instead of having the ball pitched to them), he said to you, "You can tell how far they'll hit the ball by how tall they are." To give him a little practical lesson in statistics, you decide to test his hypothesis. You gather data from 30 players, measuring their height in inches and their longest of three hits in feet. The following are the data. Notice that data for five players are listed on one line:

```
50 110   49 135   48 129   53 150   48 124
50 143   51 126   45 107   53 146   50 154
47 136   52 144   47 124   50 133   50 128
50 118   48 135   47 129   45 126   48 118
45 121   53 142   46 122   47 119   51 134
49 130   46 132   51 144   50 132   50 131
```

The following program reads the data and performs the regression analysis. It also produces a plot of the data, along with the regression line assuming that SAS/GRAPH is installed:

```
DATA hits;
   INFILE 'c:\MyRawData\Baseball.dat';
   INPUT Height Distance @@;
* Perform regression analysis, plot observed values with regression line;
PROC REG DATA = hits;
   MODEL Distance = Height;
   PLOT Distance * Height;
   TITLE 'Results of Regression Analysis';
RUN;
```

In the MODEL and PLOT statements, Distance is the dependent variable, and Height is the independent variable. The output from the above program is shown and discussed in section 7.6.

7.6 Reading the Output of PROC REG

The output from each REG procedure has several parts. The analysis of variance section and the parameter estimates usually print on the same page. Some optional statements, like PLOT, produce additional output on separate pages.

The output shown in this section is the result of the following PROC REG statements from the preceding section:

```
PROC REG DATA = hits;
   MODEL Distance = Height;
   PLOT Distance * Height;
   TITLE 'Results of Regression Analysis';
RUN;
```

The first section of output is the analysis of variance section, which gives information about how well the model fits the data:

```
                  Results of Regression Analysis                    1

                         The REG Procedure
                         Model: MODEL1
                    Dependent Variable: Distance


                       Analysis of Variance

                              Sum of      ❷ Mean
    Source        ❶ DF        Squares       Square   ❸ F Value  ❹ Pr > F

    Model             1    1365.50831   1365.50831     16.86     0.0003
    Error            28    2268.35836     81.01280
    Corrected Total  29    3633.86667


          ❺ Root MSE            9.00071    R-Square    0.3758
            Dependent Mean    130.73333  ❼ Adj R-Sq    0.3535
          ❻ Coeff Var           6.88479
```

❶ DF   degrees of freedom associated with the source
❷ Mean Square   mean square (sum of squares divided by the degrees of freedom)
❸ F value   F value for testing the null hypothesis (all parameters are zero except intercept)
❹ Pr>F   significance probability
❺ Root MSE   root mean square error
❻ Coeff Var   the coefficient of variation
❼ Adj R-sq   the R-square value adjusted for degrees of freedom

The parameter estimates follow the analysis of variance section and give the parameters for each term in the model, including the intercept:

Parameter Estimates					
Variable	**❶** DF	Parameter Estimate	Standard Error	**❷** t Value	**❸** Pr > |t|
Intercept	1	-11.00859	34.56363	-0.32	0.7525
Height	1	2.89466	0.70506	4.11	0.0003

❶ DF	degrees of freedom for the variable
❷ t Value	*t* test for the parameter equal to zero
❸ Pr > |t|	two-tailed significance probability

From the parameter estimates you can construct the regression equation:

```
Distance = -11.00859 + 2.89466 * Height
```

The following figure shows the results of the PLOT statement. By default, when you have SAS/GRAPH, REG will plot the data points and the regression line. It will also print the regression equation at the top of the plot, along with some of the regression statistics along the right-hand side.

Results of Regression Analysis

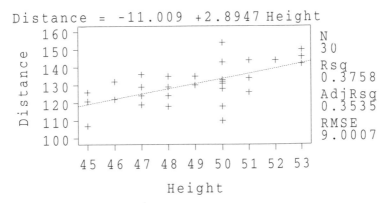

In this example, the distance the ball was hit did increase with the player's height. The model is significant (significance probability = .0003) but the relationship is not very strong (R-square = 0.3758). Perhaps age or years of experience are better predictors of how far the ball will go.

7.7 Using PROC ANOVA for One-Way Analysis of Variance

The ANOVA procedure is one of several in the SAS System that perform analysis of variance. PROC ANOVA is part of SAS/STAT software, which is licensed separately from base SAS. PROC ANOVA is specifically designed for balanced data—data where there are equal numbers of observations in each classification. If your data are not balanced, then you should use the GLM procedure, whose statements are almost identical to those of PROC ANOVA. Although we are only discussing simple one-way analysis of variance in this section, PROC ANOVA can handle multiple classification variables and models that include nested and crossed effects as well as repeated measures. If you are unsure of the appropriate analysis for your data, or are unfamiliar with basic statistical principles, we recommend that you seek advice from a trained statistician or consult a good statistical textbook.

The ANOVA procedure has two required statements: the CLASS and MODEL statements. The following is the general form of the ANOVA procedure:

```
PROC ANOVA;
   CLASS variable-list;
   MODEL dependent = effects;
```

The CLASS statement must come before the MODEL statement and defines the classification variables. For one-way analysis of variance, only one variable is listed. The MODEL statement defines the dependent variable and the effects. For one-way analysis of variance, the effect is the classification variable.

As you might expect, there are many optional statements for PROC ANOVA. One of the most useful is the MEANS statement, which calculates means of the dependent variable for any of the main effects in the MODEL statement. In addition, the MEANS statement can perform several types of multiple comparisons tests including Bonferroni *t* tests (BON), Duncan's multiple-range test (DUNCAN), Scheffe's multiple-comparison procedure (SCHEFFE), pairwise *t* tests (T), and Tukey's studentized range test (TUKEY). The MEANS statement has the following general form:

```
MEANS effects / options;
```

The effects can be any main effect in the MODEL statement (no crossed or nested effects), and options include the name of the desired multiple comparisons test (DUNCAN for example).

Example Your friend says his daughter complains that it seems like the girls on all the other softball teams are taller than her team. You decide to test her hypothesis by getting the heights for all the girls and performing analysis of variance to see if there are any differences among teams. You have the team name and each girl's height for players on five different teams. Notice that there are data for six girls on each line:

```
red   55 red   48 red   53 red   47 red   51 red   43
red   45 red   46 red   55 red   54 red   45 red   52
blue  46 blue  56 blue  48 blue  47 blue  54 blue  52
blue  49 blue  51 blue  45 blue  48 blue  55 blue  47
gray  55 gray  45 gray  47 gray  56 gray  49 gray  53
gray  48 gray  53 gray  51 gray  52 gray  48 gray  47
pink  53 pink  53 pink  58 pink  56 pink  50 pink  55
pink  59 pink  57 pink  49 pink  55 pink  56 pink  57
gold  53 gold  55 gold  48 gold  45 gold  47 gold  56
gold  55 gold  46 gold  47 gold  53 gold  51 gold  50
```

Because each team has exactly 12 girls, the data are balanced and you can use the ANOVA procedure. You want to know which, if any, teams are taller than the rest, so you use the MEANS statement in your program and choose Scheffe's multiple-comparison procedure to compare the means. Here is the program to read the data and perform the analysis of variance:

```
DATA soft;
   INFILE 'c:\MyRawData\Softball.dat';
   INPUT Team $ Height @@;
* Use ANOVA to run one-way analysis of variance;
PROC ANOVA DATA = soft;
   CLASS Team;
   MODEL Height = Team;
   MEANS Team / SCHEFFE;
   TITLE "Girls' Heights on Softball Teams";
RUN;
```

In this case, Team is the classification variable and also the effect in the MODEL statement. Height is the dependent variable. The MEANS statement will produce means of the girls' heights for each team, and the SCHEFFE option will test which teams are different from the others. The output from the above program is shown and discussed in section 7.8.

7.8 Reading the Output of PROC ANOVA

PROC ANOVA has at least two parts to its output. First it prints a table giving information about the classification variables: number of levels, values, and number of observations. Next it prints the analysis of variance table. If you use optional statements like MEANS, then their output will follow.

The example from section 7.7, where we wanted to test to see if there are differences in the heights among softball teams, used the following PROC ANOVA statements:

```
PROC ANOVA DATA = soft;
   CLASS Team;
   MODEL Height = Team;
   MEANS Team / SCHEFFE;
   TITLE "Girls' Heights on Softball Teams";
RUN;
```

The first page of the output gives information about the classification variable:

```
               Girls' Heights on Softball Teams                  1

                      The ANOVA Procedure

                   Class Level Information

         Class          Levels    Values

         Team                5     blue gold gray pink red

                 Number of observations    60
```

Here the CLASS variable is Team. It has five levels with values blue, gold, gray, pink, and red representing the five teams. There are a total of 60 observations in the data set.

The second part of the output is the analysis of variance table:

```
                    Girls' Heights on Softball Teams                  2
                          The ANOVA Procedure
   Dependent Variable: Height
```

❶ Source	❷ DF	❸ Sum of Squares	❹ Mean Square	❺ F Value	❻ Pr > F
Model	4	228.0000000	57.0000000	4.14	0.0053
Error	55	758.0000000	13.7818182		
Corrected Total	59	986.0000000			

❼ R-Square	❽ Coeff Var	❾ Root MSE	❿ Height Mean
0.231237	7.279190	3.712387	51.00000

Source	DF	Anova SS	Mean Square	F Value	Pr > F
Team	4	228.0000000	57.0000000	4.14	0.0053

Highlights of the output are

❶ `Source`   source of variation
❷ `DF`   degrees of freedom for the model, error, and total
❸ `Sum of Squares` sum of squares for the portion attributed to the model, error, and total
❹ `Mean Square`   mean square (sum of squares divided by the degrees of freedom)
❺ `F value`   F value (mean square for the model divided by the mean square for the error)
❻ `Pr > F`   significance probability associated with the F statistic
❼ `R-Square`   R-square
❽ `Coeff Var`   coefficient of variation
❾ `Root MSE`   root mean square error
❿ `Height Mean`   mean of the dependent variable

Because the model is significant (significance probability = .0053), we conclude that not all the teams are the same height. The SCHEFFE option in the MEANS statement compares the heights between the teams. Letters are used to group means, and means with the same letters are not significantly different from each other (at the 0.05 level). The following results show that your friend's daughter is partially correct—one team (PINK) is taller than her team (RED) but not all the teams are taller.

```
              Girls' Heights on Softball Teams                  3

                    The ANOVA Procedure

                 Scheffe's Test for Height

     NOTE: This test controls the type I experimentwise error rate.

              Alpha                                0.05
              Error Degrees of Freedom               55
              Error Mean Square                  13.78182
              Critical Value of F                2.53969
              Minimum Significant Difference      4.8306


        Means with the same letter are not significantly different.

        Scheffe Grouping           Mean      N    Team

                         A        54.833     12    pink
                         A
                    B    A        50.500     12    gold
                    B    A
                    B    A        50.333     12    gray
                    B
                    B             49.833     12    blue
                    B
                    B             49.500     12    red
```

7.9 Introducing the Analyst Application

The Analyst application is relatively new software from SAS Institute, first becoming available as an add-on to Release 6.12 of the SAS System. Analyst is a graphical user interface (GUI) to many of the statistical capabilities available in the SAS System. It allows you to take advantage of the statistical procedures without writing any SAS programs. You can enter and manipulate data within Analyst, or you can read data into Analyst from a number of different sources. Then you can choose from a wide variety of statistical tasks for your analysis including hypothesis tests, analysis of variance, linear models, regression, correlation, principal components analysis, and much more. All statistical tasks include a graphical component.

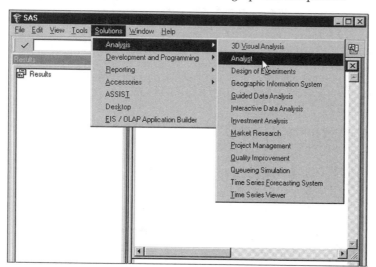

Starting Analyst
Start Analyst from the Solutions pull-down menu. Select `Analysis`, then `Analyst`.

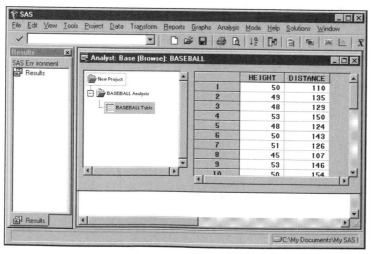

Entering data When you first invoke Analyst, you get a project tree on the left and a data table on the right. You can enter your data directly into the data table, read your data from a SAS data set, or import data from delimited or CSV files. If you have SAS/ACCESS for PC File Formats, you can also read Excel, Lotus, and dBase files.

Producing results

Once you have your data in Analyst, you can make transformations to your data (edit, recode, create new variables, and combine data files), produce reports and graphs, and perform a number of analyses. Your results will display in a separate window and they will also appear as nodes in the project tree. If, for example, you run a regression analysis on your data, you will see the same results as you would if you ran the REG procedure. The reason

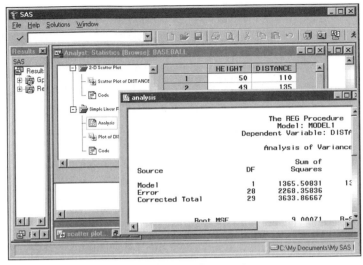

for this is that Analyst uses the very same procedures that you use if you write your own programs. If you like, you can also have your results displayed in HTML.

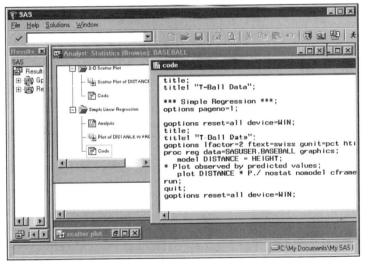

Generating SAS code

Analyst is designed to give you easy access to the statistical features of the SAS System. But Analyst can also be used as a learning tool for the rest of the SAS statistical procedures. For every analysis you perform with Analyst, it writes a SAS program. You can look at and save for future reference the programs that Analyst writes. When you run your analyses, in addition to your results, you will also get the code in your project tree. You can look at the code generated by Analyst, and you can save it in a file if you want to run the program over again, or modify it for future analysis outside of the Analyst application.

Requirements The Analyst application requires that you have base SAS installed as well as SAS/STAT, SAS/GRAPH, and SAS/ASSIST. In addition you will probably want to install SAS/FSP (if you want to enter data within Analyst), and SAS/ACCESS for PC File Formats (if you want to import Excel and other data types into Analyst). The Analyst application is included with Version 7 of the SAS System for PCs and UNIX workstations.

8 ►

" **P**roblems that go away by themselves come back by themselves. "

MARCY E. DAVIS

CHAPTER 8

Debugging Your SAS® Programs

8.1   Writing SAS Programs That Work

It's not always easy to write a program that works the first time you run it. Even experienced SAS programmers will tell you it's a delightful surprise when their programs run on the first try. The longer and more complicated the program, the more likely it is to have syntax or logic errors. But don't despair, there are a few guidelines you can follow that can make your programs run correctly sooner and help you discover errors more easily.

Make programs easy to read   One simple thing you can do is develop the habit of writing programs in a neat and consistent manner. Programs that are easy to read are easier to debug and will save you time in the long run. The following are suggestions on how to write your programs:

♦   Put only one SAS statement on a line. SAS allows you to put as many statements on a line as you wish, which may save you some space in your program, but the saved space is rarely worth the sacrifice in readability.

♦   Use indention to show the different parts of the program. Indent all statements within the DATA and PROC steps. This way you can tell at a glance how many DATA and PROC steps there are in a program and which statement belongs to which step. It's also helpful to further indent any statements between a DO statement and its END statement.

♦   Use comment statements generously to document your programs. This takes some discipline but is important, especially if anyone else is likely to read or use your program. Everyone has a different programming style, and it is often impossible to figure out what someone else's program is doing and why. Comment statements take the mystery out of the program.

Test each part of the program   You can increase your programming efficiency tremendously by making sure each part of your program is working before moving on to write the next part. If you were building a house, you would make sure the foundation was level and square before putting up the walls. You would test the plumbing before finishing the bathroom. You are, by law, required to have each stage of the house inspected before moving on to the next. The same should be done for your SAS program. But you don't have to wait for the inspector to come out; you can do it yourself.

If you are reading data from a file, use PROC PRINT to print the SAS data set at least once to make sure it is correct before moving on. Sometimes, even though there are no errors or even suspicious notes in your SAS log, the SAS data set is not correct. This could happen because SAS did not read the data the way you imagined (after all it does what you say, not what you're thinking) or because the data had some peculiarities you did not realize. For example, a researcher who received two data files from Taiwan wanted to merge them together by date. She could not figure out why they refused to merge correctly until she printed both data sets and realized one of the files used Taiwanese dates, which are offset by 11 years.

It's a good habit to print all the SAS data sets you create in a program at least once to make sure they are correct. As with reading raw data files, sometimes merging and setting data sets can produce the wrong result even though there were no error messages. So when in doubt, use PROC PRINT.

Test programs with small data sets Sometimes it's not practical to test your program with your entire data set. If your data files are very large, you may not want to print all the data and it may take a long time for your programs to run. In these cases, you can test your program with a subset of your data.

If you are reading data from a file, you can use the OBS= option in the INFILE statement to tell SAS to stop reading when it gets to that line in the file. This way you can read only the first 50 or 100 lines of data or however many it takes to get a good representation of your data. The following statement will read only the first 100 lines of the raw data file Mydata.Dat:

```
INFILE 'Mydata.Dat' OBS = 100;
```

You can also use the FIRSTOBS= option to start reading from the middle of the data file. So, if the first 100 data lines are not a good representation of your data but 101 through 200 are, you can use the following statement to read just those lines:

```
INFILE 'Mydata.Dat' FIRSTOBS = 101 OBS = 200;
```

Here FIRSTOBS= and OBS= relate to the records of raw data in the file. These do not necessarily correspond to the observations in the SAS data set created. If, for example, you are reading two records for each observation, then you would need to read 200 records to get 100 observations.

If you are reading a SAS data set instead of a raw data file, you can use the OBS= and FIRSTOBS= data set options in the SET, MERGE, or UPDATE statements.[1] This controls which observations are processed in the DATA step. For example, the following DATA step will read the first 50 observations in the CATS data set. Note that when reading SAS data sets OBS= and FIRSTOBS= truly do correspond to the observations and not to data lines:

```
DATA sampleofcats;
    SET cats (OBS = 50);
```

Test with representative data Using OBS= and FIRSTOBS= is an easy way to test your programs, but sometimes it is difficult to get a good representation of your data this way. You may need to create a small test data set by extracting representative parts of the larger data set. Or you may want to make up representative data for testing purposes. Making up data has the advantage that you can simplify the data and make sure you have every possible combination of values to test.

Sometimes you may want to make up data and write a small program just to test one aspect of your larger program. This can be extremely useful for narrowing down possible sources of error in a large complicated program.

The Enhanced Editor At the time this book was written, the Enhanced Editor was not yet released. Ordinarily we would not write about a feature that is not yet a part of the SAS System, but the Enhanced Editor is so promising that we feel it is worth mentioning here. This editor color codes your program as you write it. SAS keywords appear in one color, variables in another. All text within quotes is given the same color, so it is immediately obvious when you forget to close your quotes. Similarly, missing semicolons are much easier to discover because the colors in your program are not right. If the Enhanced Editor is not a part of SAS at your site, ask if it is available. It may be experimental for your platform, or it may be available in some future release of SAS. Either way, watch for the Enhanced Editor.

---

[1] Data set options are discussed in section 5.9.

8.2 Fixing Programs That Don't Work

In spite of your best efforts, sometimes programs just don't work. More often than not, programs don't run the first time. Even with simple programs it is easy to forget a semicolon or misspell a keyword—everyone does sometime. If your program doesn't work, the source of the problem may be obvious like an error message with the offending part of your program underlined, or not so obvious as when you have no errors but still don't have the expected results. Whatever the problem, here are a few guidelines you can follow to help fix your program.

Read the SAS log The SAS log has a wealth of information about your program. In addition to listing the program statements, it tells you things like how many lines were read from your raw data file and what were the minimum and maximum line lengths. It gives the number of observations and variables in each SAS data set you create. Information like this may seem inconsequential at first but can be very helpful in finding the source of your errors.

The SAS log has three types of messages about your program: errors, warnings, and notes.

Errors These are hard to ignore. Not only do they come up in red on your screen, but your program will not run with errors. Usually errors are some kind of syntax or spelling mistake. The following shows the error message when you accidentally add a slash between the PROC MEANS and DATA= keywords. SAS underlines the problem (the slash) and tells you it doesn't recognize the symbol.

```
1    PROC MEANS / DATA = one;
                -
                200
ERROR 200-322: The symbol is not recognized.
```

The location of the error is easy to find, because it is usually underlined, but the source of the error can sometimes be tricky. Sometimes what is wrong is not what is underlined but something else earlier in the program.

Warnings These are less serious than errors because your program will run with warnings. But beware, a warning may mean that SAS has done something you have not intended. For example, SAS will attempt to correct your spelling of certain keywords. If you misspell INPUT as IMPUT you will get the following message in your log:

```
WARNING 1-322: Assuming the symbol INPUT was misspelled as IMPUT.
```

Usually you would think, "SAS is so smart—it knows what I meant to say," but occasionally that may not be what you meant at all. Make sure that you know what all the warnings are about and that you agree with them.

Notes These are less straightforward than either warnings or errors. Sometimes notes just give you information, like telling you the execution time of each step in your program. But sometimes notes can indicate a problem. Suppose, for example, that you have the following note in your SAS log:

```
NOTE: SAS went to a new line when INPUT statement reached past the end of a line.
```

This could mean that SAS did exactly what you wanted, or it could indicate a problem with either your program or your data. Make sure that you know what each note means and why it is there.

Start at the beginning Whenever you read the SAS log, start at the beginning. This seems like a ridiculous statement—why wouldn't you start at the beginning? Well, if you are using the SAS windowing environment, the SAS log rolls by in the log window. When the program is finished, you are left looking at the end of the log. If you happen to see an error at the end of the log it is natural to try to fix that error first—the first one you see. Avoid this temptation. Often errors at the end of the log are caused by earlier ones. If you fix the first error, often most or all of the other errors will disappear. If your lawnmower is out of gas and won't start, it's probably better to add gas before trying to figure out why it won't start. The same logic applies to debugging SAS programs; fixing one problem will often fix others.

Look for common mistakes first More often than not there is a simple reason why your program doesn't work. Look for the simple reason before trying to find something more complicated. The remainder of this chapter consists of sections discussing the most common errors encountered in SAS programming. When you see this little bug in the upper-right corner of a section, you'll know that the material deals with how to debug your program. Some programming errors produce error messages, some just notes. If your SAS log contains an error or a suspicious note, look in this chapter for a section which discusses your error or note.

Sometimes error messages just don't make any sense. For example, you may get an error message saying the INPUT statement is not valid. This doesn't make much sense because you know INPUT is a valid SAS statement. In cases like these, look for missing semicolons in the statements before the error. If SAS has underlined an item, be sure to look not only at the underlined item but also at the previous few statements.

Finally, if you just can't figure out why you are not getting the results you expect, make sure you add PROC PRINT statements everywhere you create a new SAS data set. This can really help you discover errors in your logic, and sometimes uncover surprising details about your data.

Check your syntax If you have large data sets, you may want to check for syntax errors in your program before processing your data. Do this by telling SAS not to process any data when you submit your program. Add the following line to your program and submit it in the usual way:

```
OPTIONS OBS=0 NOREPLACE;
```

The OBS=0 option tells SAS not to process any data, while the NOREPLACE option tells SAS not to replace existing SAS data sets with empty ones. Once you know your syntax is correct, you can resubmit your program without the OPTIONS statement in batch mode, or replace the OPTIONS with the following if you are using the SAS windowing environment.

```
OPTIONS OBS=MAX REPLACE;
```

Remember that this syntax check will not uncover any errors related to your data or logic errors.

8.3 Searching for the Missing Semicolon

Missing semicolons are the most common source of errors in SAS programs. For whatever reason, we humans can't seem to remember to put a semicolon at the end of all our statements. (Maybe we all have rebellious right pinkies—who knows.) This is unfortunate because, while it is easy to forget the semicolon, it is not always easy to find the missing semicolon. The error messages produced are often misleading, making it difficult to find the error.

SAS reads statements from one semicolon to the next without regard to the layout of the program. If you leave off a semicolon, you in effect concatenate two SAS statements. Then SAS gets confused because it seems as though you are missing statements, or it tries to interpret entire statements as options in the previous statement. This can produce some very puzzling messages. So, if you get an error message that just doesn't make sense, look for missing semicolons.

Example The following program is missing a semicolon on the comment statement before the DATA statement:

```
* Read the data file ToadJump.dat using list input
DATA toads;
    INFILE 'c:\MyRawData\ToadJump.dat';
    INPUT ToadName $ Weight Jump1 Jump2 Jump3;
RUN;
```

Here is the SAS log after the program has run:

```
1     * Read the data file ToadJump.dat using list input
2     DATA toads;
3         INFILE 'c:\MyRawData\ToadJump.dat';
          ------
          180

ERROR 180-322: Statement is not valid or it is used out of proper order.

4         INPUT ToadName $ Weight Jump1 Jump2 Jump3;
          -----
          180

ERROR 180-322: Statement is not valid or it is used out of proper order.

5     RUN;
```

In this case, DATA toads becomes part of the comment statement. Because there is now no DATA statement, SAS underlines the INFILE and INPUT keywords and says, "Hey these statements are in the wrong place; they have to be part of a DATA step." This doesn't make much sense to you because you know INFILE and INPUT are valid statements, and you did put them in a DATA step (or so you thought). That's when you should suspect a missing semicolon.

Example The next example shows the same program, but now the semicolon is missing from the DATA statement. The INFILE statement becomes part of the DATA statement, and SAS tries to create a SAS data set named INFILE. SAS also tries to interpret the filename, 'c:\MyRawData\ToadJump.dat' as a SAS data set name, but the .dat extension is not valid for SAS data sets. It also gives you an error saying that there is no CARDS or INFILE statement. In addition, you get some warnings about data sets being incomplete. This is a good example of how one simple mistake can produce a lot of confusing messages:

```
32   * Read the data file ToadJump.dat using list input;
33   DATA toads
34      INFILE 'c:\MyRawData\ToadJump.dat';
35      INPUT ToadName $ Weight Jump1 Jump2 Jump3;
36   RUN;

ERROR: No CARDS or INFILE statement.

ERROR: Memtype   field is invalid.
NOTE: The SAS System stopped processing this step because of errors.
WARNING: The data set WORK.TOADS may be incomplete.  When this step was stopped
there were 0 observations and 5 variables.
WARNING: The data set WORK.INFILE may be incomplete.  When this step was stopped
there were 0 observations and 5 variables.
NOTE: DATA statement used:
      real time            1.09 seconds
```

Missing semicolons can produce a variety of error messages. Usually the messages say that either a statement is not valid, or an option or parameter is not valid or recognized. Sometimes you don't get an error message, but the results are still not right. If you leave off the semicolon from the last RUN statement when submitting programs in the SAS windowing environment, you won't get an error. But SAS won't run the last part of your program either.

The DATASTMTCHK system option A new system option can make some missing semicolons, such as the one in the last example, easier to find. The DATASTMTCHK system option controls what names you can use for SAS data sets in a DATA statement. By default it is set so that you cannot use the words: MERGE, RETAIN, SET, or UPDATE as a SAS data set name. This prevents you from accidentally overwriting an existing data set just because you forget a semicolon at the end of a DATA statement. You can make all SAS keywords invalid SAS data set names by setting the DATASTMTCHK option to ALLKEYWORDS. The partial log below again shows a missing semicolon at the end of the DATA statement, but this time DATASTMTCHK is set to ALLKEYWORDS:

```
1    OPTIONS DATASTMTCHK=ALLKEYWORDS;
2    * Read the data file ToadJump.dat using list input;
3    DATA toads
4       INFILE 'c:\MyRawData\ToadJump.dat';
        ------
        57
ERROR 57-185: INFILE is not allowed in the DATA statement when option
DATASTMTCHK=ALLKEYWORDS. Check for a missing semicolon in the DATA statement, or
use DATASTMTCHK=NONE.

5       INPUT ToadName $ Weight Jump1 Jump2 Jump3;
6    RUN;
ERROR: Memtype   field is invalid.
```

8.4 ▶ Note: INPUT Statement Reached Past the End of the Line

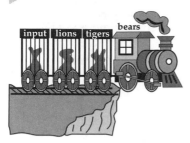

The note "SAS went to a new line when INPUT statement reached past the end of a line" is rather innocent looking, but its presence can indicate a problem. This note often goes unnoticed. It doesn't come up in red or even green lettering. It doesn't cause your program to stop. But look for it in your SAS log because it is a common note that usually means there is a problem.

This note means that as SAS was reading your data, it got to the end of the data line before it read values for all the variables in your INPUT statement. When this happens, SAS goes by default to the next line of data to get values for the remaining variables. Sometimes this is exactly what you want SAS to do, but if it's not, take a good look at your SAS log and output to be sure you know why this is happening.

Look in your SAS log where it tells you the number of lines it read from the data file and the number of observations in the SAS data set. If you have fewer observations than lines read, and you planned to have one observation per line, then you know you have a problem. Print the SAS data set using PROC PRINT. This can be very helpful in determining the source of the problem.

Example The following shows what can happen if you are using list input, and you don't have periods for missing values. You have the following data from the toad-jumping contest, where the toad's number is followed by its weight and distances for each of three jumps. When a toad was disqualified from a jump, no entry was made for that jump:

```
13   65 1.9 3.0
25 131 2.5 3.1 .5
10 202 3.8
8  128 3.2 1.9 2.6
3  162
21  99 2.4 1.7 3.0
```

The following is the SAS log from a program that reads the raw data using list input and prints the results using PROC PRINT:

```
1    DATA toads;
2       INFILE 'c:\MyRawData\Toadjmp2.dat';
3       INPUT ToadNumber Weight Jump1 Jump2 Jump3;

NOTE: The infile 'c:\MyRawData\Toadjmp2.dat' is:
      File Name=c:\MyRawData\Toadjmp2.dat,
      RECFM=V,LRECL=256

❶ NOTE:  6 records were read from the infile 'c:\MyRawData\Toadjmp2.dat'.
         The minimum record length was 6.
         The maximum record length was 18.
❸ NOTE:  SAS went to a new line when INPUT statement reached past the end of a line.
❷ NOTE:  The data set WORK.TOADS has 3 observations and 5 variables.
   NOTE:  DATA statement used:
          real time            0.86 seconds
4    PROC PRINT;
5       TITLE 'SAS Data Set Toads';
```

❶ Notice that there were six records read from the raw data file.

❷ But, there are only three observations in the SAS data set.

❸ The note, "INPUT statement reached past the end of a line," should alert you that there may be a problem.

A look at the results of the PROC PRINT confirms that there is a problem since the numbers don't look at all correct. (Can a toad jump 128 feet?)

```
                         SAS Data Set Toads                          1

              Toad
    Obs      Number     Weight     Jump1     Jump2     Jump3

     1         13          65        1.9        3       25.0
     2         10         202        3.8        8      128.0
     3          3         162       21.0       99        2.4
```

Here SAS went to a new line when you didn't want it to. To fix this problem, the simplest thing to do is use the MISSOVER option of the INFILE statement. MISSOVER instructs SAS to assign missing values to any variables for which there were no data instead of going to the next line for data. The INFILE statement would look like this:

```
INFILE 'c:\MyRawData\Toadjmp2.dat' MISSOVER;
```

Possible causes Other reasons for receiving the note informing you that the INPUT statement reached past the end of the line include

♦ You planned for SAS to go to the next data line when it ran out of data.

♦ Blank lines in your data file, usually at the beginning or end, can cause this note. Look at the minimum line length in the SAS log. If it is zero, then you have blank lines. Edit out the blank lines and rerun your program.

♦ If you are using list input and you do not have a space between every value, you can get this note. For example, if you try to read the following data using list input, SAS will run out of data for the Gilroy Garlics because there is no space between the 15 and the 1035. SAS will read it as one number, then read the 12 where it should have been reading the 1035, and so on. To correct this problem, either add a space between the two numbers, or use column or formatted input.

```
Columbia Peaches     35  67  1 10  2  1
Gilroy Garlics       151035 12 11  7  6
Sacramento Tomatoes  124  85 15  4  9  1
```

♦ If you have some data lines which are shorter than the rest, and you are using column or formatted input, this can cause a problem. If you try to read a name, for example, in columns 60 through 70 when some of the names extend only to column 68, and you didn't add spaces at the end of the line to fill it out to column 70, then SAS will go to the next line to read the name. To avoid this problem, use the TRUNCOVER option in the INFILE statement (discussed in section 2.15). For example:

```
INFILE 'c:\MyRawData\Addresses.dat' TRUNCOVER;
```

8.5 ▶ Note: Lost Card

Lost card? You thought you were writing SAS programs, not playing a card game. This note makes more sense if you remember that computer programs and data used to be punched out on computer cards. A lost card means that SAS was expecting another line (or card) of data and didn't find it.

If you are reading multiple lines of data for each observation, then a lost card could mean you have missing or duplicate lines of data. If you are reading two data lines for each observation, then SAS will expect an even number of lines in the data file. If you have an odd number, then you will get the lost-card message. It can often be difficult to locate the missing or duplicate lines, especially with large data files. Printing the SAS data set as well as careful proofreading of the data file can be helpful in identifying problem areas.

Example The following example shows what can happen if you have a missing data line. The raw data show the normal high and low temperatures and the record high and low for the month of July for each city. The last city is missing the last data line:

```
Nome AK
55 44
88 29
Miami FL
90 75
97 65
Raleigh NC
88 68
```

The following shows the SAS log from a program which reads the data, three lines per observation:

```
1    DATA highlow;
2       INFILE 'c:\MyRawData\Temps.dat';
3       INPUT City $ State $ / NormalHigh NormalLow/ RecordHigh RecordLow;

NOTE: The infile 'c:\MyRawData\Temps.dat' is:
      File Name=c:\MyRawData\Temps.dat,
      RECFM=V,LRECL=256

NOTE: LOST CARD.
City=Raleigh State=NC NormalHigh=88 NormalLow=68 RecordHigh=. RecordLow=.
_ERROR_=1 _N_=3
NOTE: 8 records were read from the infile
      'c:\MyRawData\Temps.dat'.
      The minimum record length was 5.
      The maximum record length was 10.
NOTE: The data set WORK.HIGHLOW has 2 observations and 6 variables.
NOTE: DATA statement used:
      real time           1.27 seconds
```

In this case, you get the lost-card note, and SAS prints the values of the variables it read for the observation with the lost card. The observation is not included in the SAS data set. You can see from the log that SAS read eight records from the file (it should have been a multiple of three) but the SAS data set has only two observations. The last partial observation was not included.

Example It is very common to get other messages along with the lost-card note. The invalid-data note is a common byproduct of the lost card. If the second line were missing from the temperature data, then you would get invalid data as well as a lost card because SAS will try to read Miami FL as the record high and low. The following shows the invalid-data note from the SAS log:

```
Nome AK
88 29
Miami FL
90 75
97 65
Raleigh NC
88 68
105 50
```

```
NOTE: Invalid data for RecordHigh in line 3 1-5.
NOTE: Invalid data for RecordLow in line 3 7-8.
RULE:      ----+----1----+----2----+----3----+----4----+----5----+----6----+
3          Miami FL
City=Nome State=AK NormalHigh=88 NormalLow=29 RecordHigh=. RecordLow=.
_ERROR_=1 _N_=1
```

Example In addition to getting the lost-card note, it is also common to get a note indicating that the INPUT statement reached past the end of a line. If you forgot the last number in the file, as in the following example, then you would get these two notes together:

```
Nome AK
55 44
88 29
Miami FL
90 75
97 65
Raleigh NC
88 68
105
```

Because the program uses list input, SAS will try to go to the next line to get the data for the last variable. Since there isn't another line of data, you get the lost-card note. The following is part of the SAS log showing these two messages together:

```
NOTE: LOST CARD.
City=Raleigh State=NC NormalHigh=88 NormalLow=68 RecordHigh=105 RecordLow=.
_ERROR_=1 _N_=3
NOTE: 9 records were read from the infile
      'c:\MyRawData\Temps3.dat'.
      The minimum record length was 3.
      The maximum record length was 10.
NOTE: SAS went to a new line when INPUT statement reached past the end of a line.
NOTE: The data set WORK.HIGHLOW has 2 observations and 6 variables.
```

For this example, the solution is to add the missing data to the raw data file and rerun the program.

8.6 Note: Invalid Data

The typical new SAS user, upon seeing the invalid-data note, will ignore it, hoping perhaps that it will simply go away by itself. That's rather ironic considering that the message is explicit and easy to interpret once you know how to read it.

Interpreting the message The invalid-data note appears when SAS is unable to read from a raw data file because the data are inconsistent with the INPUT statement. This note almost always indicates a problem. For example, one common mistake is typing in the letter O instead of the number 0. If the variable is numeric, then SAS is unable to interpret the letter O. In response, SAS does two things; it sets the value of this variable to missing and prints out a message like this for the problematic observation:

```
❶  NOTE: Invalid data for IDNumber in line 8 1-5.
❷  RULE:----+----1----+----2----+----3----+----4----+----5----+----6----+
❷  8    007  James Bond    SA341

❸  IDNumber=. Name=James Bond Class=SA Q1=3 Q2=4 Q3=1 _ERROR_=1 _N_=8
```

❶ The first line tells you where the problem occurred. Specifically, it states the name of the variable SAS got stuck on and the line number and columns of the raw data file that SAS was trying to read. In this example, the error occurred while SAS was trying to read a variable named IDNumber from columns 1 through 5 in line 8 of the input file.

❷ The next line is a sort of ruler with columns as the increments. The numeral 1 marks the tenth column, 2 marks the twentieth, and so on. Below the ruler, SAS dumps the actual line of raw data so you can see the little troublemaker for yourself. Using the ruler as a guide, you can count over to the column in question. At this point you can compare the actual raw data to your INPUT statement, and the error is usually obvious. The value of IDNumber should be zero-zero-seven, but looking at the line of actual data you can see that a careless typist has typed zero-letter O-seven. Such an error may seem minor to you, but you'll soon learn that computers are hopelessly persnickety.

❸ As if this weren't enough, SAS prints one more piece of information: the values of each variable for that observation as SAS read it. In this case, you can see that IDNumber equals missing, Name equals James Bond, and so on. Two automatic variables appear at the end of the line: _ERROR_ and _N_. The _ERROR_ variable has a value of 1 if there is a data error for that observation, and 0 if there is not. In an invalid-data note, _ERROR_ always equals 1. The automatic variable _N_ is the number of times SAS has looped through the DATA step.

Unprintable characters Occasionally invalid data contain unprintable characters. This can happen if data are entered into some other software such as a spreadsheet or word processor and then input in SAS without being properly imported. In such cases, SAS also prints the raw data in hexadecimal format.

This invalid-data note contains unprintable characters:

```
NOTE: Invalid data for IDNumber in line 10 1-5.
RULE:----+----1----+----2----+----3----+----4----+----5----+----6----+
❶   C..    Indiana Jones PI83.
❷   Z012224666666246667254332222222222222222222222222222222222222222222
❷   NDB0009E491E10AFE5300983E0000000000000000000000000000000000000000000
IdNumber=. Name=Indiana Jones Class=PI Q1=8 Q2=3. _ERROR_=1 _N_=10
```

- ❶ As before, SAS prints the line of raw data that contains the invalid data.

- ❷ Directly below the line of raw data, SAS prints two lines containing the hexadecimal equivalent of your data. You needn't understand hexadecimal values to be able to read this. SAS prints the data this way because the normal 10 numerals and 26 letters don't provide enough values to represent all computer symbols uniquely. Hexadecimal uses two characters to represent each symbol. To read hexadecimal, take a digit from the first line together with the corresponding digit from the second line. In this case, a form-feed and a carriage-return-line-feed slipped into columns 1 to 2 and appear as two harmless-looking periods in the line of data. In hexadecimal, however, the periods are translated as 0D and 1B, while a real period in column 24 is 2E in hex.[1]

Possible causes Common reasons for receiving the invalid-data note include

- ◆ using the letter O instead of the number zero

- ◆ forgetting to specify that a variable is character (SAS assumes it is numeric)

- ◆ incorrect column specifications producing embedded spaces in numeric data

- ◆ list-style data with two periods in a row and no space in between

- ◆ missing data not marked with a period for list-style input causing SAS to read the next data value

- ◆ using special characters such as carriage-return-line-feed and form-feed

- ◆ using the wrong informat such as MMDDYY. instead of DDMMYY.

- ◆ invalid dates (such as September 31) read with a date informat.

---

[1] The codes for form-feed and carriage-return-line-feed vary among operating environments, so yours may be different.

8.7 Note: Missing Values Were Generated

The missing-values note appears when SAS is unable to compute the value of a variable because of preexisting missing values in your data. This is not necessarily a problem. It is possible that your data contain legitimate missing values and that setting a new variable to missing is a desirable response. But it is also possible that the missing values result from an error and that you need to fix your program or your data. A good rule is to think of the missing-values note as a flag telling you to check for an error.

Example Here again are the data from the toad-jumping contest including the toad's name and the distance jumped in each of three trials:

```
Lucky   1.9   .   3.0
Spot    2.5  3.1  0.5
Tubs     .    .   3.8
Hop     3.2  1.9  2.6
Noisy   1.3  1.8  1.5
Winner   .    .    .
```

Notice that several of the toads have missing values for one or more jumps. To compute the average distance jumped, the program in the following SAS log reads the raw data, adds together the values for the three jumps, and divides by three:

```
1       DATA toads;
2           INFILE 'c:\MyRawData\Jump.dat';
3           INPUT ToadName $ Jump1 Jump2 Jump3;
4           AverageJump = (Jump1 + Jump2 + Jump3) / 3;
5       RUN;

NOTE: The infile 'c:\MyRawData\Jump.dat' is:
      FILENAME=c:\MyRawData\Jump.dat,
      RECFM=V,LRECL=132

NOTE: 6 records were read from the infile 'c:\MyRawData\Jump.dat'.
      The minimum record length was 18.
      The maximum record length was 18.

NOTE: ❶Missing values were generated as a result of performing an
      operation on missing values.
      ❷Each place is given by: (Number of times) at (Line):(Column)
      3 at 4:21    3 at 4:29    3 at 4:38

NOTE: The data set WORK.TOADS has 6 observations and 5 variables.
```

Because of missing values in the data, SAS was unable to compute AverageJump for some of the toads. In response, SAS printed the missing-values note which has two parts:

❶ The first part of the note says that SAS was forced to set some values to missing.

❷ The second part is a bit more cryptic. SAS lists the number of times values were set to missing. This generally corresponds to the number of observations that generated missing values, unless the problem occurs within a DO-loop. Next SAS states where in the program it encountered the problem. In the preceding example, SAS set three values to missing: at line 4, column 21; then at line 4, column 29; and again at line 4, column 38. Looking at the program, you can see that line 4 is the line which calculates AverageJump. In column 21, the variable Jump1 is added to the variable Jump2; in column 29, the variable Jump2 is added to the variable Jump3; and in column 38 the sum of the jumps is divided by 3. Looking at the raw data, you can see that three observations have missing values for Jump1, Jump2, or Jump3. Those observations are the three times mentioned in the missing-values note.

Finding the missing values   In this case it was easy to find the observations with missing values. But if you had a data set with hundreds, or millions, of observations, then you couldn't just glance at the data. In that case, you could subset the problematic observations with a subsetting IF statement, and print them with a program like this:

```
DATA missing;
   INFILE 'Jump.dat';
   INPUT ToadName $ Jump1 Jump2 Jump3;
   AverageJump = (Jump1 + Jump2 + Jump3) / 3;
   IF AverageJump = .;

PROC PRINT DATA = missing;
   TITLE 'Observations with Missing Values Generated';
RUN;
```

Your output would look like this:

```
        Observations with Missing Values Generated        1
            Toad                                  Average
   Obs      Name       Jump1     Jump2     Jump3   Jump
    1       Lucky       1.9        .        3.0     .
    2       Tubs         .         .        3.8     .
    3       Winner       .         .         .      .
```

Using the SUM and MEAN functions   You may be able to circumvent this problem when you are computing a sum or mean by using the SUM or MEAN function instead of an arithmetic expression. In the preceding program, you could remove this line:

```
AverageJump = (Jump1 + Jump2 + Jump3) / 3;
```

And substitute this line:

```
AverageJump = MEAN(Jump1, Jump2, Jump3);
```

The SUM and MEAN functions use only non-missing values for the computation. In this example, you would still get the missing-values note for one toad, Winner, because it had missing values for all three jumps.

8.8 ▶ Note: Numeric Values Have Been Converted to Character (or Vice Versa)

Even with only two data types, numeric and character, SAS programmers sometimes get their variables mixed up. When you accidentally mix numeric and character variables, SAS tries to fix your program by converting variables from numeric to character or vice versa, as needed. Programmers sometimes ignore this problem, but that is not a good idea. If you ignore this message, it may come back to haunt you as you find new incompatibilities resulting from the fix. If, indeed, a variable needs to be converted, you should do it yourself, explicitly, so you know what your variables are doing.

Example   To show how SAS handles this kind of incompatibility, here is the log from a program that mixes the two types of data:

```
1    DATA numchar;
2        VarA = 5;
3        VarB = '5';
4        VarC = VarA * VarB;
5        VarD = 98;
6        VarE = SUBSTR(VarD, 2, 1);
7    RUN;
NOTE: Character values have been converted to numeric
      values at the places given by: (Line):(Column).
      4:12
NOTE: Numeric values have been converted to character
      values at the places given by: (Line):(Column).
      6:15
NOTE: The data set WORK.NUMCHAR has 1 observations and 5 variables.
NOTE: DATA statement used:
      real time            0.16 seconds
```

In this program the variable VarA is numeric because it is equal to the number 5; VarB is character because it is equal to 5 enclosed in quotes. VarC is the product of VarA and VarB. Since character variables cannot be used in arithmetic expressions, SAS converts VarB to numeric and prints the values-have-been-converted note. This note tells you where in your program SAS found an incompatibility. In this case, the problem occurred at line 4, column 12. The variable name, VarB, appears at line 4, column 12, so you know that SAS converted VarB from character to numeric.

The variable VarD is numeric because it is equal to the number 98. However, in line 6 of the program, VarD is used in the SUBSTR function, which requires a character variable. To rectify the problem, SAS converts VarD to character and prints a note saying that numeric values were converted to character at line 6, column 15.

Converting variables To convert variables from character to numeric, you use the INPUT function. To convert from numeric to character, you use the PUT function. Most often, you would use these functions in an assignment statement with the following syntax:

Character to Numeric	**Numeric to Character**
newvar = INPUT(*oldvar, informat*);	*newvar* = PUT(*oldvar, format*);

These two slightly eccentric functions are first cousins of the PUT and INPUT statements. Just as an INPUT statement uses informats, the INPUT function uses informats; and just as PUT statements use formats, the PUT function uses formats. These functions can be confusing because they are similar but different. In the case of the INPUT function, the informat must be the type you are converting to—numeric. In contrast, the format for the PUT function must be the type you are converting from—numeric.[1] To convert the troublesome variables in the program that mixes character and numeric variables, you would use these statements:

Character to Numeric	**Numeric to Character**
NewB = INPUT(VarB, 1.);	NewD = PUT(VarD, 2.);

If you rerun the preceding program with functions added to convert the variables, you will receive a log like this:

```
10     DATA numchar;
11        VarA = 5;
12        VarB = '5';
13        NewB = INPUT(VarB, 1.);
14        VarC = VarA * NewB;
16        VarD = 98;
17        NewD = PUT(VarD, 2.);
10        VarE = SUBSTR(NewD, 2, 1);
19     RUN;

NOTE: The data set WORK.NUMCHAR has 1 observations and 7 variables.
NOTE: DATA statement used:
      real time           0.11 seconds
```

Notice that this version of the program runs without any suspicious messages, and uses slightly less CPU time.

---

[1] In this discussion, we are talking about converting variables from numeric to character or vice versa, but you can also use the PUT function to change one character value to another character value. When you do this, *oldvar* and *newvar* would be character variables, and the format would be a character format.

8.9 ▶ DATA Step Produces Wrong Results but No Error Message

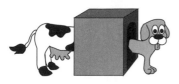

Some of the hardest errors to debug aren't errors at all, at least not to SAS. If you do complex programming, you may write a DATA step that runs just fine—with no errors or suspicious notes—but produces the wrong results. The more complex your programs are, the more likely you are to get this kind of error. Sometimes it seems like a DATA step is a black box. You know what goes in, and you know what comes out, but what happens in the middle is a mystery. This problem is actually a logic error; somewhere along the way SAS got the wrong instruction.

Example Here is a program that illustrates this problem and how to debug it. The raw data file below contains information from a class. For each student there are three scores from tests, and one score from homework:

```
Linda    53 60  66 42
Derek    72 64  56 32
Kathy    98 82 100 48
Michael  80 55  95 50
```

This program is supposed to select students whose average score is below 70, but it doesn't work. Here is the log from the wayward program:

```
1       * Keep only students with mean below 70;
2       DATA lowscore;
3          INFILE 'c:\MyRawData\Class.dat';
4          INPUT Name $ Score1 Score2 Score3 Homework;
5          Homework = Homework * 2;
6          AverageScore = MEAN(Score1 + Score2 + Score3 + Homework);
7          IF AverageScore < 70;
8       RUN;

NOTE: The infile 'c:\MyRawData\Class.dat' is:
      FILENAME=c:\MyRawData\Class.dat,
      RECFM=V,LRECL=132

NOTE: 4 records were read from the infile 'c:\MyRawData\Class.dat'.
      The minimum record length was 20.
      The maximum record length was 20.
NOTE: The data set WORK.LOWSCORE has 0 observations and 6
      variables.
```

First, the DATA step reads the raw data from a file called Class.dat. The highest possible score on homework is 50. To make the homework count the same as a test, the program doubles the value of Homework. Then the program computes the mean of the three test scores and Homework, and subsets the data by selecting only observations with a mean score below 70. Unfortunately, something went wrong. The LOWSCORE data set contains no observations. A glance at the raw data confirms that there should be students whose mean scores are below 70.

Using the PUT statement to debug To debug a problem like this, you have to figure out exactly what is happening inside the DATA step. A good way to do this is with PUT statements. Elsewhere in this book, PUT statements are used along with FILE statements to write raw data files and custom reports. If you use a PUT statement without a FILE statement, then SAS writes the data in the SAS log. That is just fine for debugging. PUT statements can take many forms, but for debugging, a handy style of PUT statement is

```
PUT _ALL_;
```

SAS will print all the variables in your data set: first the variable name, then the actual data value, with an equals sign in between. If you have a lot of variables, you can print just the relevant ones this way:

```
PUT varname = varname = ;
```

Without the equals signs, SAS would print just the data values. Adding the equals signs tells SAS to label the data so that you know which data values are which.

The DATA step below is identical to the one shown earlier except that a PUT statement was added. In a longer DATA step, you might choose to have more than one PUT statement. In this case, one will suffice. This PUT statement is placed before the subsetting IF, since in this particular program the subsetting IF eliminates all observations:

```
9     * Keep only students with mean below 70;
10    DATA lowscore;
11       INFILE 'c:\MyRawData\Class.dat';
12       INPUT Name $ Score1 Score2 Score3 Homework;
13       Homework = Homework * 2;
14       AverageScore = MEAN(Score1 + Score2 + Score3 + Homework);
15       PUT Name= Score1= Score2= Score3= Homework= AverageScore=;
16       IF AverageScore < 70;
17    RUN;

NOTE: The infile 'c:\MyRawData\Class.dat' is:
      FILENAME=c:\MyRawData\Class.dat,
      RECFM=V,LRECL=132

Name=Linda Score1=53 Score2=60 Score3=66 Homework=84 AverageScore=263
Name=Derek Score1=72 Score2=64 Score3=56 Homework=64 AverageScore=256
Name=Kathy Score1=98 Score2=82 Score3=100 Homework=96 AverageScore=376
Name=Michael Score1=80 Score2=55 Score3=95 Homework=100 AverageScore=330

NOTE: 4 records were read from the infile 'c:\MyRawData\Class.dat'.
      The minimum record length was 20.
      The maximum record length was 20.
NOTE: The data set WORK.LOWSCORE has 0 observations and 6
      variables.
```

Looking at the the log, you can see the result of the PUT statement. The data listed in the middle of the log show that the variables are being input properly, and the variable Homework is being adjusted properly. However, something is wrong with the values of AverageScore; they are much too high. There is a syntax error in the line that computes AverageScore. Instead of commas separating the three score variables in the MEAN function, there are plus signs. Since functions can contain arithmetic expressions, SAS simply added the four variables together, as instructed, and computed the mean of a single number.

8.10 The DATA Step Debugger

If you use interactive SAS, then you have another choice when it comes to debugging logic errors. Instead of the PUT statements discussed in section 8.9, you can use the DATA step debugger.

To understand the DATA step debugger, you have to know that SAS runs every program in two phases. To the person running the program, it looks like one action, but in reality SAS first compiles your program, then SAS executes your program. Errors can occur during either phase, but they are different types of errors. Syntax errors and some data errors (such as numeric-to-character-conversion) occur at compile time. Other errors such as logic errors and some data errors (such as missing-values-were-generated) compile just fine, but cause you to get bad results at execution.

The DATA step debugger does its work at execution time. That means you can't use the DATA step debugger to find compile-time errors such as missing semicolons. (You don't really need it for these errors since they always generate messages in your log.) However, if you have an execution-time error, then the DATA step debugger may be a big help.

Example To show how the DATA step debugger compares to the traditional method using PUT statements to debug logic errors, this example uses the same program as section 8.9. The raw data file below contains five variables—student's name, scores from three tests, and score from homework:

```
Linda    53 60  66 42
Derek    72 64  56 32
Kathy    98 82 100 48
Michael  80 55  95 50
```

Starting the debugger The following program is supposed to select students whose average score is below 70, but it doesn't work. To invoke the debugger, simply add the DEBUG option to the end of your DATA statement, and submit the DATA step from the SAS windowing environment.

```
* Keep only students with mean below 70;
DATA lowscore / DEBUG;
   INFILE 'c:\MyRawData\Class.dat';
   INPUT Name $ Score1 Score2 Score3 Homework;
   Homework = Homework * 2;
   AverageScore = MEAN(Score1 + Score2 + Score3 + Homework);
   IF AverageScore < 70;
RUN;
```

The debugger windows After you submit the DATA step, two windows will appear: the DEBUGGER LOG window and the DEBUGGER SOURCE window. The DEBUGGER LOG window contains messages from the debugger and a command line. The DEBUGGER SOURCE window contains your DATA step statements with the current line highlighted.

One nice bonus of the DATA step debugger is the ability to watch SAS executing a DATA step line-by-line and observation-by-observation. Since the highlighting in the DEBUGGER SOURCE window marks each line as SAS executes it, the debugger provides a graphic illustration of the structure of a DATA step. For a beginner, this alone could be very enlightening. You may even want to take a DATA step that works just fine, and run it through the DATA step debugger just to see this.

Executing debugger commands

You can control the debugger in two ways—using pull-down menus or typing commands at a command line. Once you invoke the DATA step debugger, you will see some new menu options. The View, Run, and Breakpoint menus contain debugger commands. If you prefer to type commands, you can type them after the arrow at the bottom of the DEBUGGER LOG window. In the DEBUGGER LOG window to the right, the STEP command has been typed at the command line. The following table shows the most common commands:

Menu Path	Command Line	Description
Run-Step	`<return>`	executes one statement
	`STEP n`	executes *n* statements, where *n* is a number
View-Examine values	`EXAMINE variable-list`	prints the values of variables
View-Set values	`SET variable = expression`	assigns a value to a specified variable for the current observation
Run-Quit	`QUIT`	ends the debugger and finishes executing the DATA step

In this DEBUGGER LOG window you can see the programmer has pressed the return key until SAS stepped to line 6 of the program. Then the programmer typed EXAMINE _ALL_, and SAS listed all the variables and their values. Looking at the data values, you can see the value of AverageScore is much too high. There is a logic error in the line that computes AverageScore. The plus signs should be commas. Once you find the error, quit the debugger, recall your program, and correct the error, remembering to remove the DEBUG option.

8.11   Error: Invalid Option, Error: The Option Is Not Recognized, or Error: Statement Is Not Valid

If SAS cannot make sense out of one of your statements, it stops executing the current DATA or PROC step and prints one of these messages:

```
ERROR 22-7: Invalid option name.
ERROR 202-322: The option or parameter is not recognized.
ERROR 180-322: Statement is not valid or it is used out of proper order.
```

The invalid-option message and its cousin, the option-is-not-recognized message, tell you that you have a valid statement, but SAS can't make sense out of an apparent option. The statement-is-not-valid message, on the other hand, means that SAS can't understand the statement at all. Thankfully, with all three messages SAS underlines the point at which it got confused so you know where to look for the problem.

Example   The SAS log below contains an invalid option:

```
1     DATA class (ROP = Score1);
                    ---
                    22
ERROR 22-7: Invalid option name ROP.

2         INFILE 'c:\MyRawData\Scores.dat';
3         INPUT  Name $ Score1 Score2 Score3 Homework;
4     RUN;

NOTE: The SAS System stopped processing this step because of errors.
NOTE: DATA statement used:
      real time           0.15 seconds
```

In this DATA step, the word DROP was misspelled as ROP. Since SAS cannot interpret this, it underlines the word ROP, prints the invalid-option message, and stops processing the DATA step.

Example   The following log contains an option-is-not-recognized message:

```
5     PROC PRINT
6         VAR Score2;
          --- ------
          202 202
ERROR 202-322: The option or parameter is not recognized.
7     RUN;

NOTE: The SAS System stopped processing this step because of errors.
NOTE: PROCEDURE PRINT used:
      real time           0.32 seconds
```

SAS underlined the VAR statement. This message may seem puzzling since VAR is not an option, but a statement, and a valid statement at that. But if you look at the previous statement, you will see that the PROC statement is missing one of those pesky semicolons. As a result, SAS tried to interpret the words VAR and Score2 as options in the PROC statement. Since no options exist with those names, SAS stopped processing the step and printed the option-is-not-recognized message.

Example   Here is a log with the statement-is-not-valid message:

```
8    PROC PRINT;
9        SET class;
         ---
         180
ERROR 180-322: Statement is not valid or it is used out of proper order.
10   RUN;

NOTE: The SAS System stopped processing this step because of errors.
NOTE: PROCEDURE PRINT used:
      real time           0.04 seconds
```

In this case, a SET statement was used in a PROC step. Since SET statements can be used only in DATA steps, SAS underlines the word SET and prints the statement-is-not-valid message.

Possible causes   Generally, with these error messages, the cause of the problem is easy to detect. You should check the underlined item and the previous statement for possible errors. Possible causes include

- a misspelled keyword

- a missing semicolon

- a DATA step statement in a PROC step (or vice versa)

- a RUN statement in the middle of a DATA or PROC step (this does not cause errors for some procedures)

- the correct option with the wrong statement

- an unmatched quote

- an unmatched comment.

8.12 Note: Variable Is Uninitialized or Error: Variable Not Found

If you find one of these messages in your SAS log, then SAS is telling you that the variable named in the message does not exist:

```
NOTE: Variable X is uninitialized.
WARNING: Variable X not found.
ERROR: Variable X not found.
```

Generally, the first time you get one of these messages, it is quite a shock. You may be sure that the variable does exist. After all, you remember creating it. Fortunately, the problem is usually easy to fix once you understand what SAS is telling you.

If the problem happens in a DATA step, then SAS prints the variable-is-uninitialized note, initializes the variable, and continues to execute your program. Normally variables are initialized when they are read (via an INPUT, SET, MERGE, or UPDATE statement) or when they are created via an assignment statement. If you use a variable for the first time in a way that does not assign a value to the variable (such as on the right side of an assignment statement, in the condition of an IF statement, or in a DROP or KEEP option) then SAS tries to fix the problem by assigning a value of missing to the variable for all observations. This is very generous of SAS, but it almost never fixes the problem, since you probably don't want the variable to have missing values for all observations.

When the problem happens in a PROC step, the results are more grave. If the error occurs in a critical statement such as a VAR statement, then SAS prints the variable-not-found error and does not execute the step. If the error occurs in a less critical statement such as a LABEL statement, then SAS prints the variable-not-found error message, and attempts to run the step.

Example Here is the log from a program with missing-variable problems in both a DATA and a PROC step:

```
1     DATA highscore (KEEP = Name Total);
2        INPUT Name $ Score1 Score2;
3        IF Scor1 > 5;
4        Total = Score1 + Score2;
5        DATALINES;

NOTE: Variable Scor1 is uninitialized.
NOTE: The data set WORK.HIGHSCORE has 0 observations and 2 variables.
NOTE: DATA statement used:
      real time           2.19 seconds

8      ;
9
10    PROC PRINT DATA = highscore;
11       VAR Name Score2 Total;
ERROR: Variable SCORE2 not found.
12    RUN;

NOTE: The SAS System stopped processing this step because of errors.
NOTE: PROCEDURE PRINT used:
      real time           0.32 seconds
```

In this DATA step, the INPUT statement reads three variables: Name, Score1, and Score2. But a misspelling in the subsetting IF statement causes SAS to initialize a new variable named Scor1. Because Scor1 has missing values, none of the observations satisfies the subsetting IF, and the data set HIGHSCORE is left with zero observations.

In the PROC PRINT, the VAR statement requests three variables: Name, Score2, and Total. Score2 did exist but was dropped from the data set by the KEEP= option in the DATA statement. That KEEP= option kept only two variables, Name and Total. As a result, SAS prints the variable-not-found error message, and does not execute the PROC PRINT.

Possible causes Common ways to "lose" variables include

+ misspelling a variable name

+ using a variable that was dropped at some earlier time

+ using the wrong data set

+ committing a logic error, such as using a variable before it is created.

If the source of the problem is not immediately obvious, PROC CONTENTS can often help you figure out what is going on. PROC CONTENTS, which is discussed in section 2.8, gives you information about what is in a SAS data set including variable names.

8.13   SAS Truncates a Character Variable

Sometimes you may notice that some, or all, of the values of a character variable are truncated. You may be expecting "peanut butter" and get "peanut b" or "chocolate ice cream" and get "chocolate ice." This usually happens when you use IF statements to create a new character variable, or when you are using list-style input and you have values longer than eight characters.

All character variables have a fixed length determined by one of the following methods.

INPUT statement   If a variable's values are read from a raw data file, then the length is determined by the INPUT statement. If you are using list-style input, then the length defaults to 8. If you are using column or formatted input, then the length is determined by the number of columns, or informat. The following shows examples of INPUT statements that read values for the Food variable and the resulting lengths of Food:

INPUT statement	Length of Food
`INPUT Food;`	8
`INPUT Food $ 1-10;`	10
`INPUT Food $15.;`	15

Assignment statement   If you are creating the variable in an assignment statement, then the length is determined by the first occurrence of the new variable name. For example, the following program creates a variable, Status, whose values are determined by the Temperature variable:

```
DATA summer;
   SET temps;
   IF Temperature > 100 THEN Status = 'Hot';
      ELSE Status = 'Cold';
RUN;
```

Because the word Hot has three characters and that is the first statement which uses the variable, Status has a length of 3. Any other values for that variable would be truncated to three characters (Col instead of Cold for example).

LENGTH statement   The LENGTH statement in a DATA step defines variable lengths and, if it comes before the INPUT or assignment statement, will override either of the previous two methods of determining length. The following LENGTH statement sets the length of the Status variable to 4 and the Food variable to 15:

```
LENGTH Status $4 Food $15;
```

ATTRIB statement   You can also assign variable lengths in an ATTRIB statement in a DATA step where you can associate formats, informats, labels, and lengths to variables in a single statement. Always place the LENGTH option before a FORMAT option in an ATTRIB statement to ensure that the variables are assigned proper lengths. For example, the following statement assigns the character variable Status a length of 4 and the label Hot or Cold:

```
ATTRIB Status LENGTH = $4 LABEL = 'Hot or Cold';
```

Example The following example shows what can happen if you let SAS determine the length of a character variable (in this case, using the assignment statement method). You have the following data for a consumer survey of car color preferences. Age is followed by sex (coded as 1 for male and 2 for female), annual income, and preferred car color (yellow, gray, blue, or white):

```
19 1 14000 Y
45 1 65000 G
72 2 35000 B
31 1 44000 Y
58 2 83000 W
```

You want to create a new variable, AgeGroup, which has these values: Teen for customers under 20, Adult for ages 20 through 64, and Senior for those 65 and over. In the following program, a series of IF-THEN/ELSE statements create AgeGroup:

```
DATA carsurvey;
   INFILE 'c:\MyRawData\Cars.dat';
   INPUT Age Sex Income Color $;
   IF Age < 20 THEN AgeGroup = 'Teen';
      ELSE IF Age < 65 THEN AgeGroup = 'Adult';
      ELSE AgeGroup = 'Senior';
PROC PRINT DATA = carsurvey;
   TITLE 'Car Color Survey Results';
RUN;
```

The following results of the PROC PRINT show how the values of AgeGroup are truncated to four characters—the number of characters in Teen.

```
                    Car Color Survey Results                    1


                                                    Age
         Obs    Age    Sex    Income    Color      Group

          1      19     1      14000      Y         Teen
          2      45     1      65000      G         Adul
          3      72     2      35000      B         Seni
          4      31     1      44000      Y         Adul
          5      58     2      83000      W         Adul
```

The addition of a LENGTH statement in the DATA step, as follows, would eliminate the truncation problem:

```
DATA carsurvey;
   INFILE 'c:\MyRawData\Cars.dat';
   INPUT Age Sex Income Color $;
   LENGTH AgeGroup $7;
   IF Age < 20 THEN AgeGroup = 'Teen';
      ELSE IF Age < 65 THEN AgeGroup = 'Adult';
      ELSE AgeGroup = 'Senior';
RUN;
```

8.14 SAS Stops in the Middle of a Job

One of the most disconcerting errors encountered by SAS users is having SAS stop in the middle of a job. It's as if your program has suddenly dropped dead without so much as an error message to act as a smoking gun. Without an error message, you are left to sleuth this problem on your own. Often the problem has nothing to do with SAS. Instead the operating environment may have stopped your program in its tracks. Other times the problem results from programming errors that prevent SAS from seeing the entire job.

A number of completely unrelated reasons can cause SAS to stop in the middle of a job. They are listed below, starting with the most general problems and ending with the ones that are specific to certain execution modes or operating environments.

An unmatched quote Unmatched quotation marks wreak havoc on SAS programs, including making SAS stop in the middle of a job. In this case, SAS stops because, in effect, it thinks the remainder of the job is part of a quote. In batch or non-interactive mode, the solution is simple enough. Insert the missing quotation mark and resubmit the program. In the SAS windowing environment you can't just resubmit the program because SAS is still waiting for the other quote. The solution is to submit a sacrificial quote like this:

```
';
RUN;
```

Then recall your program, correct the problem (remembering to delete the extra quote and RUN statement at the end), and rerun the program. Some prefer to exit SAS and start over. If you do, just remember to recall and save your program before exiting.

An unmatched comment Unmatched comments can cause SAS to stop in the middle of a program, much like unmatched quotes. The problem is that SAS can't read the entire program because part of it is accidentally stuck in a comment. This isn't so likely to happen if you use the kind of comment that starts with an asterisk and ends with a semicolon since programs contain many semicolons, and any semicolon will do to end a comment. But if you use the style of comment that starts with /* and ends with */, and you forget to include the last */, then SAS will assume that the remainder of your job is one long comment. The solution, in batch or non-interactive mode is to insert the missing end-of-comment and resubmit the program. In the SAS windowing environment, the solution is to submit a lone end-of-comment like this:

```
*/;
RUN;
```

Then recall your program, correct the problem (remembering to delete the extra end-of-comment and RUN statement at the end), and rerun the program. Some prefer to exit SAS and start over. If you do, just remember to recall and save your program before exiting.

No RUN statement at the end of a program This problem occurs only in interactive SAS. In non-interactive or in batch mode there is an implicit RUN statement at the end of every SAS job. The problem is that in interactive mode SAS has no way of knowing when it is time to execute your last step unless you tell it with a RUN statement. The solution is to submit the wayward statement.

```
RUN;
```

Not sure what the problem is? If you are working in the SAS windowing environment, and you think you have an unmatched quote, unmatched comment, or missing RUN statement, but you're not sure, you may want to submit the following set of statements:

```
*';
*";
*/;
RUN;
```

Together these statements form a sort of universal terminator for SAS programs. If the program has no problems, these statements do nothing since the first three would then be comments, and an extra RUN statement between steps does nothing. That means you can submit these without fear of causing any harm.

Out of time Batch systems often have time limits, measured in CPU seconds, for computer jobs. These limits are set locally by your systems programmers. And these limits are helpful because they allow small jobs to be submitted to a special queue with a higher priority. That way your short job doesn't have to wait for some mega-job to finish processing. Time limits may also be set to stop jobs that accidentally get into an infinite loop. If your job stops in the middle, and you are running in batch mode, and you can find no unmatched quotes or comments, then you should consider whether your job might have stopped because it ran into a time limit. To find out how to fix this problem, talk to your local SAS Support Consultant or systems programmer.

/* in the first column Under OS/390 there is a unique hazard. Recall that one style of SAS comment starts with a slash-asterisk (/*). Batch jobs under OS/390 use Job Control Language (JCL). In JCL a /* starting in column one signals the end of your program file. So if SAS programmers start a comment with a /* in column one, they inadvertently instruct the computer to stop right then and there. SAS never even sees the remainder of the job. The solution, of course, is to move the comment out of column one or to change to a comment starting with an asterisk (*) and ending with a semicolon (;).

8.15 SAS Runs Out of Memory or Disk Space

What do you do when you finally get your program running, and you get a message that your computer is out of memory or disk space? Well, you could petition to buy a bigger computer, which isn't really such a bad idea, but there are a few things you can try before resorting to spending money. Because this issue is very system dependent, it is not possible to cover everything you might be able to do in this section. However, this section describes a few universal actions you can take to remedy the situation. If none of these things work, then seek out your site's SAS Support Consultant for advice.

It is helpful, in trying to solve the problem, to know why it happens. Usually when you run out of memory, it's when you are doing some pretty intensive computations or sorting data sets with lots of variables. The GLM procedure (General Linear Models), for example, can use lots of memory when your model is complicated and there are many levels for each classification variable. You run out of disk space because SAS uses disk to store all its temporary working files, including temporary SAS data sets, and the SAS log and output. If you are creating many large temporary SAS data sets during the course of a SAS session, this can quickly fill up your disk space.

Memory and disk space One thing you can do to help decrease disk storage is decrease the number of bytes needed to store data. This can also help memory problems that arise when sorting data sets with character data. Since all numbers are expanded to the fullest precision while SAS is processing data, changing storage requirements for numeric data will not help memory problems. Both character (if you are using list input), and numeric variables have a default storage requirement of 8 bytes. This works for most situations. But if memory or disk space is at a premium, you can usually find some variables which require fewer bytes.

For character data, each character requires one byte of storage. The length of a character variable is determined by one of the following: the INPUT statement, the LENGTH or ATTRIB statement, or, if it is created in an assignment statement, the length of the first value. If you are using list input, then variables are given a length of 8. If your data are only one character long, Y or N for example, then you are using eight times the storage space you actually need. You can use the LENGTH statement before the INPUT statement to change the default length. For example, the following gives the character variable Answer a length of one byte:

```
LENGTH Answer $1;
```

If you are using column input, then the length is equal to the number of columns you are reading; if you are using formatted input, then the length is equal to the width of the format. You can change the lengths of variables in existing SAS data sets by using a LENGTH statement between a DATA statement and a SET, MERGE, or UPDATE statement.

Disk space If you are running out of disk space, in addition to shortening the lengths of character variables, you may also be able to decrease the lengths of numeric variables. Numeric data are a little trickier than character when it comes to length. All numbers can be safely stored in 8 bytes, and that's why 8 is the default. Some numbers can be safely stored in fewer bytes, but which numbers depends on your operating environment. Look in the SAS Companion documentation for your operating environment to determine the length and precision of numeric variables. For example, under Windows and UNIX, you can safely store integers up to 8,192 in 3 bytes. In general, if your numbers contain decimal values, then you must use 8 bytes. If you have small integer values, then you can use 4 bytes (in some operating environments 2 or 3 bytes). Use the LENGTH statement to change the lengths of numeric data:

```
LENGTH Tigers 4;
```

This statement changes the length of the numeric variable Tigers to 4 bytes. If your numbers are categorical, like 1 for male and 2 for female, then you can read them as character data with a length of 1 and save even more space.

Another thing you can try if you are running out of disk space is to decrease the number and size of SAS data sets created during a SAS session. If you are going to use only a fraction of your data for analysis, then subset your data as soon as possible using the subsetting IF statement. For example, if you needed observations only for females, then use the following statement in your DATA step:

```
IF Sex = 'female';
```

If you need to look at only a few of the variables in your data set, then use the KEEP= (or DROP=) data set option to decrease the number of variables. For example, if you had a data set containing information about all the zoo animals, but you wanted to look at only the lions and tigers, then you could use the following statements to create a data set with only the Lions and Tigers variables:

```
DATA partial;
   SET zooanimals (KEEP = Lions Tigers);
```

The SAS log and output also take up disk space. If you are using the SAS windowing environment, then clear the SAS log and output often.

It is also possible to compress SAS data sets. Compressing may save space if your data have many repeated values. But beware, compressing can in some cases actually increase the size of your data set. Fortunately SAS gives a message in your log window telling you the change in size of your data sets. You can turn on compression by using either the COMPRESS=YES system option, or the COMPRESS=YES data set option. Use the system option if you want all the SAS data sets you create to be compressed. Use the data set option when you want to control which SAS data sets to compress. For example:

```
DATA compressedzooanimals (COMPRESS = YES);
   SET zooanimals;
```

If you have more than one disk on your system, then you might be able to have SAS store its working files in a different location where there is more space. See the SAS Companion documentation for your operating environment, or check with your site's SAS Support Consultant for more information on how to do this.

Memory If memory is your problem, then do what you can to eliminate other programs that are using your computer's memory. If you are using a windowing environment to run your SAS programs, try running in batch or non-interactive mode instead. The windows takes quite a lot of memory, and on a personal computer it can be a significant fraction of the total available memory. Also, see the SAS Companion documentation for your operating environment for potential ways to make more memory available on your system.

If you have tried all of the above, and you are still running out of memory or disk space, then you can always try finding a bigger computer. One of the nice things about SAS is that the language is the same for all operating environments. To move your program to another operating environment, you would only need to change a few statements like INFILE, which deal directly with the operating environment.

> "The riders in a race do not stop short when they reach their goal. There is a little finishing canter before coming to a standstill. There is time to hear the kind voice of friends and to say to one's self: 'The work is done.' But just as one says that, the answer comes: 'The race is over, but the work never is done while the power to work remains.'"

JUSTICE OLIVER WENDELL HOLMES, JR.

From a radio address on the occasion of his 90th birthday, March 8, 1931. *Bartlett's Familiar Quotations* 13th edition, by John Bartlett, copyright 1955 by Little, Brown & Company. Fair use consent by the publisher.

APPENDICES

Appendix A Where to Go from Here

The goal of this book is to get you started using SAS and to teach you basic principles of SAS programming. For some of you, this book may be all you need. Others, however, may need to go beyond this book. This section lists sources for other training and information about the SAS System. Contact SAS Institute for more information on any of the following items. You may also have additional sources of information, developed locally, at your site. Check with your site's SAS Support Consultant for more information.

SAS Online Documentation

The SAS Online Documentation is your complete reference material for the SAS System. It is included with the SAS System, and should be available on your computer. The documentation appears on a separate CD and can be either copied to your system, or run directly off the CD. The documentation is in HTML (Hypertext Markup Language) format so that it may be accessed through a Web browser. The online documentation gives detailed information and examples of all aspects of the SAS System, and includes documentation for all products even if you do not have those products licensed. Much of the online documentation is also available in book form.

SAS System Help

SAS System Help is available from within your SAS session, and can be accessed through the Help pull-down menu or by typing the word HELP in the command line area on your display. SAS System Help gives you access to tutorials, sample programs, general information, and specific syntax. The information you will find here is generally more terse than what you would find in the online documentation.

SAS Manuals

SAS Institute publishes many manuals about its software. They fall into several general categories: introduction, reference, user's guides, examples books, and syntax. The introductory books are designed to get you started using a particular piece of SAS software. The reference books are for looking up information about SAS procedures and statements. All statements are discussed in the reference manuals, and the syntax is given. The user's guides are designed to be more instructive than the reference books—giving many examples and explanations. The examples books provide practical examples that you can adapt and apply to your own work. The syntax books are small books giving just syntax. The *SAS Publications Catalog*, which is available both online at the SAS Web site or in book form, gives a complete listing of all the SAS manuals available.

Books by Users

There are many titles in the Books by Users series offered by SAS Institute. These books are written by users of SAS software, and thus offer a different perspective from the SAS documentation. Topics range from very general and introductory to very specific. The Books by Users are listed at the end of this book and in the *SAS Publications Catalog*.

SAS/TUTOR

SAS/TUTOR is a product of SAS Institute and is licensed separately. These online courses are highly interactive and cover a broad range of topics from general introduction to specialized areas. You can license each course individually or the whole library.

SAS Institute Training Courses

The Institute offers courses on SAS software covering many topics and varying in length and cost. You can also arrange to have on-site training for many of the courses. In addition to the instructor-based courses, SAS also offers video-based courses. Contact the Institute for more information about either of these training opportunities.

SAS User Groups

SAS has a network of user groups which spans the globe. There are in-house groups, local groups, and regional and international groups. The regional and international groups generally meet once a year for several days. Talks are given by users and SAS employees; there are workshops and training opportunities and usually vendor exhibits. SAS Users Group International (SUGI) is the largest user group. Local and in-house groups usually meet more frequently for a shorter duration. These user-group meetings can be a great source of information about SAS software. More information about SUGI and the regional user groups can be found at the SAS Web site.

SAS Communications and *Observations*

These two magazines published by SAS Institute are good sources of information. *SAS Communications* is available to all SAS users at no extra cost. It covers news items like capabilities of new releases of SAS software, has articles of general interest, and has some technical information. *Observations* is a technical journal for SAS software users. *Observations* was published in printed form, but is now available exclusively online. You can find *Observations* at the SAS Web site.

SAS-L

SAS-L is an electronic mailing list of SAS users all over the world. (With electronic mailing lists, you send a message to the list, and a copy is sent to each person on the list.) This group helps subscribers solve SAS problems, discusses SAS philosophy, posts announcements, and discusses whatever else seems related to SAS. Contact your site's SAS Support Consultant for information on how to subscribe to this high-volume list.

SAS Institute's Web Site

Like most companies these days, SAS has a very useful Web site. You can find all sorts of information there: news and events, answers to frequently asked questions (FAQ), technical information, product descriptions, publications information, training information, year 2000 issues—the list is almost endless. If you have a question, and can't find the answer here, then try the SAS Web site. Chances are that you will find something useful at

www.sas.com.

SAS Technical Support

If you are really stuck on a SAS problem, you can contact SAS Technical Support. The various ways of contacting SAS Technical Support are covered in Appendix B.

Appendix B Getting Help from SAS Institute Technical Support

Sooner or later you will come up with a question for which you can't find the answer. With some software companies, very little technical support is available, or the support is available but only for an extra charge—not so with the Institute. SAS Institute has a policy of "free, unlimited support to all sites licensing software." In addition, SAS Institute's low employee turnover means better, more knowledgeable service for users.

If you have a question about SAS, you should first check with the people who support SAS at your own site. Every SAS site should have one or more people designated as official SAS Support Personnel. You probably have a SAS Installation Representative who receives the disks or tapes for installing new releases of SAS software, and a SAS Support Consultant, an experienced SAS user who is available to answer questions. If these people cannot answer your question, they may contact SAS Institute's Technical Support or they may ask you to contact Technical Support. While any SAS user can contact Technical Support, priority is given to people officially designated as SAS Support Personnel.

Before you contact Technical Support, you must know certain information: your site or customer number, the release of SAS you are using, and the name of your operating environment. To find out your site number and release of SAS, run a SAS program, any SAS program, or just start interactive SAS. Then look at the beginning of your SAS log to find your site number and release notes.

There are several ways to contact Technical Support including

- ♦   Telephone
- ♦   Fax
- ♦   World Wide Web
- ♦   E-mail
- ♦   FTP.

The traditional way to contact Technical Support, by phone, still works well.

Voice: (919) 677-8008 between 9 a.m. and 8 p.m. Eastern time

Fax: (919) 677-4444

Those who have access to the Internet may find it easier to contact Technical Support via SAS Institute's Web site. The address for SAS Institute's home page is

www.sas.com

If you are connected to the Internet, and you are using interactive SAS, you can connect to the Technical Support Web site with a few clicks of a mouse. With SAS running, just select SAS on the Web from the Help pull-down menu and then select Technical Support. From here you can browse tables of Frequently Asked Questions (FAQ), search release notes for known problems, and find other helpful information.

If you can't find the answer to your question, you can contact a person in Technical Support. Select `Report Problems or Ask Questions`, then select `Submit a problem/question on-line`. This selection presents you with a form so that all you have to do is fill in the blanks, and then click on `Submit this request` when you are done.

You can also submit problems to Technical Support via the Electronic Mail Interface to Technical Support (or EMITS), by sending a message to

```
support@sas.com
```

However, e-mail messages sent to this address must be in a specific format. That's why using the Web address above is so easy—it puts your message in the correct format for you. If you wish to submit a problem by e-mail, it must follow this format:

```
To:support@sas.com
From:<your email address>
Subject:<anything>

site=<your site number>
company=<your company name>
phone=<your phone number>
area=<the problem area such as PROC PRINT or install/Windows95>
release=<the release of SAS you are using>
os=<your operating environment>
A detailed description of your problem.
```

You just replace the arrows and descriptions with your information. For example,

```
release=<the release of SAS you are using>
```

could become

```
release=7.0
```

One more mode of reaching Technical Support is worth mentioning: File Transfer Protocal (or FTP). Using FTP you can download useful files such as SAS Notes and sample programs.

Appendix C An Overview of SAS Products

SAS Institute licenses many different products. This book covers elements from base SAS software, SAS/STAT software, and SAS/ACCESS for PC File Formats. You can see from the following list that there is much more to SAS than just these products. Fortunately, most of the products are integrated, so you don't have to convert data sets or start up another program to use the other products. The following is a partial list of SAS products with brief descriptions. Since the number of SAS products is constantly changing, check the SAS Web site (www.sas.com) or the most recent issue of *SAS Communications* for a current list. You must have base SAS installed on your system to run most of these products. Not all products are available for all operating environments. Contact SAS Institute for more information on any of the products:

Base SAS
must be installed on your system to run most of the other SAS products. Base SAS includes the DATA step for manipulating your data and simple statistical and utilitarian procedures.

Enterprise Miner
is a complete product in itself. It provides an easy-to-use front-end to the SEMMA (Sample, Explore, Modify, Model, Assess) process for business users.

SAS/ACCESS
allows you access to data used by other software packages. You can read and, in some cases, write data in their native formats without having to leave the SAS System. Most of the popular database software is supported, and each has its own SAS/ACCESS product.

SAS/AF
allows you to write your own interactive SAS applications. Applications written with SAS/AF allow users quick-and-easy access to information without knowing the SAS language.

SAS/ASSIST
is a menu-driven front end to SAS. You make choices from menus, and SAS writes the program for you. Programs can be stored for later use.

SAS/CALC
is a spreadsheet application.

SAS/CONNECT
connects computers running the SAS System. Data can be shared between the computers, and programs developed on one computer or operating environment can be transferred to another for processing.

SAS/EIS
allows you to develop and use custom executive information systems. Managers can use the EIS interfaces to SAS to quickly get the information they need by simply pointing and clicking (with a mouse, of course).

SAS/ETS
has many procedures for analysis of time-series data, forecasting, and business planning.

SAS/FSP
comprises full-screen products that provide interactive methods for data entry, editing, and retrieval. Custom data entry screens can be developed with error checking built in.

SAS/GIS
is a geographic information system for analyzing data with spatial relationships.

SAS/GRAPH
produces high-resolution plots, charts, and maps.

SAS/IML
Interactive Matrix Language is a programming language with an extensive set of mathematical and matrix operators.

SAS/INSIGHT
is a tool for visual analysis of your data. Statistical results are displayed graphically whenever possible and interactive manipulation of data is possible.

SAS/IntrNet
software allows you to effectively deliver your SAS applications to the Web.

SAS/LAB
is for guided statistical analysis. This product is good for people who need to analyze data but do not have a background in statistics.

SAS/MDDB
software allows you to save data in multidimensional database (MDDB) formats for use with online analytical processing (OLAP) (otherwise known as slicing and dicing your data).

SAS/OR
provides procedures for project management and operations research. Included in its capabilities are linear programming, Gantt charts, activity networks, and decision analysis.

SAS/QC
provides procedures for statistical quality improvement, including methods for experimental design, improved process, and statistical control.

SAS/SHARE
provides concurrent access to data by multiple users.

SAS/SPECTRAVIEW
is a tool for analysis and visualization of three-dimensional data.

SAS/STAT
has procedures for most types of statistical analyses including many forms of regression and analysis of variance.

SAS/TOOLKIT
enables you to write your own SAS procedures, functions, formats, informats, and engines.

SAS/TUTOR
is an online tool for learning the SAS System. There are lessons covering many different aspects of the SAS System.

SAS/Warehouse Administrator
simplifies the creation and maintenance of data warehouses.

Appendix D Coming to SAS from SPSS

More often than not, the first question asked by people who know SPSS and want to learn SAS is, "How do the two software packages compare?" No simple answer is possible since both products are continually evolving, with new releases introducing new capabilities. Nonetheless, general comparisons can be drawn.

SAS and SPSS are very similar. Compared to other statistical software, these two products (plus a few others) are similar because they are languages. Most other statistical packages are extremely rigid, lacking the flexibility of a language. Compared to other computer languages, SAS and SPSS are similar because of their powerful, built-in data handling and statistical capabilities.

Some SPSS users may not even know that SPSS is a programming language since many SPSS users use only the SPSS point-and-click interface. If you are one of these people, then you will be glad to know that SAS also has point-and-click interfaces. You should try the Analyst application, a free product discussed in section 7.9. If you are a programmer, you'll be glad to know that SAS gives you a choice of modes. You can create your program in a menu-driven interactive system, or you can write your program with an editor and submit it non-interactively or in batch.

Despite their fundamental similarities, SAS and SPSS have different styles. SAS is more diverse, especially when you consider the entire family of SAS products. Appendix C contains a listing of SAS products at the time this book was written. Most of these products are integrated, so they can be used seamlessly with base SAS. Likewise, SAS has more options. More options mean more power to get exactly what you want. People who do really complex programming find they can do things with SAS that would be impossible to do with SPSS.

Terminology Some vocabulary differences exist between SAS and SPSS. To help you translate from one language to the other, here is a brief dictionary of analogous terms:

SPSS term	Analogous SAS term
active file	*no analogous term*
no analogous term	temporary SAS data set or table
case	observation or row
command	statement
display file	log file
display file	listing or output file
file handle	libref
function	function
input format	informat
numeric data	numeric data
output format	format
portable file	SAS data set or table
system file	permanent SAS data set or table
string data	character data
value label	user-defined format
variable	variable or column
variable label	label
no analogous term	DATA step
no analogous term	PROC step

Active files The concept of an active file in SPSS has no equivalent in SAS. When you read data in an SPSS program, SPSS creates an active system file. This active file is similar to a temporary SAS data set because it exists only for the duration of the SPSS session, just as temporary SAS data sets exist only for the duration of a SAS session. However, SPSS has only one active file at a time, while SAS can have any number of temporary or permanent data sets. When you run an analysis in SPSS, the data must come from the active file. When you run an analysis in SAS, by default SAS will use the data set most recently created. But you can easily use any other SAS data set including the permanent SAS data set you created last week and haven't touched since. All SAS data sets are always active.

DATA and PROC steps The SAS language has some concepts that have no parallel in SPSS, such as DATA and PROC steps. All SAS programs are divided into these two types of steps. Basically, DATA steps read and modify data while PROC (short for procedure) steps perform specific analyses or functions such as sorting, writing reports, or running statistical analyses. SPSS programs do the same types of operations but without distinct steps.

Examples For a comparison, we provide the following two programs that perform the same operations in SPSS and SAS. We used SPSS 8.0 and SAS 7.0, both running under the Windows 95 operating environment. A radio station commissioned a market research company to survey listeners. Respondents were asked to listen to songs and rate them on a scale of 1 to 5, with 1 being dislike very much and 5 being like very much. Here is a sample of the raw data. The variables are first name, age, sex, and the ratings for five songs:

```
Gail     14 1 5 3 1 3 5
Jim      56 2 3 2 2 3 2
Susan    34 1 4 2 1 1 5
Barbara  45 1 3 3 1 2 4
Steve    13 2 5 4 1 4 5
```

The two programs below read the same raw data file and produce the same types of reports:

SPSS Program

```
DATA LIST FILE =
   'c:\MyRawData\Survey.dat'
   /Name 1-8 (A) Age 9-10
   Sex 12 Song1 TO Song5 13-22.
VARIABLE LABELS
   Song1 'Black Water/DB'
   Song2 'Bennie and the Jets/EJ'
   Song3 'Stayin Alive/BG'
   Song4 'Fire and Rain/JT'
   Song5 'Country Roads/JD'.
VALUE LABELS
   sex 1 'female' 2 'male'.
TITLE 'Music Market Survey'.
LIST.
FREQUENCIES
   VARIABLES = Song1.
CROSSTABS
   /TABLES = Sex BY Song1.
SAVE OUTFILE =
   'c:\MySPSSDir\survey.sav'.
```

SAS program

```
DATA 'c:\MySASDir\survey';
   INFILE 'c:\MyRawData\Survey.dat';
   INPUT Name $ 1-8 Age
      Sex Song1-Song5;
   LABEL Song1 = 'Black Water/DB'
      Song2 = 'Bennie and the Jets/EJ'
      Song3 = 'Stayin Alive/BG'
      Song4 = 'Fire and Rain/JT'
      Song5 = 'Country Roads/JD';
PROC FORMAT;
   VALUE sex 1 = 'female'
             2 = 'male';
TITLE 'Music Market Survey';
PROC PRINT;
PROC FREQ;
   TABLE Song1 Sex * Song1;
   FORMAT Sex Sex.;
RUN;
```

The following table shows which SPSS commands and SAS statements perform the same operations:

SPSS command	SAS statement
DATA LIST	INFILE and INPUT
VARIABLE LABELS	LABEL
VALUE LABELS	PROC FORMAT
TITLE	TITLE
LIST	PROC PRINT
FREQUENCIES and CROSSTABS	PROC FREQ
SAVE OUTFILE	DATA

SPSS display file Here are the reports from the SPSS display file output as a text file. To make the output easier to read, the system notes have been deleted.

```
List
NAME     AGE SEX SONG1 SONG2 SONG3 SONG4 SONG5

Gail      14   1    5     3     1     3     5
Jim       56   2    3     2     2     3     2
Susan     34   1    4     2     1     1     5
Barbara   45   1    3     3     1     2     4
Steve     13   2    5     4     1     4     5
Number of cases read:  5    Number of cases listed:  5

Frequencies
Statistics
Black Water/DB
------------------------
 | N | Valid   | 5 |
 |   | ------- | - |
 |   | Missing | 0 |
 | - | ------- | - |

Black Water/DB
----------------------------------------------------------------------
 |          |       | Frequency | Percent | Valid Percent | Cumulative |
 |          |       |           |         |               |   Percent  |
 |          | ----- | --------- | ------- | ------------- | ---------- |
 | Valid    |   3   |     2     |  40.0   |     40.0      |    40.0    |
 |          | ----- | --------- | ------- | ------------- | ---------- |
 |          |   4   |     1     |  20.0   |     20.0      |    60.0    |
 |          | ----- | --------- | ------- | ------------- | ---------- |
 |          |   5   |     2     |  40.0   |     40.0      |   100.0    |
 |          | ----- | --------- | ------- | ------------- | ---------- |
 |          | Total |     5     | 100.0   |    100.0      |            |
 | -----    | ----- | --------- | ------- | ------------- | ---------- |

Crosstabs
Case Processing Summary
----------------------------------------------------------------------
 |                      | Cases                                          |
 |                      | Valid         | Missing      | Total          |
 |                      | N | Percent   | N | Percent  | N | Percent    |
 | SEX * Black Water/DB | 5 | 100.0%    | 0 |  .0%     | 5 | 100.0%     |
 ---------------------------------------------------------------------

SEX * Black Water/DB Crosstabulation
Count
-------------------------------------------------
 |       |        | Black Water/DB | Total |
 |       |        |  3  | 4 | 5 |          |
 | SEX   | female |  1  | 1 | 1 |    3     |
 |       | male   |  1  |   | 1 |    2     |
 | Total |        |  2  | 1 | 2 |    5     |
```

SAS output   The following output is from the SAS program. You can see that the SAS output looks similar to the SPSS display file. One difference is that the results of SAS procedures are written to a separate file, so you don't have to sort out the notes from your results the way you do with SPSS.

```
                         Music Market Survey                              1

  Obs    Name      Age   Sex   Song1   Song2   Song3   Song4   Song5

   1     Gail       14    1      5       3       1       3       5
   2     Jim        56    2      3       2       2       3       2
   3     Susan      34    1      4       2       1       1       5
   4     Barbara    45    1      3       3       1       2       4
   5     Steve      13    2      5       4       1       4       5

                         Music Market Survey                              2

                         The FREQ Procedure

                         Black Water/DB

                                             Cumulative    Cumulative
        Song1      Frequency      Percent     Frequency      Percent

          3            2          40.00           2          40.00
          4            1          20.00           3          60.00
          5            2          40.00           5         100.00


                      Table of Sex by Song1

            Sex         Song1(Black Water/DB)

            Frequency|
            Percent  |
            Row Pct  |
            Col Pct  |3        |4        |5        |  Total

            female   |    1    |    1    |    1    |    3
                     | 20.00   | 20.00   | 20.00   | 60.00
                     | 33.33   | 33.33   | 33.33   |
                     | 50.00   |100.00   | 50.00   |

            male     |    1    |    0    |    1    |    2
                     | 20.00   |  0.00   | 20.00   | 40.00
                     | 50.00   |  0.00   | 50.00   |
                     | 50.00   |  0.00   | 50.00   |

            Total         2         1         2         5
                       40.00     20.00     40.00    100.00
```

Getting SPSS system files into SAS SAS can read SPSS data files directly. To do this you use a LIBNAME statement with this form:

```
LIBNAME libref SPSS 'filename';
```

After the keyword LIBNAME, you put the libref (similar to an SPSS file handle), then put the option SPSS followed by the name of your SPSS system or portable file. The SPSS option tells SAS to use the SPSS engine (instead of the default SAS data set engine) to read your data set. Under some operating environments (including Windows 95, Windows NT, and OS/2) SAS can read only SPSS portable files; on others it can read SPSS compressed and uncompressed system files, too. To find out what you can do, check the SAS Companion for your operating environment.

When SAS reads SPSS files, SAS preserves as much as possible. Variable names, variable labels, print formats, and the data remain the same. SPSS missing values become SAS missing values. SPSS value labels are not copied because the SAS equivalent, user-defined formats, are not stored in SAS data sets. If you want value labels, you can create user-defined formats with PROC FORMAT and then use them with FORMAT statements. See section 4.7 for an explanation of how to do this.

Example The following SAS program reads the SPSS file created by the SPSS program in the preceding example. Because this example was run under Windows 95, the SPSS file was saved as a portable file using menus and named survey.por. The LIBNAME statement tells SAS to use the SPSS engine to read the file.

First, SAS prints a copy of the SPSS portable file with PROC PRINT. Then, SAS prints a report describing the portable file with PROC CONTENTS. Last, the DATA step copies the SPSS portable file into a permanent SAS data set named SPSSSURVEY in the MySASLib directory (Windows, NT, OS/2):

```
LIBNAME myspss SPSS 'c:\MySPSSLib\survey.por';

* Print the SPSS portable file;
PROC PRINT DATA = myspss._FIRST_;

* List the contents of the SPSS portable file;
PROC CONTENTS DATA = myspss._FIRST_;

* Convert SPSS portable file to SAS data set;
DATA 'c:\MySASLib\spsssurvey';
   SET myspss._FIRST_;

RUN;
```

In this example, the name that SAS uses for the SPSS system file is MYSPSS._FIRST_. MYSPSS is the libref assigned to the SPSS portable file in the LIBNAME statement. You can use any name you wish for the libref as long as it follows the rules for valid SAS librefs (eight characters or shorter; starts with a letter or underscore; and contains only letters, numerals, or underscores). Since SPSS files don't have internal names, you can also use any name for the member name. _FIRST_ is a common member name used for reading external files, but you could use any valid SAS member name.

Here is the output.

```
                          The SAS System                        1

         Obs   NAME      AGE   SEX   SONG1   SONG2   SONG3   SONG4   SONG5
          1    Gail      14    1     5       3       1       3       5
          2    Jim       56    2     3       2       2       3       2
          3    Susan     34    1     4       2       1       1       5
          4    Barbara   45    1     3       3       1       2       4
          5    Steve     13    2     5       4       1       4       5

                          The SAS System                        2

                        The CONTENTS Procedure

Data Set Name: MYSPSS._FIRST_           Observations:           .
Member Type:   DATA                     Variables:              8
Engine:        SPSS                     Indexes:                0
Created:       12:19 Tuesday,           Observation Length:     64
               June 16, 1998
Last Modified: 14:44 Wednesday,         Deleted Observations: 0
               June 17, 1998
Protection:                             Compressed:             NO
Data Set Type:                          Sorted:                 NO
Label:

              -----Engine/Host Dependent Information-----

              ORIGSOFT: SPSS for MS WINDOWS Release 8.0
              SPSSINFO: (NONE)
              COMPRESS: NO
              SPSSTYPE: PORTFILE

          -----Alphabetic List of Variables and Attributes-----

     #   Variable   Type   Len   Pos   Format   Label
    ---------------------------------------------------------------
     2   AGE        Num     8     8    2.
     1   NAME       Char    8     0    8.
     3   SEX        Num     8    16    1.
     4   SONG1      Num     8    24    2.       Black Water/DB
     5   SONG2      Num     8    32    2.       Bennie and the Jets/EJ
     6   SONG3      Num     8    40    2.       Stayin Alive/BG
     7   SONG4      Num     8    48    2.       Fire and Rain/JT
     8   SONG5      Num     8    56    2.       Country Roads/JD
```

Appendix E Coming to SAS from a Programming Language

You can write SAS programs that do many of the tasks that standard programming languages like C++, FORTRAN, and Visual BASIC can do. There are many similarities between SAS and these languages, but there are some important differences. If you are used to programming with these types of languages, learning SAS will be easier if you remember the differences.

Built-in loop The major difference is that SAS has a built-in loop for data handling. If you read data from a file, or process SAS data sets in the DATA step, SAS automatically loops through all the data. In a programming language, you typically need to set up an array to hold the data, then use a loop (DO, WHILE, or FOR) to process the array. You may need to know how many data elements are in the file, or check for end-of-file markers. The DATA step in SAS automates this.

While SAS processes all the data, it sees only one observation at a time. All the statements in a DATA step operate on only one observation at a time. In a programming language, you can see all the observations at once, by referencing the appropriate array subscript. In SAS you can simulate this using LAG functions or other techniques, but you will find that it is seldom necessary.

Loops DO loops are present in SAS, but you must keep in mind that a DO loop in SAS is executed with each pass through the DATA step. So if your loop has 6 iterations, and you have 10 observations in your data set, the statements inside your loop will be executed 60 times—6 times for each of the 10 observations (assuming the INPUT or SET statement is not inside the loop). The built-in loop in SAS, in essence, puts a loop around your entire DATA step. Because of the built-in loop, arrays and DO loops are not used nearly as often in SAS programs as they are in other languages.

Arrays SAS does have arrays, but they are used differently from the way they are used in programming languages. An array in SAS consists of variables. You use arrays when you want to do the same thing to each variable in the array, and you don't want to write a separate statement for each variable. Arrays are temporary in SAS, existing only for the duration of the DATA step in which they are defined. Arrays provide ways to shorten and simplify your SAS programs.

Functions SAS has many functions available that help simplify your programming tasks. Functions in SAS are used in DATA steps and, therefore, operate within an observation. If you want to find the minimum value for an observation across a group of variables, for example, you would use the MIN function. SAS has many functions available in the following categories: arithmetic, array, character, date and time, financial, mathematical, probability, quantile, random number, sample statistics, state and ZIP code, trigonometric and hyperbolic, and truncation.

Procedures While functions operate across variables, SAS procedures operate across observations. If you want to find the minimum value for a variable across all observations, then use PROC MEANS. SAS procedures can do a lot in just a few statements. Results from procedures are nicely formatted and you don't have to worry about how many decimal places to print, or where to put the results on the page. A simple PROC PRINT statement, for example, will print all the data in your SAS data set, fit as many variables as it can on a page, decide on the best format for each variable, and label each variable at the top of every page. But, SAS is flexible, so if you don't like the way SAS printed your results, you can change it.

Data types Another difference between SAS and most other languages is that SAS has only two types of data: numeric and character. All numbers in SAS are assumed to be double-precision floating-point values. You don't have to declare what type of numbers you are using. You can, however, change the number of bytes used to store data using the LENGTH statement. The default length is 8 bytes, which safely stores all numbers. If you are using small integer values, you might be able to use a length of 4 or fewer depending on the computer and operating environment you are using. The SAS Companion documentation for your host will tell you which numbers you can safely store in how many bytes.

Program structure Many programming languages are particular about the layout of programs. In FORTRAN, for example, any character in column 6 indicates that the line is a continuation of the previous line. SAS has no restrictions on program layout. A statement can be indented, split on many lines, or on the same line as other statements. SAS simply reads a statement from one semicolon to another. In addition, SAS statements are not case sensitive.

Compilation and execution Most programming languages have separate compile and execute phases. SAS does have separate phases, but when you submit a SAS program it automatically compiles and executes. You can, however, save compiled SAS DATA steps using the Stored Program Facility in SAS. This facility is most useful for production type jobs with long, compute-intensive, DATA steps.

Comparison of a SAS program to a C++ program The following compares a SAS program to a C++ program. Each program reads the following data from a file and prints it. The data file has three columns for the students' names, ages, and grade-point averages:

```
Mary    19 3.45
Bob     20 3.12
Scott   22 2.89
Marie   18 3.75
Ruth    20 2.67
```

The SAS Program

```
DATA grades;
    INFILE 'c:\MyRawData\gpa.dat';
    INPUT Name $ Age Gpa;
PROC PRINT DATA = grades;
RUN;
```

The C++ Program

```cpp
#include <iostream>
#include <fstream>
#include <iomanip>
using namespace std;

const int N=100;

struct student
{
        char name[32];
        int age;
        double GPA;
};

void main(void)
{
        student grades[N];

        ifstream in("gpa.dat");
        if (in.fail())
        exit(-1);

        int i=0;
        while (!in.eof() && i<N)
        {
                in>>grades[i].name>>grades[i].age>>grades[i].GPA;
                cout<<setw(10)<<left<<grades[i].name
                        <<setw(10)<<grades[i].age
                        <<fixed<<setprecision(2)<<grades[i].GPA<<endl;
                ++i;
        }

        in.close();
}
```

In the C++ program, the variables name (character array), age (integer), and gpa (float) are grouped in a data structure called student. Then, an array of these structures, named grades, is declared with an arbitrary dimension of N. Each variable in the program must be declared both in type and dimension (if an array). The SAS program has no such section. The variables are defined as either character ($) or numeric in the INPUT statement.

Next, the C++ program opens the file and uses a while statement to read the data into grades, stopping when it reaches the end of the file marker (EOF). In the same step, the C++ program writes the data out to the standard output device. In the SAS program, the DATA step sets up the built-in loop which reads all the data in the file. The INFILE statement specifies which file to read, and the INPUT statement defines the variables. The data are stored in a SAS data set named GRADES. A simple PROC PRINT prints the contents of the GRADES data set.

Here are the results of the PROC PRINT from the SAS program.

```
                    The SAS System                        1

           Obs    Name     Age    Gpa

            1     Mary      19     3.45
            2     Bob       20     3.12
            3     Scott     22     2.89
            4     Marie     18     3.75
            5     Ruth      20     2.67
```

Here are the results from the C++ program.

```
    Mary      19      3.45
    Bob       20      3.12
    Scott     22      2.89
    Marie     18      3.75
    Ruth      20      2.67
```

Notice that SAS automatically added a default title, page number, column headings, and obervation numbers to its report. The way the C++ program was written, it printed just the data. Of course you could rewrite the C++ program to make the output look exactly like the SAS output, but it would take more programming.

Appendix F Coming to SAS from SQL

If you already know Structured Query Language (SQL), then you will be pleased to know that you can use SQL statements in SAS programs to create, read, and modify SAS data sets. There are two basic ways to use SQL with SAS:

♦   You can embed complete SQL statements in the SQL procedure.

♦   You can use WHERE statements to select rows in standard SAS DATA and PROC steps.

Both of these features are available with base SAS, so you don't have to license any other SAS software to use SQL.

Terminology Terms such table, row, and column that originated with relational databases are now standard SAS terms also. However, other terms can also be used with SAS. To help you understand SAS terminology, here is a brief dictionary of analagous terms:

SQL term	Analogous SAS term
column	column or variable
row	row or observation
table	table or data set
join	merge, set, update or modify
NULL value	missing value
alias	alias
view	view
no analogous term	DATA step
no analogous term	PROC step

SQL does not contain structures like SAS DATA and PROC steps. Basically, DATA steps read and modify data while PROC (short for procedure) steps perform specific analyses or functions such as sorting, writing reports, or running statistical analyses. In SQL, reports are written automatically whenever you use a SELECT statement; sorting is performed by the ORDER BY clause; and the operations performed by most other SAS procedures don't exist in SQL.

SAS has fewer data types than standard SQL. The character data type is the same in both languages. All other SQL data types (numeric, decimal, integer, smallint, float, real, double precision, and date) map to the SAS numeric data type.

PROC SQL The SQL procedure in SAS follows all but a few of the guidelines set by the American National Standards Institute (ANSI) for implementations of SQL. The work performed by SQL, and therefore by PROC SQL, can also be done in SAS by DATA steps, PROC PRINT, PROC SORT, and PROC MEANS. The basic form of the SQL procedure is

```
PROC SQL;
   sql-statement;
```

The *sql-statement* in PROC SQL may be any SQL statement—ALTER, CREATE, DELETE, DESCRIBE, DROP, INSERT, SELECT, UPDATE, or VALIDATE—with a semicolon stuck on the end. You can have any number of SQL statements in a single PROC SQL step.

You can use PROC SQL interactively or in batch jobs. Unlike most other SAS procedures, PROC SQL will run interactively without a RUN statement. You just need to submit the program statements. Any results from SELECT statements are displayed automatically unless you specify the NOPRINT option on the PROC statement like this:

```
PROC SQL NOPRINT;
```

An SQL view is a stored SELECT statement that is executed at run time. PROC SQL can create views, and other procedures can read views created via PROC SQL.

Example To show how PROC SQL works and to provide a comparison, here are programs using PROC SQL and other SAS statements to perform the same function.

Creating a table The first program uses PROC SQL to create and print a simple table with three columns. This program uses CREATE, INSERT, and SELECT statements in a single PROC SQL step:

```
LIBNAME sports 'c:\MySASLib';
PROC SQL;
   CREATE TABLE sports.customer
      (CustomerNumber num,
       Name            char(17),
       Address         char(20));

   INSERT INTO sports.customer
      VALUES (101, 'Murphy''s Sports ', '115 Main St.         ')
      VALUES (102, 'Sun N Ski       ', '2106 Newberry Ave.   ')
      VALUES (103, 'Sports Outfitters', '19 Cary Way          ')
      VALUES (104, 'Cramer & Johnson ', '4106 Arlington Blvd.')
      VALUES (105, 'Sports Savers    ', '2708 Broadway        ');

   TITLE 'The Sports Customer Data';
   SELECT *
      FROM sports.customer;
```

Notice that the LIBNAME statement sets up a libref named SPORTS, pointing to a subdirectory named MySASLib on the C drive (Windows, OS/2). The LIBNAME statement may be different for your operating environment. See sections 2.9 and 2.10 for more information about LIBNAME statements. This program creates a permanent SAS table named CUSTOMER in the MySASLib subdirectory. No RUN statement is needed; to run this program you simply submit it to SAS. Here is the output.

```
               The Sports Customer Data              1


           Customer  Name              Address
           Number

           ---------------------------------------------------

                101  Murphy's Sports   115 Main St.
                102  Sun N Ski         2106 Newberry Ave.
                103  Sports Outfitters 19 Cary Way
                104  Cramer & Johnson  4106 Arlington Blvd.
                105  Sports Savers     2708 Broadway
```

The next program uses standard SAS statements to create the same table. Notice that the LIBNAME statement, the table name, and the TITLE statement are identical in both programs. LIBNAME statements stay in effect for the duration of a session or job. So, if you ran these programs in a single session or job, you would not have to repeat the LIBNAME statement. It is repeated here only for the sake of completeness.

```
LIBNAME sports 'c:\MySASLib';
DATA sports.customer;
   INPUT CustomerNumber Name $ 5-21 Address $ 23-42;
   DATALINES;
101 Murphy's Sports   115 Main St.
102 Sun N Ski         2106 Newberry Ave.
103 Sports Outfitters 19 Cary Way
104 Cramer & Johnson  4106 Arlington Blvd.
105 Sports Savers     2708 Broadway
   ;
PROC PRINT DATA = sports.customer;
TITLE 'The Sports Customer Data';
RUN;
```

Here is the output from the standard SAS program. It looks a little different from the previous report, but it contains the same information.

```
                    The Sports Customer Data                    2

        Obs    Customer    Name                Address
                 Number

         1       101       Murphy's Sports     115 Main St.
         2       102       Sun N Ski           2106 Newberry Ave.
         3       103       Sports Outfitters   19 Cary Way
         4       104       Cramer & Johnson    4106 Arlington Blvd.
         5       105       Sports Savers       2708 Broadway
```

Reading an existing table The next two programs read the CUSTOMER table and select one row. Here is the PROC SQL version of this program:

```
LIBNAME sports 'c:\MySASLib';
PROC SQL;
   TITLE 'Customer Number 102';
   SELECT *
      FROM sports.customer
      WHERE CustomerNumber = 102;
```

The PROC SQL output looks like this.

```
                  Customer Number 102                    3

        Customer  Name                Address
          Number
        -------------------------------------------------
             102  Sun N Ski          2106 Newberry Ave.
```

The following program uses SAS DATA and PROC steps to select and print the same row from the CUSTOMER table:

```
LIBNAME sports 'c:\MySASLib';
DATA sunnski;
   SET sports.customer;
   IF CustomerNumber = 102;
PROC PRINT DATA = sunnski;
   TITLE 'Customer Number 102';
RUN;
```

Here is the PROC PRINT output.

```
                  Customer Number 102                    4

        Obs   Customer     Name          Address
                Number

         1       102     Sun N Ski    2106 Newberry Ave.
```

Using the Query window to build a query There is another way to write PROC SQL statements: the Query window. You can open the Query window by selecting `Query` from the Tools menu. The Query window guides you through the process of building a query and then executes your query. You can see the SQL statements created by the Query window by selecting either `Show Query...` or `Preview Window...` from the Tools pull-down menu.

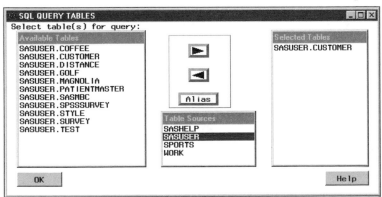

WHERE statement   The WHERE statement in SAS is modeled after the WHERE clause of SQL, and is similar to a subsetting IF statement. However, there are some differences in how a WHERE statement and a subsetting IF work. While subsetting IFs can appear only in DATA steps, WHERE statements can be used in DATA or PROC steps. WHERE statements are generally more efficient than subsetting IF statements, especially when they allow you to eliminate a DATA step by subsetting directly in a procedure. When WHERE statements are used in a DATA step, SAS applies WHERE statements earlier than IF statements. This has several repercussions:

♦   The WHERE statement is more efficient than a subsetting IF because it avoids reading unwanted rows.

♦   The WHERE statement can select rows only from existing SAS tables. The IF statement, however, can select rows from SAS tables or from raw data files being read with INPUT statements.

♦   With a WHERE statement, you can select rows based only on the values of columns being read. With a subsetting IF statement, you can select rows based on the value of a column created in the current DATA step.

♦   The WHERE and IF statements may produce different results when two tables are combined in a MERGE, SET, or UPDATE statement. Operations that occur after SAS applies WHERE statements but before SAS applies IF statements may cause the statements to select different rows.

Examples   To show how the WHERE statement works and to provide a comparison with the IF statement, here are programs using WHERE and IF statements to perform the same functions. All three of these programs read the CUSTOMER SAS table created by the previous programs. The goal of these programs is to select and print one row from an existing SAS table:

Subsetting IF   This program uses a subsetting IF statement to select one row:

```
LIBNAME sports 'c:\MySASLib';
DATA outfitters;
   SET sports.customer;
   IF Name = 'Sports Outfitters';
PROC PRINT DATA = outfitters;
RUN;
```

Here is the output.

```
                    The SAS System                       1

        Obs     Customer        Name            Address
                 Number
         1        103       Sports Outfitters   19 Cary Way
```

WHERE statement in a DATA step The next program uses a WHERE statement in the DATA step and then prints the results with PROC PRINT:

```
LIBNAME sports 'c:\MySASLib';
DATA outfitters;
   SET sports.customer;
   WHERE Name = 'Sports Outfitters';
PROC PRINT DATA = outfitters;
RUN;
```

The output looks like this.

```
                        The SAS System                      2

            Obs     Customer        Name          Address
                    Number

             1        103     Sports Outfitters  19 Cary Way
```

WHERE statement in a PROC step The last program uses a WHERE statement directly in the PROC PRINT:

```
LIBNAME sports 'c:\MySASLib';
PROC PRINT DATA = sports.customer;
   WHERE Name = 'Sports Outfitters';
RUN;
```

Here is the output.

```
                        The SAS System                      3

            Obs     Customer        Name          Address
                    Number

             3        103     Sports Outfitters  19 Cary Way
```

Notice that the row number for the first two reports is 1 while the row number for the last report is 3. This happens because the first two programs create a table with one row and then print it. In contrast, the last program never creates a table; it simply reads the existing table by searching for the right row, which happens to be number 3.

Index

Call your local SAS® office to order these other books and tapes available through the Books by Users℠ program:

An Array of Challenges — Test Your SAS® Skills
by **Robert Virgile**...................................Order No. A55625

Applied Multivariate Statistics with SAS® Software
by **Ravindra Khattree**
and **Dayanand N. Naik**.........................Order No. A55234

Applied Statistics and the SAS® Programming Language, Fourth Edition
by **Ronald P. Cody**
and **Jeffrey K. Smith**............................Order No. A55984

Beyond the Obvious with SAS® Screen Control Language
by **Don Stanley** ....Order No. A55073

Carpenter's Complete Guide to the SAS® Macro Language
by **Art Carpenter** ....Order No. A56100

The Cartoon Guide to Statistics
by **Larry Gonick**
and **Woollcott Smith**............................Order No. A55153

Categorical Data Analysis Using the SAS® System
by **Maura E. Stokes, Charles S. Davis,**
and **Gary G. Koch** ....Order No. A55320

Common Statistical Methods for Clinical Research with SAS® Examples
by **Glenn A. Walker**..............................Order No. A55991

Concepts and Case Studies in Data Management
by **William S. Calvert**
and **J. Meimei Ma**.................................Order No. A55220

Efficiency: Improving the Performance of Your SAS® Applications
by **Robert Virgile**..................................Order No. A55960

Essential Client/Server Survival Guide, Second Edition
by **Robert Orfali, Dan Harkey,**
and **Jeri Edwards**..................................Order No. A56285

Extending SAS® Survival Analysis Techniques for Medical Research
by **Alan Cantor** ....Order No. A55504

A Handbook of Statistical Analysis using SAS®
by **B.S. Everitt**
and **G. Der** ....Order No. A56378

The How-To Book for SAS/GRAPH® Software
by **Thomas Miron** ....Order No. A55203

In the Know ... SAS® Tips and Techniques From Around the Globe
by **Phil Mason** ....Order No. A55513

Learning SAS® in the Computer Lab
by **Rebecca J. Elliott** ....Order No. A55273

Mastering the SAS® System, Second Edition
by **Jay A. Jaffe** ....Order No. A55123

The Next Step: Integrating the Software Life Cycle with SAS® Programming
by **Paul Gill** ....Order No. A55697

Painless Windows 3.1: A Beginner's Handbook for SAS® Users
by **Jodie Gilmore** ....Order No. A55505

Painless Windows: A Handbook for SAS® Users
by **Jodie Gilmore** ....Order No. A55769

Professional SAS® Programmers Pocket Reference, Second Edition
by **Rick Aster** ....Order No. A56646

Professional SAS® Programming Secrets, Second Edition
by **Rick Aster**
and **Rhena Seidman** ....Order No. A56279

Professional SAS® User Interfaces
by **Rick Aster** ....Order No. A56197

Programming Techniques for Object-Based Statistical Analysis with SAS® Software
by **Tanya Kolosova**
and **Samuel Berestizhevsky** ....Order No. A55869

Audio Tapes

100 Essential SAS® Software Concepts (set of two)
by **Rick Aster** ....Order No. A55309

A Look at SAS® Files (set of two)
by **Rick Aster** ....Order No. A55207

JMP® Books

Basic Business Statistics: A Casebook
by **Dean P. Foster, Robert A. Stine**
and **Richard P. Waterman** ....Order No. A56813

Business Analysis Using Regression: A Casebook
by **Dean P. Foster, Robert A. Stine**
and **Richard P. Waterman** ....Order No. A56818

JMP® Start Statistics, Version 3
by **John Sall** and **Ann Lehman** ....Order No. A55626

*Welcome * Bienvenue *Willkommen *Yohkoso * Bienvenido*

SAS Publishing Is Easy to Reach

Visit our Web site located at support.sas.com/pubs

You will find product and service details, including

- **companion Web sites**
- **sample chapters**
- **tables of contents**
- **author biographies**
- **book reviews**

Learn about

- **regional users group conferences**
- **trade show sites and dates**
- **authoring opportunities**
- **e-books**

Explore all the services that Publications has to offer!

Your Listserv Subscription Automatically Brings the News to You

Do you want to be among the first to learn about the latest books and services available from SAS Publishing? Subscribe to our listserv **newdocnews-l** and, once each month, you will automatically receive a description of the newest books and which environments or operating systems and SAS® release(s) each book addresses.

To subscribe,

1. Send an e-mail message to **listserv@vm.sas.com**.

2. Leave the "Subject" line blank.

3. Use the following text for your message:

   subscribe NEWDOCNEWS-L *your-first-name your-last-name*

   For example: subscribe NEWDOCNEWS-L John Doe

You're Invited to Publish with SAS Institute's Books by Users Press

If you enjoy writing about SAS software and how to use it, the Books by Users program at SAS Institute offers a variety of publishing options. We are actively recruiting authors to publish books and sample code.

If you find the idea of writing a book by yourself a little intimidating, consider writing with a co-author. Keep in mind that you will receive complete editorial and publishing support, access to our users, technical advice and assistance, and competitive royalties. Please ask us for an author packet at **sasbbu@sas.com** or call 919-531-7447. See the Books by Users Web page at **support.sas.com/bbu** for complete information.

Book Discount Offered at SAS Public Training Courses!

When you attend one of our SAS Public Training Courses at any of our regional Training Centers in the United States, you will receive a 20% discount on any book orders placed during the course. Take advantage of this offer at the next course you attend!

SAS Institute Inc.
SAS Campus Drive
Cary, NC 27513-2414
Fax 919-677-4444

E-mail: sasbook@sas.com
Web page: support.sas.com/pubs
To order books, call SAS Publishing Sales at 800-727-3228*
For product information, consulting, customer service, or training, call 800-727-0025
For other SAS Institute business, call 919-677-8000*

* Note: Customers outside the United States should contact their local SAS office.

The Power to Know.

SAS Publishing